BLISS IS IT!

THE TEACHERS OF THE HIGHER PLANES

Sixth Book of Wisdom

Ruth Lee, *Scribe*

LeeWay
PUBLISHING

LeeWay
PUBLISHING

This book is an updated and revised version of the 2012 edition originally published by AuthorHouse.

LeeWay Publishing
Naples, Florida USA
www.LeeWayPublishing.com

ISBN: 978-0-9970529-5-4
Library of Congress Control Number: 2016963466
Printed in the United States of America
First Printing 2017

Cover design by Sarah Barrie of Cyanotype.ca
Internal Design by Alfredo Sarraga Jr.

More Books by **Ruth Lee**

Other **Books of Wisdom** From
The Teachers of the Higher Planes

We Are Here

The Work Begins

The Art of Life ~ *Living Together in Harmony*

Now is The Time

Bliss is It!

The Word of The Maya

The Making of a Scribe - *How to Achieve a Life You Can Write About*

Writing in Spirit Workbook

Writing in Spirit Notebook

Can You Pray? *We Are All Here to Seek the Way*

Novels by Ruth Lee

Angel of The Maya

Within the Veil: *An Adventure in Time*

Writing in Spirit ~ *Jeanne's Story*

Follow your bliss!

If you do follow your bliss, you put yourself on a kind of track that has been there all the while waiting for you, and the life you ought to be living is the one you are living.

When you can see that, you begin to meet people who are in the field of your bliss, and they open the doors to you.

I say, follow your bliss and don't be afraid, and doors will open where you didn't know they were going to be.

If you follow your bliss, doors will open for you that wouldn't have opened for anyone else.

--~Joseph Campbell (1904-1987)

BLISS IS IT!

THE TEACHERS OF THE HIGHER PLANES

Sixth Book of Wisdom

Ruth Lee, *Scribe*

LeeWay
PUBLISHING

Introduction

What takes place between your heart, mind, and faith is not easy to define. You either have a sense of who you are and what you believe—or feel lost when others talk about spiritual work, other times, or past lives. This can and often does lead to arguments between otherwise good friends, but it need not. You do not have to believe anything!

If you could sit down and talk to someone about what you want from life, who would you choose and what would you say? I ask, because that happened to me! Suddenly I was working in a way that defied everything I believed until then. Suspending judgment, I began to write in ways that defy logic—unlike anything I had ever done. Could you do it? Would you have listened to this call: *'No need to understand, just write.'* I did, thus began the most amazing journey of my life.

Once you gain peace of mind, you find others espouse things you cannot believe, yet they accept you as you are without understanding you. How can anyone read a book written by a spiritual scribe and believe it happened as she wrote? I decided I did not care! I believed—and it became my way of life. You decide if you can accept such advice or not.

Who wants to read a book some say the author did not write? Who admits they read such work? Stop wondering about how others changed their lives, gained peace of mind, and study little else. Instead, see for yourself—read ***The Books of Wisdom****!*

Bliss is It! is not intended to induce you to read, teach, or preach wisdom freely given by teachers from another dimension. It merely offers a change of view and helps you open to another world or two—ignoring more and more what it means to live in a world populated by those who do not love you, care about you, nor are interested in why you are here.

Discover why you are *you* and how to enjoy life as you are now, while aspiring to rise until you ascend at the end of this life and move into a better, more wonderful *you* than appears in this view. Take your time, **Bliss is It!** presents views of much you cannot see while living in a way you maintain is not *your way*—but truly is.

'We are here to help you' came through the first time *The Teachers of the Higher Planes* arrived in *The Scribe's* life, and thus they remain for all time. Are you ready for a new *you* and a better world than what you maintain now? This book can help you realize life is what it is and—*this is bliss!*

Chapter One

Today is not the first day of your life—regardless of what others might say or pray will happen. It is just another day in an extremely long continuum of time you may or may not understand now—but will understand by the time you finish reading **Bliss is It!**

Today you are who counts. To deny it is to subscribe to the idea *you* are not here to be you, nor here to do whatever you wish and then leave, and we are not here to teach you now. This is the last time we will attempt to help human beings become who they are meant to be—not imitations of those limited by what is not done or provided by others—plus all manner of limiting ideas that make no sense to anyone with a brain.

Whatever your life,
You choose to live this way!

You can state emphatically you cannot do what you want, but that is nonsense. You will discover later—if not now, that you are lying to yourself and no one else sees you as you do. We would not arrive in a huff and blow much fluff so all feel great and never become what they are meant to be now. Many spend their lives hypnotized by men and women ignorant of life—yet making money by telling others how to live well. Some even see themselves as divine gods of some kind or doing work God gives to them alone. That is not true, and you must know that before judging what is given by *The Scribe,* as we dictated through time to all ready to move beyond this world now.

No one is going to tell you your life is a waste of time, but your mind tallies and keeps score and reminds you when you spend too much, got incorrect change, or could not explain what you meant, and so on. We know the mind is not only a brain that functions much like you trained computers to arrange things for you, yet is not mechanically-inclined enough to use as a computer without getting confused. Does this make sense, or have you truly forgotten that nothing can replace your mind?

Now you want friends, family, and others who will stick by you no matter what you say, do, or even believe, but most do not think it will happen. Why? You do not talk to friends about what ails you, tires your mind, or even what you believe. Instead, you talk nonsense, inserting little words or big ideas into drunken tirades in hopes you feel better about your world on the morrow. We are here to help you reveal who you are and what you feel so you can let others know you believe in God—and remain popular!

If you stand up and proclaim you believe in a higher being or someone greater than you, what will happen? Are you going to be stoned or buried alive? Is the worst possible thing going to happen—that you are ridiculed by those who could not possibly be friends if they laughed then? Try to imagine what you fear most and it comes down to your ego getting bruised, your thoughts being crushed, or your hopes being dashed. That is all—not that you lose your life or never able to have a good friend again.

You worry you may look like a fool!

Who but a fool would deny what is most accurate and true about life? The fool who pretends to not believe in *'God'* is trying to raise a few eyebrows. We base this on what we observed over the past years working on Earth. Such pretentious nonsense to say you believe this is it, and you are an atomic structure that will blow up or continue to function as such. You must realize you sound stupid to those who know more than you will ever comprehend while living this life.

Before leaving to find a book easier to read, think about what you want and what you get when you frown or look down on others. Do you arrogantly grab what another has in hand, or peek over your shoulder and glance away if anyone notices you browsing through what you do not wish to pay for then? You may always be a browser and never get to the gist of anything you read, but at least you seek. That is how it begins.

The foolish never do much but look about—and keep hunting for whatever others say is profound, but cannot figure out. You are browsing now! Perhaps seeking to determine if this book is better than another in **The Books of Wisdom** series created by *The Teachers of the Higher Planes,* using Ruth Lee to trance-scribe what is found in the sunlight of this planet now—and assumed by some to be difficult to read? You will find this book easy to read! Admit it and get over the idea that whatever comes through a medium or channel cannot be easy to understand or will not help you achieve success and increase your belief in whatever you think bliss is now.

Quietly assess all that is...

If you do this, you find you are never without a friend—even when stone-cold sober, yet uttering complete nonsense. Someone, probably female, will say you are nice and have a good life. Think about it. Why would anyone surround themselves with tripe and the impolite when they hold higher visions of the world than *'this is it'*? You must not feel all you do is ignored or boring? Perhaps it is, but someone will enjoy it and want to hear it.

As you accept that bliss is not exactly what you expected it would be when you arrived in the village that exists around you wherever you are now, realize bliss exists for you to use and experience, but not abuse. We hope you enjoy life, but some are determined to undermine everything done to ease their suffering, pain, or worries. Why?

We do not have time, nor do we care to explain their motives. We are here to help you ascend to a higher plane of life now. We have no interest in prolonging the misery of those who deny bliss exists!

Chapter Two

Rich and famous is the antithesis of being in a state of bliss, yet many reading this are seeking that kind of existence. Why would anyone who can be all they are here to be seek to be different, yet not use what they create and believe—in order to follow the dollar or pound sign to another life. In such times God is forbidden to be called upon, prayed to, or even thought about. Why and how do people decide to create new gods now?

If you never felt worthy of another or clever with much to say to others, you probably would not write a book at any point in life. Right? That was the rule until recently when fools decided that to look clever or competent with much to share, they should write books and dare others to compare them to what is already out there. What a life—and what a way to spend your time when you are not born to write!

Assume you are *you,* doing what you like to do, would you want others to follow and do exactly what you do? If so, you can teach, preach, even write about what you do as if a recipe for others to follow. Will it not take you away from who you are today? Will it not make you pause and repeat whatever you said or did when different from who you are now? If all you want is happiness and a feeling of contentment that only comes from within, why write about your life?

When you remain silent, not speaking about what you intend to do, are you out of sync with others or being polite and letting them later discover how unwise it was to have condemned what you did then? If you let others speak and never correct their impressions of you, are you condemning them or making fun of them? We would ask you to speak if others dare say they know you and do not. We would say it is false to let people speak of you in terms that mislead others into believing you are someone you will never be or want to be, even when you act the part.

How long and how often do you talk now? Do you let others speak for you rather than speak up and mention your problems or doubts? Perhaps you set others up to do whatever, rather than speak your thoughts? If so, you cause yourself no end of problems and probably lose friends by expecting them to cater to your whims and risk the chance of their being disliked by your enemies.

Who would you like to be if not you?

When you see others abandoning rules you were brought up to accept and possibly believe to be blessed, are you sick with envy or upset that they are disrespectful? Think on it and make amends for anything you may have said when you attacked their stand once they left the premises. Many want to be loved, but few respect all others. Why? It is unfashionable to be kind now.

Read three things thoroughly to understand them—then read again. Decide what they can be, will be, or were in the past. Read and understand at least three decent, helpful things that provide meaningful thoughts and dreams. If you cannot find anything worthy of your intelligent mind after reading something three times, you must be out of line with your time.

We suggest you begin re-reading **The Books of Wisdom** we created years ago upon arriving here to help you save planet Earth. Begin at the beginning and read, study, and let it become a philosophy you can teach if you believe it is helpful, thus you help others, too.

Who teaches you now? How do they get through your outer shell to the inner wonder of your mind? Are you full of selfish thoughts—not interested in anyone else? If so, you will do okay in the modern world of today, but you will never star. Instead, you will be accepted as acting the way everyone behaves, with nothing exceptional to say. Why? It happens when you do not accept life as a wondrous adventure—preferring instead to be someone who has no need for others.

How can you let go of the past without floating free endlessly? Simply think about what you want to be. Once done, you begin to realize you cannot change your life if you believe you cannot become someone other than this one. If you came to Earth to be *you*—no one else, but once here got caught up in a family convinced it was the only family to be whatever or do something new, you likely became arrogant, too. However, every family has at least one who differs from all others. Maybe you are that one?

Quickly assess your work on this plane and see if you can rise on your own or require more and more help from everyone who came before you to this world. If you read and built a fictional life based on what someone else conceived as an ideal life, most likely you do not feel like you belong in this world. Right? You might feel you belong to a place, situation, family, or whatever different from what you experience in this place and time. If you continue this fiction, or decide it is better than whatever you conceive in your mind, you will not feel better.

Whatever you do now, make whatever you create yours. Why? A slave rises daily and does a job. Jobs are set up by others to keep people occupied doing trivial pursuits that require no degree of integrity or ingenuity. If it is a difficult task, generally the one hiring such people gets involved, may even become well-versed in how it works in order to take over the business. He does not seek out slaves to do his work!

A slave will stay a slave, wondering why anyone would want to do such work and not hate it. When you slave away at cutting grass or doing small tasks, do you ask yourself if it is necessary to do commonplace tasks to become a success? You may be surprised, but most people believe slaving away at some point in the day or during their lives is helpful in deciding what they do not wish to do with their time. By the way, they are right!

Whatever you decide you can be or succeed at believing is what you assume everyone likes or would want to do, too. If you limit your mind to such thoughts during this life, you have no imagination. Assume whatever you do is done well enough to let go and not repeat again. If you constantly review and redo, going over and over whatever you know, you cannot grow.

Three times three is a number not as developed as some might believe nine to be. If you classify your life as a '9' and repeat that '9' is the culmination of many lives, and you chose to live again in order to come to this world a more perfect being, you are making it up and cannot decide why you would accept it as truth rather than think it absurd. If you often play that kind of mind game, think about why you do it. Stop doing it as soon as you realize you cannot gauge or guess why you returned to paradise.

Yes, you are in paradise without realizing why it is a paradise or how much energy you need to be here and live as if on fire. It is a gift! You have been living here for years, yet still cannot understand what you did to be here now. Right or not, you are here to do a job called *life*. You are also here to develop your line as far as you can without losing your mind.

A mind is not a gift so much as a tool given to you to use to align your life with time and whatever else you are here to do. Yes, it is a bit confusing, but English is that way today. You use words over and over again without changing the way they are spoken or how they appear. To decide why you do that is for another time and another life. Now you will concentrate on why you want to live like another who has much more than you ever thought you required.

What does it take to please you today?

When you create and deliver imagination to others in ways they cannot create on their own, you are paid large sums. Right or wrong? Usually an artist must wait for the common mind to determine if their art is acceptable to the population around them before they are supported. So, what pays today?

The absurd notion that you are paid to do something new or unique is completely erased when you look at the richest entertainers on your planet today. The flashy, insincere, addicted, and unable to hide their fears, are paid more than others. Why? They make up for a commonplace life. They help individuals feel better about themselves, or provide an acceptable social reason to gamble away whatever they make. It is not payment made to help another do better in life, rather a way to watch others lose their integrity and slip from grace, while not being judged badly by others for having succeeded.

If your idea of making money is to earn so much you can play God and give it away later in life, you will not be honored or given much credit for doing it. If you honor others along the path—helping them get ahead and not expecting payment, you may be honored at some point, but probably not. If you consider these two extremes, which do you lean toward now and why? If you lean toward exploiting everyone in order to be Number One, you are not alone and will find many who will honor you for cutting others' throats, thus not allowed to own everything Earth produces now. However, if you choose to help and respect your fellow occupants of this planet, you may not have to come back again, and can leave before everything is damaged by rain, fire, and famine.

Whatever you choose to be or choose to see is what makes you a better judge of character—or does not. If you never size up others or study psychology, are not gifted with psychic insights, and believe in nothing, you are lost. A guide is not always noticed until those lost cannot figure out what to do and begin blaming God for it. That is why so many run about now seeking gurus and shamans who will say they are making progress. Progress? What is that, when you talk about God?

Tuesday of each week is a good time to sit back and do very little. Right? Tuesday is as good as any day to decide when you will rest your weary body and mind and let Spirit preside. You need only decide what day works best for you, then religiously follow it to found a new belief system which others who lack imagination will follow to their graves.

Why lead—or follow others, when you know *your* path is open and easy to see? All you need do is put one foot in front of the other and believe you are here to be you, then follow your talents to some work you want to do as long as you are here. When you decide to take over and rule others, you have no idea what you are doing, but discover if you have no ability to rule that you will be beheaded or worse before you leave Earth. Why then get involved in taking over and ruling others? All that goes back to wanting riches and fame!

By the time you finish reading this book, you will discover all is yours once you figure out who you are—nothing else can substitute for being you! This is neither a good time nor a bad time to be alive, yet some will say daily it was better in the past or things will be better tomorrow. Are you locked into those extreme mindsets? Are you depressed and angry because you cannot release the past, or anxiety-ridden because you fear what will arrive after you leave or happen day-after-tomorrow?

Take time to sit and think of nothing that comes to mind. Whatever bothers your rest, shake it off. Do not let any thought nest in your mind now.

Whatever happens to you while resting—doing nothing but easing your mind, helps you heal and feel real. Rest is meant to be a state of bliss, but few reach it. Thus your mind is described as idling in order to let God figure out what you are up to now and can do better.

Try letting God guide you. This is good advice! It will help more than anything you tried in the past when seeking advice on how to feel great and not worry about life.

Chapter Three

In the future of *you* are many places and things you do not realize are active in your surreal world today, thus causing you to select and make choices that one day soon will prove you created this life and did a fine job. When you believe you can see things that are about to happen, you are not clairvoyant! In your own way, you are experiencing life as an exclusive being who can see what you want to be, thus setting your internal course to achieve it. You create it, because you saw it!

Every few miles along your path you will find others waiting to meet or link with you and share what they are doing now, however, you usually travel alone. You may believe you have babies who will always be with you, but they are not yours—only your responsibility to raise and help them understand who created this life.

In the forecast for today and tomorrow, or whatever you choose to label your daily life, you will find all is done before such time arrives. You merely live it out. Can it be you created a down-and-glum life or an accident of fate, because you did something in another time now required to be played out again?

Many explanations suggest you must pay for what you do wrong, while others explain it as having been ethical or moral in the past, you come back because you want to return. Whatever, since you chose to come back, tackle this life and attempt to deny your mind another opportunity to become someone else. At the end of this life, ask to go on and ascend to live in another way, instead of repeating human behavior and a life similar to what you have now.

If you could be another, Who would you be?

You would still be *you*—exactly as you are now! No matter what you say or want to believe, *you* created this being who sees you, looks beyond you, and wants to be like others. You are who decided to study and work hard—or not, to understand the science of modern man or incur greater knowledge you could experiment with in order to reach a higher knowledge of this life.

You choose! No one can keep a brilliant mind from accomplishing whatever it wants. You may try to alibi out and say you are not as accomplished as many others, because you are not as bright. We would laugh at the idea, and you would be wise to do the same. You choose what you do and with whom you associate. All that is done with your mind agreeing to do it for *you*.

Some want to say they were not given credit when young, thus they never developed enough confidence to reach out and change their lives or move beyond what their parents did. That is incorrect and not supported by those who know you now or knew you since birth. You showed interest in something, then practiced it, thus creating a way to measure you against others the same age. After repeated efforts you gave up in disgust, because you could not do it better than others, or you decided you were great and did something else. This became a pattern of learning you carry with you and can now erase.

Whatever you do, do it for you! If it benefits another, wonderful! You are asked to exist as is now and enjoy your bliss, but first you must understand what bliss is and what you get from it.

If your work is demeaning or unclean, others may pay you much to do it for them. Why not? It is good work if it hurts no other, including beings not categorized as humans. A simple law of life: Anything not beneficial to anyone will not benefit you to work on it! Before trying to figure out how to evade laws, explore why they need not be obeyed.

Who will be a woman or man of greatness who detests the family that raised them? You may be aware many overcame family situations that kept them down, only to create the same kind of family. Why? Unwilling to change or experiment, they followed a way they hoped would be excused as their not being responsible for whatever if ever told off. You cannot accept that kind of view today. You must realize everyone who ever lived beyond age 21, or younger in many societies now, had a chance to give of self. As an adult, to say you cannot live your life as you wish is to lie and accept it. Change your life so as not to be dependent upon others.

When free, enjoy your time here—
This is bliss!

To blame another for what you did not want to change about yourself is unreasonable and of little interest to others observing your life. You must agree or be dismissed as a fraud? You are seen by others as unwilling to accept responsibility for who you are and how you live.

When a child unguarded by adults falls, that child may be injured and harmed in ways that cannot be changed by events encountered later in life. Having said that, you were not socially harmed or you would not be reading this book and trying to discover a short-cut to bliss. You would be in a prison of your making or jailed by the public at large. It takes time to build a case for insanity today, because everyone is trying to make this world a safer place.

In some countries developing a work ethic is not pursued enough, as well as recognizing the need to protect the sick, weak, and young. This will be held against all their adults, regardless of what they established as great work on Earth. According to what you were given and did not need, you will be held accountable for your resurrection this life. Yes, you are a resurrected being—not a re-established mind and body, or even a soul new to this planet. *You* are a bit of each and every thing you can imagine as being alive and part of the entire universe of your world.

You are not unique? You are now the essence of whatever came together when conceived and, due to the circumstances of that event, cannot be repeated by anyone ever again. Try as you may, you cannot create the same genes in the same way between a pair of participants who wanted or did not wish it to end in conception then.

Having established enough facts to help you move on to what we are here to teach you now, we would appreciate *you* keeping your work at a level you understand. Try to rise higher than you can physically grasp, while keeping it under your hair longer than a ten-minute lecture that you can float and accept life is not perceptible now. According to your terminology, life is, was, and will be. Life is, but bliss is not what you get from living a life over time that is unworthy of your mind or inspired intentions.

When ready to do something great,
Do it!

Don't stop and talk about your life and why you aspired to do this work or do something new. Do it! Get on with the work of providing copies others can read or not.

Once you do what you have in mind, other work will arrive in time that suits your individual mind and thought process. Yes, your mind does change, but not as much as you say it does. You have to physically collapse some waves or do something drastic to change the way you think and use your brain—or simply read a book that changes your ideas about life.

Once again, we gather together to give you a lesson on how to live for *you* without harming others. Do we want you to be happy? We see nothing unique about wanting to be happy or enjoying life without strife, but now all continually seek people who will never agree with them—or obviously are trying to make fools of everyone. Why? You want to pass your lives without having to work hard, ending up doing more work than otherwise if you had followed the path you were given at birth.

If given a path at birth and parents who worked to help you get ahead, or not, you are where now? You used people—not the other way around, as so many paint parents of the past now. You used them in order to one day walk away and not support them in ways they sacrificed to give you, or they pay the price of never having joy again. Bliss is not something you get, rather something that fits in and helps you forgive and live well every day of your life.

If you harm a child,
You cannot feel great!

Having worked on what you did as a child to get this far, you probably measured over and over again what neighbors did and what your parents neglected to do, but most people do not think enough about how the village helped them get well when ill, or educated them when their parents had no time or were ignorant of the subjects required to ace life, and so on. List the benefits you received at times from living where you did or being raised as you were. List everything, then laugh as you enter it into your mind and let it stay for all time.

Bliss is not consistent—and not something you can give to others. It is what you are, believe, and conceive whenever you convene a meeting with another who appears to think as you do, or is much aware of your perfections and ignores what you do not do well, as well as other such conceits. Bliss is greater than all of this! Bliss is the state in which you exist when all is in balance.

Chapter Four

There is no way you can criticize others without feeling betrayed when you later hear the same said about you. You may believe you spotted something wrong that others were unaware of created a way for them to be saved from similar situations you stumbled upon, but most likely you will never be the same as anyone else, so do not talk a lot about what you spot as being wrong, instead emphasize what you see as right. Why the long, long winding sentence to reach the simple conclusion that it is better to be positive than negative when discussing another? Because it is easier to spot what is wrong than what is done perfectly or right all the time.

The mind does not want you to be complacent, without work, so it constantly reminds you of your imperfections—thus you criticize others. The critical mind is the enemy of bliss. Right? Maybe not, but it does little to help you feel confident and able to fit in with the crowd around you most of the time. Once you deliberately shut down the critic, you may slip and not do much better—even drop your work performance to less than it was when you were eager to correct and improve your life.

There is a place and time to submit to the critic, and that time and place is whenever you set out to learn something new. Never believe you were born to be a tennis ace or rock performer, thus all you need is a few hours of hard work and you will be a star accepting everyone's adoration. It does not happen like that! You may wish to say some are talented and gifted from the moment they arrive on earth—unaware they are stars, but you would be admitting you failed to realize you are a star, too.

When unaware you were born a star, you may not want to be someone worthy of love, or advise others on how to survive, but God is in the details and helps you survive and thrive when you finally decide to follow your Guides and live as you might if you wished to exist in bliss. Yes, bliss is when you are on your own, working alone, doing what you came to be!

Explaining it easily is not what sticks with you, so we continue to construct continuous sentences that progress with difficulty until you suddenly see what we mean. That is when the light becomes much brighter and you see signs of intelligent life all around you—and you want to know who is in the next world.

Can you exist in bliss and not realize it?

Before we go further and discuss what you can be, who you are, and why you are on Earth, why not rest a bit and think about it? You are not ready to think or rest! You want to read easily-explained lessons, so you can get on with your life. That is why you buy a book to read or borrow it from another.

If you buy the work, do you value the lesson more or do you love it as much as when someone else pays for it? You may argue all you like, but paying for your education is always best, gaining help along the way from those who furnish it at prices not beyond what you can earn.

You must participate to become part of a work. That work then frees you from being dependent upon another or many others. Once dependency ends, you feel the urge to do it again and again, but do not yield to it. Instead, once you understand exactly who you are and why you are here, create your life and share it with others.

The love you can give others who do not love their work and life in this time is greater than if you try to lift and help people by giving all your love to those who will never understand the sacrifice you made for them. When you subscribe to being a martyr for another or for a cause, you are not remembered later with envy or pride, even if people say you saved the tribe or caused others to live better lives. You are here to do what you came to do and then leave! This may sound like you have little to do, but do not underestimate the pride and ego that resides within and around this life.

If you live in a society that loves money more than people, you are urged to beat others at whatever—and do whatever to compete full-time. Do not speak evil of capitalistic people, because all on Earth are participating in resurrecting such a way of life for their tribe or country and want money now. How can a faulty system benefit you and create bliss? It does not exist!

When confirmed as a student of the world, you alone may see you as unable to link or connect with another or be happily married, but you can change. However, if you live in a place governed by those who are dead set against what you want to do, learn patience or end up dead—without any way to make progress in what you originally sought to follow. Why seek to be born into such a society or country again?

You may not want to move up now, but when your time is over and done, you must ask to ascend to a higher level of development. We are here now to help you work hard on what makes you a good guide to others who cannot find their way out of this life. If you are a teacher or preacher, please do not paraphrase what we write and how we work with *The Scribe*. Instead, produce a work of art or piece of work that means much to you and use it as an example of living and enjoying bliss without hurting others.

Why do so many seek recognition and fame?

You may not believe some behave badly—guaranteed to be imprisoned early in life due to such behavior, but it happens and is not being taken seriously enough by parents who have too much. You must nip bad behavior early and keep children in check when young, so they can grow straight, but you do not need to keep them in place and tie yourself in knots to keep your family growing tall and wise. You merely have to take steps when required—not ten years later.

Work hard when a baby develops into a healthy child. Do not forget your child or let another take over your work of disciplining, educating, feeding, and whatever else is required until your child can leave home and not come back again. Yes, that outcome is definitely not what some want to hear about now, but you must do enough while raising children to be able later in life to enjoy bliss.

If all you do exists and has been proven to work well for all others, is it a risk for you to do it? Why do you doubt such a view? Are you resistant or lazy and unwilling to take charge and do what was proven best for whatever? When you barely have enough time to live your life using all that is provided now, why reinvent everything? Be assured, doing things badly is not a way to extend life. It does not create a state of bliss!

Whatever you do, enjoy it! Time will pass and another world will come forward, but progress will be dependent upon what you did last. Does this make sense? If not, you need to make sure you are up-to-date on all you came to create. Prove you do work you like, and do it well. Once you update your views of *you*, perhaps you will work harder, too?

Did we create our book, **The World of Tomorrow,** so you would want to move ahead and become another you? You may not have read what we said, but this book teaches how to live in modern times in ways that provide support, while educating your mind about what is to come after this life. If you cannot figure out what you require by the time you expire, reread **The World of Tomorrow**.

Chapter Five

By the time you read this line you are half-way to deciding if you can complete this book, and if it is worth your time, and so on. Life is not like that, so why would a book about living life to the fullest be judged that way? What you are, how you live, and why you believe in what you seem to see and talk about is difficult to describe, let alone how to change what is blocking your path. Your path is always there, but there are ways and means of ignoring it without realizing you are.

We want you to score!

To do what you came to Earth to do requires you to pay attention to how you are created. If you ignore you are not particularly athletic, yet intend to set records, you either take too much for granted or not enough. Instead, try to figure out what suits you best and be ahead of all others in your style of life or running your kind of race. You feel much better about the world once you work in accord with how your body is coordinated.

Whatever you do—be You!

As you read those words, do you smile and acknowledge the wisdom of doing what you are here to do—following through now with what you are physically and mentally designed to do? If you never test our thoughts on yourself, this would be a good time to decide why you resist and do not comply. When you know who you are and always aspire to be another, you learn a lot about your mind—even a bit about how you are designed to live now.

What if one you love hates something about you now? Are you aware you decided to ignore that the other is not totally in love with you, thus forgiving anything that is not perfect as far as he sees. You may realize that it need not stay that way. It may be a habit such as ignoring others, or not taking into consideration how others perceive you to be, or maybe something you eat or do not like. Change whatever, but never change your body to suit another human! Be you and take the first step in self-acceptance by acknowledging others have bodies better or worse than yours—and it is of no consequence if their bad habits are disliked by others, too.

To favor others' appearance over your body type is natural and common among the small of mind. However, as you develop physically and your body changes, hopefully your mind compensates for whatever your adolescent personality once sought as ideal, rather than what you God gave you. You may not want to be bald or tall or without anyone saying you are beautiful or handsome now, but better that than being told you are ignorant, unfeeling, and evil.

If all you seek is to camouflage or change the physical manifestation of your self-hatred, you cannot do anything to rid yourself of the mindset that determined you were inadequate. You can change your attitude and work, but not your brain, so do what you can and accept what you cannot change.

Who would you favor if told you were like a parent? Would you claim to be the one of the same sex or the other? Psychologists today say you must favor the parent of the same sex and accept that you have similar mindset and flaws. Do you agree or fight such designations in order to downgrade all who practice psychology, or because it does not agree with what you perceive to be you now?

Who you are psychologically and physically is not what others usually recognize when studying you and what you do. If you change perceptions, you become them. Thus you merely disguised your life and changed over time into another. That is why we succeed now!

We describe a life in which bliss is something you can easily acquire and live with. However, you want bliss without perspiring or changing anything about your life. Try doing things our way for a while, see what happens.

Within a week of having read this line you will be different in various ways—yet not changed a lot. Why would you change if you did not get the message or do not wish to change? It may force you to deny it, thus become cemented in a lie or belief you did not accept until now.

You want to be different from everyone else. So you change and become the same as everyone else! Accept it and get on with being you, thus attaining the unique state of being unlike everyone else.

Whatever is to happen did and will and was, thus nothing you can do about it now? That is certainly a complicated way of stating you exist in many dimensions and see things differently in each of them, but to say you do not change would be a mistake. You change with every brainwave and every belief change you decide to make.

The way to change work now is to accept it as being easy. Accept that you make things more difficult than they are in order to expect exorbitant pay and extras in the way of benefits not deserved. You make work appear to be exceptional and difficult in order to deserve what you make in your state of mind. That having been said, you can work hard and deserve more by staying at home and assuming the full role of whatever you were to be when you came on board.

Who are you?

How many times have you asked that of another when you should have been answering it instead? You may ask your best friends to describe themselves and be shocked at what they see, but probably not. If you know them more than a few days this life, along the way you assimilated what they thought of themselves and have little to change now. Why then ask them to describe who they are? You may have changed and want them to ask about it. You may notice friends are no longer as close or into what you do as they once were, and you wish to know if they changed or you did. All it takes is a bit of interest to learn what is different, but for many it takes too long to determine they do not care enough to keep up with those they call friends.

What is a friend, if you never want to be close? A friend may never be heard or seen—even be in the same scene, but you know them. You know who will help you with your work and who would not. Do you favor those who help, even if you never help them? You bet, and you may even spend your life trying to find them. Why? Takers are always on the prowl, unwilling to stop and notice how few givers are available now to take any for granted or abuse.

If you never abuse anyone, will you be immune to it? Probably not. You may be okay, but then again you probably never feel it is real when others talk behind your back or call you names, because you do not hear it then. When you do, you may blame the one who reveals others are not true friends—not in love with you or hoping you succeed, too. Perhaps you cannot tell the difference between gold and brass, but you must learn who is a friend if you are to gain control of your life and live in bliss.

Take this to heart and never stop working on it all this life: You deserve someone who is like you! If you do not believe it, you will rue the day you did not accept it as a fact of life.

Why would you not want someone better than you? You would always be catering to them, learning from them, or taking abuse, in order to stay with them full-time. You know you have no intention of doing that, so begin trying to be as smart as you can be now and love others enough that they can depend on what you say.

Chapter Six

What you desire can determine how you will change the being you are or came here to be. Blame Mom, Dad, brother, or others, but you are who you are, and you change because you want what others are or have. Once you understand that, you can begin returning to the path you left to become someone other than who you are, or understand your whims and how they offend and demand more than you can ignore.

You have to ignore much when in a store that supplies all your needs in life, but not nearly as much as when surrounded by things that mean nothing to your eternal being. What do you do when you shop for things you require? Do you make a list and stick to it or listlessly pursue whatever comes close to what you think you need? The way you shop affects what you buy and how you live. You may not want to save or do things others deem wise, but with limited time, energy, and money, what else is there to do but use them wisely?

Once you decide life provides everything you require in the way of constant movement and interesting work, you begin to realize you need not do anything—or you can do whatever you like. How old are you when that thought makes sense? At age 10, are you able to outline your entire life and provide your mind with an adequate education that hopefully enables you to do necessary work or, deceived by your mind, will you wait until 45 to decide you will live *your* life now? If you never before in this life decided to be whom you are and do what you like, decide now!

The essence of being you is not easy to describe, but you will figure it out when you lay down to die. You will not leave without figuring out how you were deceived by the mind into believing you would live for a long time and be loved by others, even if you never cared for them. If you are wise, decide now to understand how and why people love others and what makes you one they will want to be around or not.

Take the long path round the mountain and enjoy your time away from the crowds of life. Be yourself and let others realize you are not going to harm them, nor do you expect they are out to get you now. Be aware, but do not share your complaints, unless they relate to what others can appreciate. Be aware you perspire only when working hard—not because you tell many lies.

Who will identify you as never being honest? The one who cares that much resides within your house. If you lie a lot, you are never believed—and what you say is not taken seriously. That is your bonus in life. You go through life without anyone believing you or wanting to be you, thus a liar can make up things and believe them—accepting that others are wise not to follow these lines. That is not something the wise admire or desire, yet how many do not realize that is how they are described by the crowd around them now?

Lying to your mother and unaware she is onto you is a way of beating the system when young, but many continue to believe others never mind a lie or two as long as they normally act nice. Why would you accept such a premise? You would not, but never give it much thought, thus you feel a lack of bliss whenever permitted to get one over on the crowd or cheat a friend who has no reason to not love you until now.

Some say: *"Whatever is said in a crowd is not that hurtful."* We know it is dishonest to not have the courage to stand and speak of what is in your heart. From now on, imagine you are alone when shouting and no one hears a word you say—all they will hear is what you yell loud and clear. Can you do that and feel great about the impression you make? If so, move on friend, you are cleared to go!

There are times when a miracle occurs and you are unsure if you saw or heard whatever, but are clever enough not to dispute it or say you believe it. Why would you think it a miracle if it were not true? Are you in the habit of lying all the time? We want you to understand that lying to *you* is more than interesting to us. It is bad and will not help you ascend at the end!

You must be honest to rise in the world of commerce, or be discovered sooner than expected that you stupidly tried to fool those as dishonest as you wished to be. All who cheat gravitate toward the street. Dreams are cheap on the paved highway to no other destination than making much money.

When you figure out commerce is fun only if everyone gets the point of doing business as a group, you may be retired or unhappy you got fired. You may never be aware that to do business with a crowd you must get along with them--none can be too greedy or pushy to succeed. This takes time! Most who succeed within corporations were helped since birth to understand how companies work.

Corporations are dead—
And no one is aware of it!

Why would a good idea die? You begin doubting it is a good idea! You must believe in the good of others to work together on anything cooperatively for a common purpose. If you doubt others work hard, you idle and create a void. They then begin to wonder if you are ill or neglecting your duties. Once seen as a slacker or dreamer, you are always doubted, and then rooted out by the group.

Why are no corporations founded on economy now—helping a nation become greater than it was? Because you doubt—disbelieve others could conceive of such great things. You do not want to trust others, thus you doubt all!

Once doubt moves in, confidence wanes. You start refraining from speaking openly. You lie to save time, or so you say. You tell exaggerated tales about what another does, caring not if it rips apart their heart. This is the trail of tears you carry with you, causing serious dismay when you arrive on the other side of this life. Do not do that!

Think about what you reveal and why you want to talk about what others hide. It could be you one day! You, would feel you were not given a fair trial, too.

Those who lie say they never do and do not like liars. Why? Being a liar does not make you immune to what others think of you. In fact, the bigger the lie, the more often it is based on a belief that truth would not be impressive enough to sway others to think highly of them.

Whatever you see and believe is not always believed, so make sure someone understands and likes you now. Why would we propose you build bridges to others and cater to their whims in order to be respected and loved? It is how you live. You never tried any other way to get beyond who you are now, so we propose you stay as is today. You can change when you rearrange your molecules and have another go at being human or passing into the ether and becoming another.

If you are seriously interested in beating your competition without losing sight of what you want in life, all is fun and games. If you decide to seriously compete with others, you begin to change within. Your mind unwinds and becomes asinine or juvenile—less than adult—equally as uncoordinated as most under age 9. Why slip back into the past?

Some have never been young! Too quickly they were allowed to act older than their age. You cannot allow it! If allowed, you will embarrass your parents at a time when they would like to retire and forget they ever knew you as a child.

Take care of how you behave and not talk about your neighbors. There is a difference between being loved and being hated, and you cannot be both. You cannot be hated if all you do is be you and intentionally harm no one else, even if inclined to make haste and tread on the feelings of family and loved ones in order to impress others. The difference between the two extremes is small, but most believe they are leagues apart now. When you intend to destroy another's life, take care not to slip into the abyss—thinking you can back out without leaving traces of your past. It will not work out!

Today we found several ways to block your path and described them as if for a laugh or on a dare, because we want you to compare how you live now to how you will live in the future *you*—if you decide to ascend and live in bliss. You take it from here, but whatever you do, you choose and become what you believe you will be.

We do not share in your daring feats. However, we know you all care and wish to be honest, loved, and respected by others. The wonder is that you cannot figure out how to accomplish it easily now!

Chapter Seven

If you are ready to move into a new *you*—one who is attractive and happy, sign up for a class on how to be you now. Read a book until you know what to do, perhaps decide to enter the spiritual path of doing business and asking another to look into the future and tell you what to do now. No matter what you try, there is a time when you must sit within You and decide what *you* want to do. All other pursuits are merely a way to shift blame in the event it becomes difficult to begin or start over being all you ever wanted to be now.

Can you be you without thinking on it?

Yes, and it is not any easier than analyzing your entire life and erasing pages—trying to eliminate strife from a stormy marriage or raising a child who no longer respects his parents. To enter the hallowed halls of your spiritual world and come out all right on the other side, provided with enough insights to live a more nearly perfect life, you have to be disciplined and eager to work hard. Life is not without work, but most prefer to do what comes easily rather than what they would do if wise, considering their assets and the need to move quickly.

What if you decide to take the easy route? Who would criticize you for taking the quick way to another life, or doing what you like and neglecting everyone and everything you do not want or like? You are not allowed to skip ahead!

It is written in the clouds that you are not alone or without something to own as you now become this personality. When you meet honest folks, or talk to those who are and have been wise for quite some time, never forget: *You must be you*. However, you can cry and weep—claiming you were cheated, not given what others needed to get ahead, feel neglected, and so on. We do not weep or wail and we suspect you feel no empathy from others, too, when you prevail upon those who are much deeper than you seem to be to help you feel better.

What if you decide to meditate an hour a day and upon trying it out, you discover it takes a lot of time? Hello!! Are you awake or asleep—unable to understand living means you thrive when you can do what you want and can succeed at what others claim is difficult or impossible? That should be all the incentive most need to meditate for several hours at a time—and do it more than once a month.

What if no one knows you meditate and cannot appreciate it? That is when you make progress being yourself! You are doing what you want—and doing it for no better reason than it helps you see inside the confusing life you lead. It helps you become more appreciative of everyone.

Who would ask you to never seek God or find another to love? If you ever find such a person in your crowd, walk away and never look back. Honestly, who is going to project such a black cloud on a crowd and not be rooted out and expelled to find another place to practice their angry, ignorant, and unlovable crafts now? Take time to be you and realize your view of life is not shared by others—because you are unique!

Once you feel you are unique and not a freak, you can sing and think about anyone you love without worrying if others might dislike it. You begin living within your income and seeing others as friends, instead of immediately deciding they must be enemies. You are now aware paranoia exists when someone is unhappy with whom he or she may be. You know they never stop to think about what they contribute to their belief they are not living as well as many others—or they deserve to be upset due to how they live their lives.

Whatever you do or say reaps something later. It may not be noticed until the crops are counted and you find yourself starving with no one wanting you around them then. You have to grow your community now to lean on later when you may not be as easy to love and support as you believe yourself to be now. If your work is not good enough, take it home and do it over. Do not sabotage others so you appear to be working to the same degree as they are.

All we can add is: *Be yourself and make this a happy day for others! Sooner—rather than later, you will experience bliss and surround yourself with it then.*

Whatever you decide is wise may or may not be, according to others, but you decided! It is what you believe and not to be divided or changed without careful thought as to how it might affect others who believe as you do now. If you thrive in a new place and climate, it may not be great for everyone else you like, but it is not your decision to make.

It is never your decision what another adult might do or not. However, you will be held accountable for harming a child related to you or bred in your bed and given life support now. You have no business having relationships not respected enough to give life and love to what might come of its love or simulation of it.

To love others is not enough…

You must love what comes to you as you work—and how you feel now. You are who you are, based on what you say and how others believe you to be, but mostly it is what you did that creates the foundation for your bliss now. Believe you are loved and always did well by others, you probably sleep well and enjoy life. To be able to share your life with others and enjoy their respect is, however, as close as you get to feeling happy now.

Bliss is not what you get from being yourself, but close enough that you sense what it is and can emulate it to be filled with it now. Try to be yourself and you will not fit in with your crowd. Instead, live as you are and everyone can judge if you fit in with what they are now and wish to continue to be in years to come.

All is stagnant now, but it will start moving in another direction within a short time of you being you and noticing how many others enjoy life, too. Whoever says you cannot be you and enjoy life is wrong and cannot be considered a strong supporter of *The Lord*. All who promise that you will be saved on the final day have no way of knowing if they are saved—let alone you or anyone else.

Try to stay away from crowds when praying. You can be more easily swayed then into behaving in ways not you—that make you feel unrelated to what is happening in your life. Instead, pray alone and let God enter your thoughts and overcome whatever upset you enough to seek help then.

All devoted to others will discover they built a life around serving man rather than God, and are no better off or further ahead than the man or woman who does a good job, works hard, and is kind. Daily you have opportunities to help another and you either shun these things or seek them out, but it is what you think and believe that determines whether you serve God or not. To serve man in order to help others contribute to those starving is an honorable job. Those who do it well will always be guided to a better life when that work is over. Those who cheat or use what is given by another to help others will be cheated and regret it by the time they reach the end of this life.

Nothing said now is new to most of you, but for anyone who never thought about such work and how to live a life that pays you back in ways you can understand—you are now in awe! Awe is a way of helping you gain perspective and realize you are not the only one who knows God or always works hard. In the days ahead, you may start thinking that way, but you are never alone—without others to support your work if you serve what you believe is the means and ends of your inner life, as well as with humankind and in God's way.

All believe what they see

Some immediately say they do not agree and precisely outline what they believe and how it does not agree with whatever is said or in print. They are ignored more and more. Why? The one making the statement is over it, has moved away, and is talking about something else now. Thus to argue about what was said in the past is a waste of breath. Instead, when you first hear it take time to raise your objection—rather than wait, hoping to find others to back you and deny it if you are seen as an enemy.

Who would you rather be in a movie: the hero, the martyr, the enemy of man? You always decide what road you will walk this life. For most it is much harder to steer a course toward what is condemned by God and man, so why not take the easy route and be nice and kind, and loving toward others?

Chapter Eight

Time will not give you what you want. If you ignore time more than ever before, you must figure it out and define what it is. We can help you with it now!

We know you made an effort to read about time and assimilate our lines on it, but some never get it! How can you define a life if you cannot figure out time? How do you know if you can survive to live another life if you believe this is all there is? Everything is about time now!

If you take off a day from your usual trade, you may be able to behave in a way completely different from whatever you normally do, but probably not. Why? Habit! If you form a way of being you today and keep at it for three months or more, forget about adapting quickly to something in conflict with it. You cannot. You try for a while, then give up and do not do it again unless you are afraid, in love, or totally aware of what you are doing every moment of this life.

Can you be so aware of time that you do nothing with it? We have prepared several ways to identify *you* in another dimension, but most cannot see it now. Why? You cannot think for yourself.

You read what others say about movies, rather than checking out who acts in it, wrote it, and how long it runs. If that provides no clue, then perhaps it is up to you to decide if you want to view it or not. Once you find a script good enough to follow and view, why change your way of looking for movies after that? You decide what happens, even if you do not see it now.

If you could be anyone,
Who would you be?

We want you to realize *you* would not change even if you had to become like another you want to be. You would choose only good things—or perversely, the difficult things, but not everything—not the boring, tedious, unlovely things the other does. You want to be someone else without taking time to develop a life that fits those requirements. Once you decide to become someone other than who you are now, what happens? Knowing it can be done, you would work very hard to change.

Let us applaud anyone reading that last line who decides to become a better person than you are now. Let our applause follow you all your days. May you feel the hand of God on your back even now—helping you stand taller, straighter, and breathing more deeply. Actually, that is all it takes to change the way you feel today and how others see you. It really is that easy!

If evil, you do deceitful things, believing it to be great fun. You are seen by others as someone they cannot trust. That lack of trust builds until one day you are cast out or put down and cannot have fun with anyone you once believed thought as you all had agreed to believe.

Can you follow the adolescent way of believing everyone wants to put down others and enjoys it? Think again about your mind and where you based your everyday behaviors. If they are less than great, think about how you behaved at age 8. If you were smarter and better behaved at 8 than you are today, you are in trouble!

If it takes time to figure out why you can rise to the top of your crowd without putting anyone else down, you probably cannot do it. Why? That type of mind does not rise.

The calculating mind is never content to let others do what they want, like, or do well. Calculators want to excel, but not let others know them well. If you are one who adds and divides crowds, you cannot star. It is those who multiply their talents—accepting that others want to be stars as well, who take the crowd by chance and land on top. It is never that grand a challenge to be a star when everyone is content with garbage; but when you decide you are better than you are, you may never again rest for a moment on this star.

All of this is about bliss,
But not all there is to it!

You must know who you are and why you want so much now—plus everything you stick in a jar or publish in articles, although at the end of the day it is never that way. You are who you are! So love you enough to stick with it and define this life well or change and improve what you thought you were. Change will not give you peace of mind, but sticking to the same old thing is not perceived as bliss, either.

What bliss is this when you cannot find peace of mind, and wherever you go others tell you what they know, want, or desire? You have your way of being happy or are trying to figure it out—which gives you a bit of bliss and helps you decide what it is, but you still have to attain bliss to know it!

When you think about your partner this life—everyone dreams of falling in love with someone and being accepted for who they are, along with all their faults. You, too, expect the other to be perfect and do whatever you want. Can you now define love based on those kinds of expectations? Once you figure out who you like, you have to decide why you cannot decide what is wise. It is easier to work that way than figure out life from back-to-front, rather than the other way around.

Who would you be if you married at a different time? Who would you be now, if you had not married one you came to hate or one you love to this day? When you place romance above common sense, all things are seen in this light.

You may not believe you are romantic, but if your society dreams of being molested and bedded against their wishes, permitting it to be acted out on stage and screen, you probably believe it now. That is how you can tell if you are walking, thinking, and believing wisely or not. Do you ever want to lose your virginity and not have anything make sense when you think of it again? You may, yet this may never be your choice.

All who take upon themselves activities that force others to unwillingly do things are not going to ascend at the end. They will be humbled by others and made to return and do it over again. Yes, that sounds silly to some, but everyone else gets it now!

Try to stay in your lifelines and not take over others' lives by becoming overbearing and terrible to live with. Do that and you shall be popular the rest of your life here. Why do you want to be loved by those you will never talk to, meet, or know more than superficially? If you are rootless and want to fly without developing wings of any kind, you crave it.

Flattery that comes with notoriety is matched by the downside of life. Be sure you want that kind of fame! Be aware many will hate you for it—and if done for money, it is not much fun.

All the work you do now is for *you*! Whatever you believe is what you conceive—not what we teach. You may not understand why we arranged this page or book this way, but by the time you read to its conclusion you will know what we mean and believe what you conceive as being helpful now.

Chapter Nine

Plan on living a full life! Do not settle for being upset and bored by others. You have legs enough to take you out of such places, and you can talk well enough to mingle with those who will stimulate your mind—perhaps bother you enough that you change a few things and think something new, too. To sit without thinking is not meditation, but you do not think when you meditate. Does that help you now?

Whatever you do and wherever you are is immaterial. Yes, it is not *you* who is there, but you in flesh and blood sit, dream, scheme, or do less. You are the sum of all work you do and all the things you learned about this life and what you came here to do now, but still not *you*. All is a mere instance or wisp of what makes up the entire being known to us and others as You.

What can you do to impress others and keep them from bothering you so much you forget who You is? You become solid, round, bounce, and do not frown. You figure out why you are here, why you are happy or not, and you do something to make it happen your way every day. You can do that!

When you think of round, solid, fat or thin, you think in dimensions, which is not the proper way to understand the shape you are in today. Whatever you see or believe you to be is not what others see. Yes, you could have a few things sag, droop, or be much too big, but it is your spirit that impresses others—not what you say today.

Working for yourself is not hard, some say, because they believe you will not have to work as hard, do as much, and so on. How stupid is the one who believes that to make a lot of money you need only be yourself and others will give all they have so you will be happy. You are now confronted with two dimensional types of ideas—with room for only one to stay longer than this present moment.

Which type did you choose? Do you know why? Quickly run through your thoughts and think about something totally different now.

Did you do it or not or only pause when asked if you changed your thoughts, because that is what we mean by *quickly*. If you take a minute to sit, change direction, think of something else, in that time you could be run over by a truck or stuck in the mud up to your axel. When you must— quickly change gears and move. Do not accept the belief that you cannot quickly do something new, too.

Once you begin to move faster than you did, you may find you cannot as easily remember what you did when living at a slower pace. Is that too difficult a concept for you to follow? If so, you are not changing, probably feel the same as when you picked up this book and started reading what we relate about your way of living today.

When you believe you can immediately change, think of someone you once loved, then mentally drop that person to a level lower than it was. If you love others, you cannot always be with them and do what they want, but you can pull them up and push them down, knowing they are always around you now. How? Do it again as we said—then repeat it. If you still cannot figure it out, let go. We will push you to another brink later—when you can elevate your mind over time and decide why some people are in your life and others are not.

Will we be with you when you cross over?

What a thought! Just when you believe you will learn to levitate, or at least how to see people in the future—or pass different tasks, you have to imagine what we will tell you and how much information you can use before You passes judgment on what you are doing now. Today, *'let go and let God'* is a phrase that means nothing. It does not imply anything wise—or within the realm of what you can expect, but it does sound wise. Does it not?

Who would let go of reality and take for granted everything would be supplied by a supreme being? Aaahh, you mention Ruth Lee. We agree she does live without visible strings of support attached to what she does, yet her humility and humanity is not without worry and sometimes concern whether she is doing enough or not—or whatever. She is human like you and not without fear her work will not help her or anyone else, but she continues to do work that makes sense to her. You need to feel that way today!

As you move into the new you and drop much that once bothered you, think about what you are doing here for others—without fussing about what they do for you in return. If you do nothing—or so little you resemble a baby everyone caters to, you will feel sluggish and sick—probably stuck in another life like this. If so, you do not want to change or you would!

Daily pains and worries come with this territory on earth. It does not mean you will die or be without money all your life. It merely explains what happens when you do not work hard at being absorbed in what you do, and happy to be you.

When the mind has nothing to do, it invents much. When your body is tired, the mind may ignore it and not let you rest—which is truly a mess, not something you should let happen. You must rule the mind and be you in Spirit long enough to keep your body happy.

When your body moans or groans, think about how little time you spend on it. When your mind is weepy, surly, upset without reason—imagine your body is getting too much attention and your mind is unhappy about it. To beat the heat or get warm when freezing to death, merely think and you can make the mind and body coordinate warming or cooling enough to stay alive. The mind can help the body adjust, but often is too demanding to be trusted to monitor your life here.

In a single day the mind and body coordinate in much the same way as they do all your life. You may not believe it now, but watch and see what we mean. Once again, give the body what it needs. Feed it when necessary and give it plenty that is pure to drink or can be easily purified, and you will run as if a gazelle until you are age 80 or more.

However, criticize and whine, saying your body is ugly and you want another's, and so on, expect the body to breakdown about 90 days from that whine.

You need to see how your thoughts affect your body to imagine how the mind affects your Spirit over time. You have to believe, or you will not feel like you belong in this life. Those who complain about not believing in God, and so on, are not merely whining about life and not getting what they need, but suggesting they do not believe in you, either. To not believe in God is a statement that you are unhappy being here now.

All who say they deserve a better life can earn one, but most are doing better than they deserve. You may not want to work, but then again, what on earth would you do here if not follow patterns established by your previous lives? You decide, but you will not be here longer than you need to be and longer than required to help you find your way back.

A path is suggested as a metaphor for solving the problems of this life. If you are unhappy, feeling lost, find your path. All are happy when you no longer bother their minds. You then find a way to move out and do something new, leaving your path behind. This time remember what you did and the steps required to get back to your path. You are then wise and realize you need never be angry or upset with anyone again.

It is the one who is lost who curses *The Lord* or others for being bored, out of control, or having nothing to show for all the time spent here and now. You cannot separate the idea from the mind, nor can you decide why another likes or does not like another. All you know is what you know you know—and probably not that much!

Today, as of now, take time to stop and think not! Stop and solve no problems or look at others, hoping they will help you. Instead, create a plan on paper and set it aside for ten days, then see what it says.

Chapter Ten

Critically analyze why you believe in others—or believe they have more than you, and you find your basic assumption is thus: *You must be perfect to feel right or be yourself.* You have come to accept that if you cannot be perfect, you will pull down or tear apart whoever is perfect in your mind. You cannot stand competition of any kind, but say your society thrives on it. Analyze why.

Whoever you may be today, or whatever you say you are, is not exactly a lie, but everything changes so rapidly under age 35 that you cannot say for sure if you will be a person of integrity until you reach 50 years. Why is that? How did it come to the point where you cannot decide if you are working hard enough to earn your living or not, or if you should change your career to make more money? What enables you to thrive—then drives you to distraction, removing what made you proud to be whoever you are? Why did you change, and when did it become an ever-growing factor in your life?

Once or twice a life it is necessary to align with your mind and complete a few inventories to determine if what you believe yourself to be matches what you do and how you react instinctively. You may want to inventory your matches over and over again to prove to yourself you are good, but what worth is it if you never change—merely rearrange what needs improved or removed? Take time to survive and you may live a long life, but let things accumulate because you want to believe you are healthy, attractive, and better than average, and you could end up dead long before planned.

Today is not the day you die. You may believe if dead on Monday and buried on Wednesday that all is fine, but that is not what happens. From the time you realize people die, you start thinking of living to an old age. You begin to whine and dream you will live to be wise, attractive—and age without anyone guessing you are. How naïve and how idiotic to believe you do not show your age at all!

When age 10 or 12, you begin thinking about what you have to take into account, but may never feel you are undergoing the signs of youth ending and adulthood beginning. You may want to play and not give away your age by sitting in a way that encourages others to want to be close to you, or you may not want to date others and see if they are good enough for those who guide you through life. You may not want to age, but the body has its way and you become an adult. You must believe it, or look silly to everyone else.

Once an adult, if you live a good life, you will reach a stage where you age little. You stay about the same until you decline and begin looking as if you may one day die. You display signs of age early in life if you do not eat correctly or take too much poison into your skin, but otherwise you live and look to be an adult—which is all others care about. However, when you believe you look younger than you are—and others believe you to be younger, you begin to think you are invincible and will never get sick, or eat too much for your skin, or enter a time when you decline. You start believing you can fool the eye, thus you will never die. It is all a lie!

Whatever is neglected tends to stick to the place you stuck it. If you eat nothing but fat and can digest it fast and easily, perhaps you can eat fat, but probably not. Why? Fat will not feed and keep your cells developed enough to fight off whatever attacks the body over the course of your life. Exercise can help. It permits greater mobility if joints are stuck or you cannot get up without much help. However, too much, extreme exercise can ruin your chances of being attractive and active many years beyond what you live now.

Moderation is not all there is to being safe, secure, and happy, but it makes more sense than driving too fast, drinking too much, smoking whatever, and doing anything you like in order to prove you can. That is when you lose sight of possible death. Take time to enjoy and appreciate the work you do now. If you hate what you do well, rethink it and design a new line—or better yet, build a new life.

Do not feel you have to be whoever you originally thought you must be or had to be, if it does not help you achieve belief in you as a human being and a child of God. If you attain the mindset that you are boss and can do anything you choose to do, all is lost. It ends in what we call anarchy, if there is any way to define the decay of ego states into what would be best called a god-less state.

If this is not it, what is Bliss?

Bliss cannot be described with a few lines, even a few lives, but you get it and keep it or chase after it until it fits and you decide this is it! What if you chase bliss and never get it? That is not to be intuitively worked on here, but it can mean you are unwilling to be pleased. It happens! It can be you are too overcome with who you are or were to want to be different from this and feel bliss.

'Creatures of comfort' means what? If you were to describe your life and how you live, would you say you are happy now, or you gave up on happiness and are content being someone others look up to instead? If you believe others want to be you, you take comfort in that idea even though it is not based on reality. No one today is eager to give away the chance that they may one day be rich and famous. It is the American dream of winning the lottery that infects the entire human race today.

Who would you be if you could design your life to be anyone else? Whatever your model—that is how you see yourself or how you behave that suits you today. If you look closely at your life and say it is fine as is, you are either old or wise. You may not have many options, based on your class and lifestyle, but money will not change it. Before you leave this world, you need to be aware of that.

When you desire money to earn or deserve something as ethereal as love and respect, you have none—and need to learn to deserve it.

Once you deserve the love and envy of others, you generally are older than 11 or 12, but could be lost in adolescence until you lose the one who loved you as you were. It is quickly becoming an effort to act one's age and live without going into debt, because all are disabled by brains untrained to work and accept discipline, thus unable to move ahead over time.

Who would you be if age 11 or 12, and knowing all you know now could change your life? Would you work hard or fool others into believing you were older or more sophisticated and able to mingle in any crowd? Who would you be if you could change who you are and be the one you wanted to be when young? Of course, all of this is dreaming! It can get you into trouble, but not when very young and eager to be someone.

Once you age and progress into the adult you are to be, plan on enjoying it then—not putting off what you get for being fully grown. To stay in childhood long after your age gives you away as being quite old and unacceptable to the young as one of them, you need to retrieve what you think you needed then, but only if you never felt it and still want it. The wave of adolescence now sweeping your age is stagnating your creativity and causing many to raise up and want to riot when you all need quiet—and time to be yourself and enjoy life.

Why is your world crowded now?

You know it is because so many want a child, or are afraid not to be blessed with one, or are raped and unable to say no. Who would you blame if you did not speak to men about their lack of restraint and how they train their sons? You obviously go to the one who knows the son—the mother. You would train her to want a better life for her daughters, as well as her sons, and not let them get away with murder or taking whatever they want for gain or raping anyone.

If a mother cannot love others as much as she wants a son, that is where the blame lies. No one can afford a society in which men rule and do not care who they rape. It begins with a few dying and ends with the society dead.

Today, all we raised is a bit of work you must believe is not the way to achieve and maintain bliss. For some, you cannot believe you create havoc—the opposite of bliss. You wish to say it was your mother, father, teacher, or brother who caused it, but it is you who need to accept responsibility if your life is not residing in bliss.

We can and will bless you with enough thoughts to fill your life and give you much to like, but you have to be yourself and not injure others. Once that becomes part of you and you believe you live with the intent of hurting no one—especially your work on earth this life, you will begin to feel bliss, even when it does not exist.

The work of the mind is to build a belief system which can handle whatever it is trained and disciplined to do. That should frighten a few, but is not our intention now. We want you to realize your mind does a job, and its job is to follow through on what you want to do.

To decide you will marry and not get away with raping another is a command that will not be followed unless it is imprinted and mentioned more than twice before you reach the age when you can impregnate another of your race. If you do that, you will feel enough remorse to take responsibility for what you did. If you do not, you will live in guilt and never feel bliss this life!

Chapter Eleven

Peace and quiet help all align in time, but some are so adept they can attend a rock concert and not be bothered by yelling, screaming, and demented beings writhing around them then. Are you able to adapt and continue being yourself, regardless of who may be acting out fantasies or lying big time—trying to get you to join and thus critically harm your belief system or commit a crime? Whatever else you might believe now, you do not need more sedatives or more medicine to calm your mind. You need quiet!

If you feel lost, you need someone who can help you discover where you left your path. Whatever else might be happening around you now, *you* are still the only one who knows what you feel. You can and will want to share, but who will hear if all you see and associate with are drunk and disorderly or bored beyond endurance? When you decide to get drunk or take a drug in order to be someone else, does it help? If you believe it does, then you cannot understand what bliss is—which is sad and probably somewhat bitter to accept, but do it.

Once you accept you are different from what you wanted to be or expected you would be, think about it. Are you better than expected? If so, congratulate yourself and imagine you are dead and everyone is saying how wonderful you were and how sad they are to be left with only memories of the great times they had with you now. If you are worse than you ever expected to be, then you need to protect what you believe you should be and start immediately to seek a way to gain that perspective today.

Whatever else you may be to others, you must be yourself so they can judge whether or not they like who you really are. By being you and attempting to communicate what you believe through everything you do and say, you begin to sense within if you are off-track or being true to the bigger You (that which is your Higher Being), and not another attempt at being here, there, and gone whenever. Being true to you is not always easy, but it pays to make the attempt. You will one day awaken to see you laying *'down there'* while others talk about you—seeing them sad, but happy to have known you and talked with you often.

If you stopped being yourself now, any day is the time to begin again. If you believe and conceive you are needed, you may not want to start a revolution or make others look to you when confused, but you will be a beacon to everyone who needs you! You are here for a reason that may not be revealed so far, but is obvious to those who guide and always work with you.

In the world above and around you are those who are not human beings—but not extraterrestrial, either. You are all here, but you are not now all clear to each other. It is not that you overcrowd others or they take over your space, but at times you may sense you are surrounded, yet you cannot see anyone or believe another is living with you. That is why you continue to believe you succeed and become someone unlike everyone else—but are never quite sure. Does that make you pure energy?

You are pure energy! What you do to keep your light bright depends upon what you were taught this life. If your light is dim, work hard and develop your life now, and begin to see things others never saw.

Who would you be if not you?

Whomever or whatever you are going to be! You are clever enough to realize it is always better to be an original than copy and become an imitation of another. You are unique!

You may be unhappy now or able to smile, but whatever—be you based on how you feel now and what you see around you. Keep in mind that today is primarily based on how you acted upon such things in the past. If you should decide to change how you behave, it takes three or more months and cannot be condensed much.

When a woman decides to become a man, unable to understand why she was made as is, men begin to wonder about it, too. Would they want to be a woman, or could a woman ever become someone like them? Why would a woman trade in all she has to be a man? That is not fascinating, but it is strange, because each sex has its own range. If you are extremely feminine, ultra-refined, gratified by flirting all day—never worrying about what you say, you would not want to give up such power to become a man, although many say you are not womanly then.

Today, and every day, you behave according to what is imprinted on the brain and engrained in your DNA. You can trivialize your ways and say you can change and become anyone you wish to be, but it remains engrained. If you do not train your mind to unwind, then retrain and learn new ways now, you will revert to the way you were born, bred, and raised. All that is you will want to return, so you have to keep at it. Some revert to how they acted when babies to train others to want them full-time; however, adults generally ignore such people and seek out those who are equal.

Having claimed you can change whenever you decide you need to, you may change, but probably not. Why? The claim is made, but no change planned. To change you must move to do anything new. Once you move and do it how you think is correct, improve the time it takes to assume that position in life, and keep at it until you think as you once hoped you would. There is no other way to describe it now—and it does take months.

When you decide your chances of surviving a holocaust of the type many believe happened in the past is low, you treat others better or are made to see how it feels at some point in your world. You must realize being evil or taking over and guiding another is not something you want to do, unless prepared for the consequences of what you created or developed that way. All comes back! You can believe it to be *karma* or a reaction, but you will see what we mean when you ascend and move beyond this time.

The end of a life is not like the life you led on this side, but then again—nothing is. All returns to the world around you then, thus you sense how much you never noticed—are totally ignorant of now, but it does not bother you. You will sense you must do what is required to live a better life or create a better place, but you cannot change whatever you did in this time.

This is the only time you live as is, and the only time you can create a perfect image of the one you wanted to be. That is not to say you perfect the body or mind, rather what you do together to create a more perfect and marvel-filled life that you can build upon when you fly.

Chapter Twelve

Outside of what you can see and what you believe, your world awaits you. Can it be you cannot open your mind to all your world offers you and others now? Yes, if you are honest and true to your belief system, you know you cannot possibly see all that is there for you as a human being.

Imagine all that awaits you when you cross over into another kind of planet, plane, or life on another side of this one. Take your time and pick one single thread of the millions that make up your life in this time and think about it for an hour. You cannot separate it right away—might be impossible within an hour if your work is so entangled you feel strangled by what you want to be as opposed to what you know you are. Take time now to untangle one strand and watch it multiply and grow.

When you can schedule your day in such a way as to plan for you and others to have a great experience filled with love at least once in your lives together, you become aware that planning is more about awareness and less about preparedness. You can plan and have nothing happen, yet learn a lot, or you can walk through a parade without once feeling you were stopped one moment by anyone else. It takes pacing, understanding, and the ability to mingle without feeling alone or merely single.

The single strand will not build up nor take down others. Once united with the entire fabric of your being, plus who you will be based on how you proceed, you can beat anything. You can stop whatever you asked to start or gave a nod to and never cared if it happened or not.

You have time now to disappear and come back into you and no one notice you were gone. You are not disappearing so much as finally making an appearance this life. Be your own guide twice—feel how great it is to connect with those who work from within your inner life guiding you to be here when you are required and elsewhere when you are tired.

Dreams are not exactly scenes you think about or are into now, but they can mix all you have been through to create a collage of about one hundred thoughts or more, ready for you to design a whole new life based upon what you want to know more about now. How can you dream and come back immediately to what you are? You do it all the time! For example, as you sit beside a friend who takes charge on a drive, your mind is free to wander and do whatever it wants. That is a dream state you create and let grow until you must talk or create the impression you are a good companion.

When you feel down on you or others, think again and believe they will win. Once you think you are lost or about to cash out without having gained anything, mentally count how many others you helped by being there and showing them they are better off not following what you did. You have talents to survive and win this life. Never fear you have not helped others because you lived a life that was less than great. People learn from everyone, but you are not always a student now.

Whatever comes through to you at night or in a dream may not be what you find outside your life, but it is yours. No one else will enter your work and take you out of a dream and introduce you to a terrible scene. You do that!

Only you need be afraid of what you see in a dream. Whatever you love to view usually returns over-and-over again time-after-time, so why not life-upon-life? It is your decision, but we would opt for the good life and happy thoughts, instead of morbid, weird, and frankly ugly things too many view now.

When you get lost in thought and upon coming back to yourself find music playing, what kind of music induces you to dream big? If it helps you erase stress and forgetfulness, play it now! Be aware that the elements of air and hair in your ears cannot live long and happy lives if you blast them with sound, especially whatever does not make you feel better about life.

To work on agitating another or stirring up many others is a plan for those intent upon living here again and coming back to what they do now. It is not a way to ascend! If you intend to harm anyone, you may as well forget about bliss and all it is! Once you make another suffer, you will never feel bliss. Instead, you will feel the need to explain or desire to blame another. It is guilt that remains with you until *you* fulfill another life like this one and relive it twice.

To quit, rather than work hard on anything, produces little in life, but it may benefit you and others. As we said, you are the teacher of many others. They can learn by observing your manner of work. If they like what you do, and you do it very well, they may excel by watching you and working beside you. However, most think if you do it as well as anyone ever did that they can do it better than you. Laugh and let them try!

Bellowing and crying, expecting others to buy whatever you sell is not a way to live a long and pleasant life. If it does not work the way you said it might, you will hear them yell at you. You will have to refund money once spent on something else, because you lied to get them to buy. To sell others well: First, design a great line, then be sure you do not lie. You have to pay for lies that sell well. If you lie, you may be unable to get better and earn enough from what you know well.

Take *your* work home and at night you will do great, but take the work of many others back to your nest and you end up hating one or the other. Feel blessed! Having said that, do what you can when you are paid to do it—then rest.

To work full-time and take on more hours to inspire others never works out well. Do what you can, then rest at home and come back refreshed, feeling blessed. Your work then goes on and on to reach those who recognize good work.

Working on several things is as if doing one project is a waste of time and money, as well as energy. One good job is worth more than ten half-done jobs or incomplete products not ready to release or sell well. Too many who want to impress others that they work hard end up tired, thus fit to be fired. Why risk your career trying to be the one to beat when it comes to working many hours? Instead, be the one who works hard and gets things done.

Those who play and pretend to know what everyone should do are frauds and will not do well in another line. You have only one single line you can excel in and do very well, but you can stretch and make it expand and appear to be an entire army of talents, if you work hard. When everything is said and done, you are one person who came to Earth to do one thing—and that is what you do now!

Chapter Thirteen

Instead of sitting about doing little to help yourself develop, why not set up a schedule that outlines your best attributes, talents, and what you can give up to develop them? Once you start thinking you can win, and see it as worthy of your life, once again you will feel wonderful and happy within. Once the process starts, it usually carries you upward into a better life than this. If not, what have you got to lose by trying?

When you decide you cannot win anything—or you can stop and do nothing, you are ready to die. Quitting is how you try it out. You give up, then decide to live or let life go. We would not decide such a fate for ourselves, but you have the capacity to do so now.

Whenever ready to move and do something new, do you worry you will have to work hard? If so, you are lazy and need to advise your mind that you cannot be lazy and land on top of the highest plateau you can achieve this life. You have to move and improve your life, because no one else will do it for you. Does that make you depressed or sad? If so, you are lazy and need to realize it now.

The sad part about being a success is you have to work and keep at your task—and cannot give up. Once you say you are tired or unwilling to work hard pursuing it, you lose. The decision was not the last idea or thought that came down from *you*, but a series of decisions you created one-day-at-a-time without thinking through any of them. Decide, then conclude you can be anyone you choose if you can develop work and have enough talent.

Once you try hard several times and it never comes to anything, you can walk away and admit you could not do it; but it is not quite as easy as that, because the talented will continue to work and develop and do whatever it takes if they have faith. Faith makes the difference in whether or not you get it!

When you are indifferent to what others expect or want, you become detached and possibly too remote to be in contact with others then. However, if you were off-track doing something you regret or will not want others to know about, you have to leave the crowd and get busy doing something else now. It is impossible to become someone new or different, if you always associate with the same people who knew you as you were.

To change sounds difficult—but is not!

Whenever you need to be a different person, because you are miserable as you are or you have no one who appreciates what you can do, you must change. You can and will change easily if you can see what hinders your progress; however, many never see what others perceive to be their weakness. You may not want to stop, or you developed a habit that has taken over your heart or mind, but you can change. You can become stronger for having developed a better mindset than what you had.

To develop a better life takes a plan and the determination to stick to it until you can move more quickly and do work that makes you feel better about you now. If you feel great and appreciate what you can create, others will, too. Yes, it does work like that! We could explain it, but why take up your day doing it now? Instead, you can test it and do what you love.

Sitting in a room full of people doomed to a life of boring detail, while you eagerly do something new, will not hold you back. Move and leave them quickly! You know you can return and find them basically the same, so feel no risk leaving home or doing something new if the work is boring and routine. By leaving, you set in motion grieving among those you left, and they may never let you return. You caused them to rethink their day, maybe why they do whatever for life, thus they are unhappy to think about you or welcome you back.

Take time to decide why you have to leave a crowd—know why, before you go. Once outside and in another way of life, never think they caused you to move or change. Remember God had a hand in changing your mind. You will better understand how Spirit moves you now, helping you create a new way of being okay.

If you feel great—and you must feel good now or change until you do, we welcome you into a new group who always open wide, smile, and say you are wise. That group exists! You only need move a bit and change your view of what others believe. Once you believe differently or become slightly open to what others do or share, you begin to sense love is all there is and bliss is what you feel when you achieve it, share it, and are loved.

All you are and have been can change in a flash, but for most it is a long, arduous task to change if enslaved by drugs or a vice now. You do not realize when first experimenting that it may end up being all you can do for the rest of your time here. Try to limit experiments to what you *know* will not take over and ruin a mind or create a way of life that is demeaning, nasty, and will take away your pride.

Pride cannot always keep you straight, but it tries. If you are unhappy or feel wild, you often get into trouble you later say made you crazy, sad, or mad—instead of revealing you gave up and thought it did not matter. When you get too upset, angry, or wild, others back away and many never come back. Do you want to lose friends and family in order to keep moving up, or do you wish to take them along for the ride? Think about it, then plan how you will do it now.

Whatever you do, think it over
Before you change!

Once you decide you need to do something new—do it! How easy is that? Not easy at all, if you do it right and think enough about your life. You cannot turn over the details of your life to another and expect to end up happy and filled with pride. By letting someone else take over the details, you end up enslaved—needing another to work hard keeping you as you were or as you believe you should be. Instead, do whatever you need and be free!

In the middle of every day is a time when you get tired and need to stop, feed the body, and sort out what the mind is stuck on then. Once you do that, you can move more quickly and succeed without bickering and talking behind another's back. We know how easy it is to get upset when you are depleted of what you need, so never again forget your Spirit requires time alone and the ability to help you confess what you know about this time, your life, and those who help you through it.

We know you can talk to God and have conversations without interruption, but apparently there are some who do not get this simple lesson even now. Why not accept the whisper or guidance you get from the middle of your middle mind? You have a lot you can rely on without having to ask another what time it is or why you should change your life, but many rely on someone else to sort out what they alone know is bothering them. Try to do your own therapy. If you resist telling the truth, it will be difficult; but once you admit to faults—and change what is not working well, you can do it all.

It takes little effort to neglect a child and let it grow wild, but to get that child back into circulation, behaving well, may take the rest of your life. If you add it up, take time now to discipline and train the child to be the kind of adult you can admire—and live to appreciate the results. If you do not train the child? Then worry you will be the one who must answer for problems you caused.

Those who work hard and think others need not are few—and far from equal. You are never given credit for work you say you can do but never develop. You can teach another to do what you do not like to do, but why? What about your current work is boring or makes you forget why you do it? If you know, change it immediately so you can enjoy life.

Work and other people are the theme of this chapter—with other people in the lead, as well as your habits that control how you proceed.

If you were given nothing at birth but a kiss and a burp, you live in a time when constantly asked if you want another kind of burden, or a better way to behave or feel great. You do not have the discipline to take on more pain.

Be able to say 'No' or die trying. Do not give up your life to those who want to own you and what you do. Try instead to be *you* and understand what makes you happy or sad. Once you know *you* well, others no longer control your life.

Who you are and how much you work are part of your life and the story you tell. Remember to be honest and not have to do this life over to provide proof you are. All you do and all you are comes to you once you accept your role. Do not believe you came here to be someone who looks like you or acts as you do, instead assume you alone know what you are here to be—then do it!

Today is not the only way to view your life, but it passes as okay to live that way. If you get to the pinnacle of your work and belief system, you will realize you always knew how to act and what to do, as well as who would never be of any help to you. It makes you sad only if you wait until the last day to realize that.

We are not here to belabor labor and how much it takes to do work that supports your life here, but we do know most of you do not believe it is necessary to take over and support your life any longer. Why? You have no one disciplining your mind or telling you that you know nothing about life. Universities are no longer training students to think and act intelligently!

You want what you see, and money achieves a dream that lasts about as long as opiates. In the end you have to return and see what you have—and alas, you may find you cannot do any task that benefits your well-developed appetite for fame and fortune. That is when you see how a child left to do nothing but what it wants lives a life of desperation, rather than having it made.

Today, try to be yourself. Only then learn to change and become another. You may be dissatisfied with how you live now or what you know, but continue to study, work, and earn another life. We accept all, but few want to follow the guidance of *their* work and inner life until they are wise.

Take your time, but be wise!

Do what you love, but work hard to make it as you wish it to be. Consider who does what and why, and you lose the thread of your life now. All are here for one reason and none can be left behind without seeing a difference in how your present life is woven on the other side.

Take time to help your fellow man! Do what you can to mend what is now tattered and torn, aware you may have to slip away and never come back. If that makes you sad, immediately do something about it. Bliss is not being alone on an isolated plain or island in the sky, but having people you love, love you back. Once you care, you will be aware of it.

This is the end of a long list that entails taking time to change your life plan and be you. It is not complete until you realize why it is needed. You are who you are, adjusting to become someone else will take *you* back to another life or off-track.

Time without guidance or having God within your heart can cause you great pain. It can also help you become a leader able to save a country or tribe. Decide now who you are!

Chapter Fourteen

I*n the future* indicates imminent change. You will feel numb, dumb, discontent, or even wretched if whatever is not pursued and done within a reasonable amount of time. So do not talk about the future, unless you are describing a goal you are working toward now.

All who talk about what they intend to do are harming themselves if they do not intend to do it then. Why? It is launched in the mind as fact, and many lines of thoughts start running constantly until it is time for all to collide in a super-conductive way of being *you* that day. Having to accept what you get, you will burst if you did not design it correctly.

How to live in bliss and believe the future is full of it? See you as blissful now! See all you can be, then plan to follow-up on everything you believe you must do. Wait and see what comes to be before you do more.

Once you gain fame and fortune, you may believe you attained it through your state of mind, but you did not. The force was there and you tapped into it when you declared you could handle fame and wealth and not lose your head or heart, or end up sick. If you are now doing all you must do to stay on top of your intentions, you do not have to work as hard as those sitting and dreaming—hoping whatever will come to be.

To believe you can see things and they will happen naturally is clairvoyance—not expected to be accurate or even happen. Many people insist they can find others to take care of them and give up *their* gifts so they can end up on top of the heap. That is not why you are here! If that is how you live now, it will never appear as you wish.

You must compete? You must complete! You have to do that. Whatever you claim you will do, do it—and do it soon. If you complain and say you can do better than others, do so immediately.

All of this sounds as if you will get stuck and have to repeat this life, does it not? That is because such thinking contributes to your lack of faith in what you are here to be and creates a state in which you cannot enjoy bliss. For that reason we decided to try once again to teach you how to live in this time on your plane, as if you will ascend without any pain at the end.

Most of you are faced with what to do and how to commit to what you intuitively believe is your work, because of your industry or what you inherited, but all are hindrances. You must be able to work and know when and how it needs to be done to advance in life; live a long and glorious life and ascend at the end of it. Notice we said *glorious life*—not prosperous or happy life.

You wish to attain too little today. You want prosperity—some tack on peace of mind, but few realize you are glorious beings who need only think of what you can be to begin the process of becoming that one. You need only believe in what you conceive and it will reward you in ways you cannot comprehend today.

Imagine the faith it takes to raise a child and experience a wave of belief that no one who is unwilling to do such work can ever know today. You believe you can conceive and help another rise in these dense times. You want to help others and become a mentor who can say she or he is responsible for much a child contributes to the world around him or her now. That is how the mind works all the time, but some never have a child, and as a result do not realize they cannot fully appreciate life.

What if you were raised to teach children—and live well, but forgot to do either? You will be hounded whenever you perceive how others raise children or do what it takes to make it this life and maintain their pride. You want to teach and mentor—probably do a good job, but you will not rise high. Why? You did not wish to multiply what you are and divide to share with a crowd.

If you have nothing to do and everyone blesses you, do you deserve to be called a guru? No, but some call themselves gurus and even wilder names—like shamans, but not you! You are wise to what the crowd likes now, realizing it will swing further right, then go all the way to the other side again—rising and falling, doing nothing to further your cause. You are who you are, and the thrill is to find *you* among all the many images others use to label you today.

The ability to rise and do whatever is asked is genius—not to be doubted. If you rise to the occasion and save another's life, you are not to be put down by those who have no degree behind their titles—or wish to say you do not know how to live or what to do. We do not admire those who crowd the field with ideas of being healers. Why? Such a field is peopled by those who give up their lives and time to study what is believed to be the best possible treatments out now, thus given gifts of healing if they are wise.

You may be given a gift and, without ever reading a book or studying widely, can facilitate what is needed to heal. That is not to say you know better or are wiser. It simply means you have a gift and must be wise and never say you alone do whatever. As you grow and develop, channeling your wealth of gifts to others, never let on you realize how little you did to deserve it. Why? Others would then say they are equally gifted and pretend to be like you.

No one healed believes it!

No one who is now richer because another healed their mood or taught them what to do to get it right will believe they did not deserve success—and did it all themselves. You may see a child state his mother helped him win, but that quickly ends when he gets to be a man. The woman who can do exactly what her mother taught is so rare that few honor her now, except on designated days. You must remember the past or learn it all over again. That is the reason so many will be left behind!

Whatever you can do, do it—and smile. If you finish whatever and are greatly renowned for having done it right or on time, then you are a savior of mankind. How many today can say they do anything that benefits others? You say they are equal to the task of finding their way back. Back? Yes, back to the past that kept them intact as they moved through the universe to be this *you*.

Once you discover how little time you have to be this one you believe to be unique—the only being who gets it now—be sure you are on track. How to keep on track is up to the mind most of the time, because modern man does not dwell in Spirit much or at all. You have now found a way to beat the crowd!

Simply meditate!

Meditate every day and you will ascend, or so some gurus say today. However, it is endless and you never quite reach the point in life when you can say with pride: *"I am saved and can take others away."* You cannot—and will not know that until it is time to go.

Whatever you believe and whomever you agree to work with until you feel bliss is of no interest to us. We are teachers who come here from a place beyond anything you can possibly agree exists—let alone conceive of its being of help to human beings. However, those who rapidly ignore the probability and methodology of our reaching you all now can smile and grasp whatever is asked. Get in line now and design a mind that accepts your tasks over time.

When ready to go back to what you had, all will be known. You will not postpone or delay your ascendancy. However, most do not know anything about how you came to Earth and who you are, which ends the game and you begin finding God within.

Thank all who teach you anything!

Know you can grow, because others share their gifts. If you could do this and write for others as *The Scribe* does full-time, what would you do? Probably not be as generous or accurate—definitely not as much past available to prove and provide context for growth now.

When ready, we too might help you prepare to do work for others that assures your growth and helps you realize the full width and height of this life, but do not count on it. All is quick to disappear! History is not used much today in order to confuse those who want to do better than they otherwise might.

It is not your time to leave if you do not know what you do in dreams. Once you understand what you do when you assume you are asleep, you can design dreams and act them out—and begin to ascend before the end. Try to figure out why you ignore the most important teachers of this world now—even those coming through to you spiritually, because you are so confused you believe gold is the tool used to ascend and become greater than you are in the end.

Believe and never grieve!

If you are prone to look down on others, you tend to feel down all the time, because so many others are richer or better off than you are. However, if you are optimistic and appreciative, you are not jealous of others and do not wish to be someone else. Make your choice and design a pattern to live by now, then quickly get on with it and make it your path to eternal life.

Chapter Fifteen

To deny you are wise is foolish—and never done by anyone who knows what is best. What to do if you are wise, but surrounded by fools? Work on making them wise—hope they copy your mindset. If you cannot change them, you know what to do to get away and share your life with others who are wise. Do it now!

Whatever you believe, someone else can say they know what you believe and add much to it. For this reason, we counsel you to hold your beliefs closely to your heart and live what you think—not talk about it all week. Whatever is easy to describe is easy to lie about and can deceive you as well as everyone you set out to please. We do not see you able to please all others, so better to find the few who accept you as wise and let you pursue it.

What is in your life now will not cause your death, unless you decide this is your time and you are not going to bother to live better, wiser, or care about your body. You participate in ending your life, but may not believe it now. Once you die, others will point out how often you could have done something that would not have taken years off your normal life span. Yes, after you arrive you live a normal term, but may want to leave before the end.

If you decide to end your life, just say you wish you were dead. When you ask to be released, this plants a seed that produces death inside seven years—even seven days. Death is then not unexpected, because you pled for that end. Likely, you do not admire what you became and cannot blame others, so you wish to bow out and not start over again. Try instead to start over before giving up. See if life is not much kinder once you are no longer blind to what went wrong the first time.

Who would come to Earth and want to leave as soon as birthed? You may not have been nervous at first, may have wanted to become someone noticed from birth, but being handicapped or without good parents was not something you wanted when confirmed you would be born to that person, body, or mind. Today you often say others can abort babies and end those lives, but that is not quite right.

The mind may be unable to handle what was planned or not wanted, but it happens if there is a way for the baby to live a few days. If there is no place in life for a child, or it would be blighted because society would ignore its life, it is not always wrong to say you hate the idea of a child arriving then. Yes, you are playing God, but you are not killing a child. Only God can take a life, and anyone who says otherwise is not wise.

In The World of Today and Tomorrow there is a slippage between time you believe ends one day and begins another. You ascend then! You do not always do it right, and at times do not make it to the next day, but try! Keep on trying until you get it right. The wave of the moment is not what dies and keeps you tied to this side, thus it helps to understand why you are here and how to ascend once again.

To side with one and not others divides your thoughts over time. You may always feel great and happy that you chose this path to continue your work, life, or marriage to another, but most people within a week of deciding whatever will think they could have done better. You are no different!

Whatever you think was a critical time will haunt your mind. If you lived again, you would change it. Why? You never give the mind credit for getting work done on time. Once again, the mind reminds you over-and-over again of whatever message or order you gave it to do and when you expect it to be done.

Over years of observing *you* and what you do, what happens to the mind? Does it expect you to bless *you*—say you are great because you obey your belief system rather than divide your time studying others taught and said to be better than yours? You decide!

Whatever you do with the new, remember to bless the old that helped you get this far. Deny others their glory and they will put you down when they get the opportunity. Credit another and they forget you in a moment or five, but will not go after you again and try to end your fame.

Whoever you are and whatever you want to do is not set before you arrive here. You have time to decide how you will conquer fear, burdens, or 'karmic' vows you took before arriving here. You can choose what you do.

We do not agree you work within a frame of good times or bad, based on whether or not you believe in God, but man does. Since that framework is in place and most of you agree with it, you need much faith to not believe and accept God. The work you do on Earth is not so desperate or different from what you do when not on this planet now. You decided before you arrived what you would do at this time.

The idea that you have total free will is not quite believed by man or anyone else, but it makes a good story when talking about how to live your life and do what you like. If you are granted *'free will',* as it is billed, you have to accept you are responsible for whatever you do and unable to blame anyone else—not even God. We do not like that concept as much as believing you are on a journey with only one stop along the way, and whatever you do now will be used to continue your trip or postpone it for a time. You can study the map and do what is wise, or jump on and off until you are through living this life. However, it is wise to determine your destination and how long it might take—then get on with it!

To do nothing you chose is unwise and will not be believed by anyone here. Why? Everyone agrees you can be anyone or anything you please, thus those who follow that philosophy do not think much of people who are not prosperous, too.

What if you were raised to believe people with money are demented, sinful, and should not be allowed to live long? You might think they live in your town now, but they do not. Only a few believe they will never succeed. Everyone else is deluded enough to think one day they will be rich and famous—and able to ascend in a crowd at the end.

Now that you have found a degree of difference from what we state and what most people appreciate, will it make you want to immediately stop reading, or are you fascinated by anyone proposing a different way to live today? You decide, but we are teachers of another life and style of living than you know now. Can our work be used by you? Obviously! Look at the channel writing this for you. Who is she? What did she do to earn this degree of trust from those not human? You can discuss and decide all you like, but we know why—and you cannot figure it out this life.

Chapter Sixteen

People who think like you are bound to disappoint you one day. Why? You are unique, thus you cannot all think as one or become the same personality as you age, so do not believe anyone will always agree with you.

Once realized, the only way to see things today is to try not to bully another or your family into following your orders or accepting your faith and all manner of other thoughts you maintain. Why? You will be the one lied to and deceived more than others—which in your world says a lot!

Deceit begins when one is stronger or appears more immovable than another or several others. If one wants to bring down an army, fight to the death—or say you will, while desperately negotiating in the tents. You know you both can die proving nothing, but you have your pride. Why? What makes pride so unwise as to lead you to death without proving anything?

Can you proudly stand up and say your religion is the only one that understands man now and will get you to the *'promised land'*? If so, you know nothing and will be uncomfortable whenever you step outside your circle of admirers or tribe. You will cling to each other and continually restate you are wise and everyone else is not. Can it be safe to feel great if no one else appreciates what you believe?

No one asks you if you cling together to support a political party, because your faith in others is such you cannot believe they exist to do what you live to do, but it is true. Whatever you do, others are probably doing it, too. Why? You are human.

You have chores that make you feel secure, happy, and healthy, thus most try to keep at them daily. If you do not work at what is, can you exist? The chore of breathing is so easy most people do it without thinking or worrying about the quality of air surrounding you anywhere—but many worry now! How can you stand it? Why are you crying you have asthma and your children cannot run, play, and burn calories as well as you did when young? Can it be the sun is changing everyone, or is it because you have not played nicely with the planet you have?

Who will stop you from burning and pillaging other villages? You! Your Higher Self will one day remind you that redemption will occur. Others will rise against you and take whatever they want or punish you in ways that make them feel safe again. If you war and take over countries for the sheer idea that your politics and religious thoughts are better than theirs, you will not be loved. You will be rejected, but it may take time before you realize all that is done against you and why.

Today, look at how you react when others bully you, then check out your town's actions and who in your county is running away with the money, then look at your city and what it does for revenue—using pity to get you to pay more than ever before to do what? Once you realize most of your taxes go directly to your locality, what does your state provide and why? All this without considering other states nearby and those far away.

Now you are angry! Why? Is it about taxes and others not obeying the same rules and laws you follow? What if it is about hating others so much you want to kill them—yet cannot? Work on that, then go back and revamp your taxes.

Once a parent strays or does not provide, the child is told lies. This happens all the time and is deemed the best way to help children live well now. Is not the child often aware some wrong was done and adults are not having fun? If so, they may refuse to mature and assume adulthood. They may decide to not marry or raise children, because adults who taught them how to live lied.

When ready to accept your role in life, it is assumed you rehearsed it many times, but what if you did not? What if you were never given time to develop a life that would sustain you when no one was around? Who taught you to cook, clean, and keep your home neat? If no one taught you, are you wise enough to learn?

When easy lessons are ignored more and more in order to get children out of the house, so parents can misbehave or labor in their own way, you find their children often do not mature at the proper stages in life. The mind ages and develops in stages, and a missed phase of being a teenager or whatever ends up later being lived through—usually quite embarrassing to all concerned, especially the parent who was not involved enough or was afraid to discipline the child.

What some call discipline others call demeaning, nasty, and so on—not wise enough to realize discipline is a word that means many things. If you raise a child as you would a dog, you would not believe the same rules apply. Right? You would raise your voice and deny they both require you to be in charge, before they obey without much pain or change? You are who must be disciplined! Decide what you want out of life and is wise—thus safe to teach your child.

If you are unsure of yourself, you might discover how to rearrange your thoughts in orderly ways while raising children and regulating the phases of the day so you all do the same thing at the same time—like phases of the moon, but probably not. Why? You believe raising a child is so easy you can devote a few minutes now and then to it and all is done—and one day when a great man or woman stands up and says you were the reason they aspired to be great, you helped them, etc., you will be famous. You wish a child to be happy only when you are ready to accept bliss as your usual state of mind. Until then, you are not any more capable than a spoiled child of achieving bliss in a stable, daily way.

Take your time, work hard, and all will turn out well. Right or not? You decide, but whatever you decide is the only way to raise a child or be you will not appeal to those who thought it out, too, and do otherwise.

Why war with tribes and countries because they worship or believe in different political actions than you? You are foolish to base wars on what you believe *you* and all in your country think is right. You will be shot down. Bullies never agree they are wrong! Those who try to terrorize others into submission never recognize it when turned back on them.

We would not mention any of this now, but you have such thoughts. You never think to stand and disagree before delivering your message, instead hoping whatever does not lead to disappointment or war of any kind. The village that lets one terrorize all is at fault as much as the ego left to its own life of hell now.

You must speak!

Never speaking up will not be a defense others accept if your country is overrun by fools—and you let it happen in silence. Dictators who rise and become despised need not ever get that far. Lovers who turn into abusers need not have learned they could abuse you and remain until others knew.

What you own or believe is the best in life will not satisfy others. Let go of ego beliefs that cause you to think you know best and you will be half-way to living in bliss!

Chapter Seventeen

In the world above and beyond what you see now are many who cannot come through the veil, but in the past entered, talked, and moved about. Why would they be allowed to do that then, but not now? It is time to decide which side of the veil you reside on and why.

Once you understand that contacting those who have departed or think only through others—not having developed their lives enough, you know you are alone. You are not related to others who once ruled your work, life, or family. You are *you*—and no one else is!

If you wanted to make a living from art, you would not develop what you alone enjoy or can interpret. However, some artists, writers, even political leaders believe only they can know what to believe and all others must be led or let go—ignoring them more and more than ever before. Do not let that happen!

Your ego is not equal to keeping you on Earth. Egoists are not here to learn from others—at least that is how they appear to most. If they are to progress and move beyond this time and sphere, they need to know who they are relative to others.

If you get stuck here, you are unclear about what you must do to ascend—to leave this world when it is time to rise. Unwind your mind now and remove all references to others. If you concentrate only on what you know or want, you will not ascend or leave this time.

Would you want to live this life again?

You might—and you might fight to stay on top of whatever game you believe you are winning now. All who fight and grapple with others to make a living, as if it is the sole reason for being here now, are stuck in this life. You could help them, but not if you are stuck, too. How to help those so mired in themselves they cannot understand life or how to live with others now and ascend when they can? You would be better off living your life, doing what you want, then trying to change an egoist—one who loves only self.

When you decide only you are to survive or thrive, you cut off all support from those closest to you and most able to reach out and save you from a tidal wave of hate, water, or whatever. Why do that when you can build relationships up to the day they take your body away? To do nothing to make friends during this life is a waste. You came here to learn and cannot learn much if you have no elders, friends your age, mentors, or teachers.

If you do not experiment and develop now, how would you grow and become all you wanted to be when you arrived? To feel bliss and kiss the life you have requires you to pay attention to all you do and say. Right?

What if life comes and goes without your knowing why? What if all you do is without effort—and grace delivers you from individuals and situations where you would be harmed or bothered a lot? You would now be a spiritual being living in a material world—it does happen.

What if all said so far does not apply to you and how you live? Could it be you are free to do anything, or are you here to teach and prepare others to disappear and become greater than they otherwise might be? If you are a Buddha, teacher, or another who appears and helps others, do you get a pass on doing what is right once you achieve that life? Absolutely!

You may never be asked to come back and help others, but if asked, you get a special age and place to take the stage. Nothing you do then will be expected to be neglected or spit upon by others. You will be given enough grace and intelligence to look over the crowd and talk as if they are one with your thoughts and not spit upon. What you say will not be neglected by those who see you twice.

Having achieved bliss, and become used to it, do you ever want to give it up? You will not laugh at this once you realize how you live daily is no different from how it was before you lived this way. Make sense yet?

You will still be a human being having challenges of the kind mankind faces. You can still get serious illness and die without anyone realizing it, plus all the other things that happen to humans, but you do not feel as much as they can. You are not as into the body or mind then.

When a word comes to mind and you let it go, are you forgetful or wise to not use every thought that flies by? It may not seem like it then, but being unable to say whatever is often the reason you are who you are, as well as how you work on planet Earth. If that is the case, you are not forgetful or without memory—merely moving about on a different level from everyone else.

This can mean you will not talk a lot to those you normally would associate with daily, but you may also dislike these people enough to not say what you believe and wish to say. Why then bother with them? Why not move away or stay clear of them every day? You may be paid to meet with them or stay in the same place every day, you then decide if the money is worth the price you pay to earn it daily.

Once the price of earning a living or keeping another working hard to maintain you in whatever you require is too high, you will end the relationship. You may be blamed for not understanding, wanting too much from others, etc., but it is your life. You need to be able to do what you came to be. If you have no serious intention of marrying anyone, change your mind for a time and be decent enough to let the other find another love or move up in the world, so they do not worry about you and can get along well with others.

This is about relationships and how they can hold you back, but not why they need to be watched and given special care all your life. You can get so into another that they replace God in your mind and heart. You then do not live for God or *The Spirit of All,* rather for a human who is corrupt and unable to love you as God does. You then cannot understand others or why they live as they do without someone like you around full-time.

If you wish to surround yourself with those who are frivolous and unwise, you may not find marriage to be an ideal state, but it can help you overcome idle curiosities that in time cause you to return for another life. Be wise! Let your Spirit guide you to what is best for all involved in your everyday life.

Once you know you are not alone—although alone here, you may wonder and grow quite concerned that you are abandoned on Earth and unable to know when to return or how to live well now. Do not worry! Your base of operations is always alive and operating throughout your time on Earth. You need not worry, but keep open ways to communicate with *God of All* or that which guides you this life.

Who has never felt the presence of a helping hand when exhausted, yet had much farther to walk or work? Who when it appeared had lost everything and would never be able to raise his head in public again has not been inspired? Who has not felt healing flow through the body when everyone thought she was so ill she would not get well—or at least not quickly?

You know you are not immortal as a human being, but also know you will not die when the end of this life arrives. Why? It is implanted within *you* and cannot be removed, regardless of what doctors learn about you now.

All you are and ever will be is in you now! Not a prototype, or even a type of gyro, that lets you levitate whenever filled with the power of God, but a mechanism that encapsulates all you are in a belief that you can live and begin again—and keeps happening!

Children—including many older than age 25, often believe they can survive by eating one thing only, or never eating meat, and so on. You smile, but they are here now and will not change until they realize they cannot stop the aging process. Why? It is in the mechanism that is you while here—just as you are guided by a type of gyro that at the end will spin and carry you to another personality or another being of a different type—but related to whatever you are now.

To understand that making a mess of life is allowed—but not advised, helps some, but bothers many others. Why? Children rebel until they understand time is passing and they are not enjoyed by others, nor do they enjoy life much.

Why not enjoy this time?

Why not do what you want and not hurt others doing the same? You must be an adult to understand how little fun it is to stay young and unaware of the benefits of responsibility and knowing why humility suits you better than arrogance.

To expect time to erase all that is wrong in a race is to say you are not responsible for who you are. That is not permitted now and will not stop you from being judged unfit to go on in this world or the next. You can get into a mess and unable to get out of it. You can totally ruin your personality with habits that drive others crazy.

Why be lazy? Why not contribute and enjoy sharing hard work with others, so you all can have fun later? This is what makes most businesses run—in any economy. If you do not like your work or those you employ, you are condemned to die too soon to appreciate what it was you wanted to be when young. You will die without any idea why you made money enough to help others and did not.

The lie protracted and driveled about now is that it is okay to lie and cheat in order to make money, if you can amass enough to share with the world later. That is vanity! You do not want to share anything while here. Realize that hoarding all you earn, or not sharing dividends with those who earned them, results in much you cannot spend alone;

thus you boast that one day you will leave others what is left once you are done with it. How can you boast and be proud when you are not a human being, rather a ghost of an ego that never developed far enough to realize life is lived now—not when you die.

Whatever you do now is not what you believe it to be. It is based on how you live now! You may believe life continues as is and you are more realized once you ascend, but that is not how it is. You are bliss when it exists—not once it disappears. That is to say, you are bliss now, or not. You may not live like this or as you appear to be once you depart, thus no bliss is like this.

Take to heart that you want to be the best you can be! Some forget and try to be better than all others. That gets you a one-way pass to neglect and hurt, so do not do it. Instead, try loving others—even when they do not deserve it. It helps you believe you deserve the best and can accept it when ready to ascend.

Chapter Eighteen

Of all the people you can be—even now, which one is the one you want to be when you die? Can you achieve it or is it a dream you intend to drop and never own? Why bother with a dream if it never changes anything?

Dreams change and you remain, but only if that is how you live now. Dreamers who move about in that state of mind can change their lives and do it all the time! Just because you deny you do not dream, or believe in what your dreams mean, does not mean they do not exist and are not present in everyone's life even now.

If an egotist, it is not easy to admit you are wrong, but it is a way to understand your limitations today. Being known as a boaster and braggart is surely easy to identify as an egotist, but what about the quiet ones who believe they alone know what is going on? Are they not idlers, dreamers, or mere egotists? Why not? Decide and write a paragraph about it in your journal now...

All through the work you do with *The Teachers of the Higher Planes* and *The Scribe* is much that needs your approval or understanding before you can move on with your group. Do it—come to your own conclusions! Do not assume you are alone or everyone believes as you do.

Compared to a tree, or a being you cannot see, you are not as unique in thinking as many believe they are. Understand what the human mind can do for *you*, figure out how little that is, then contribute more and more to your spiritual life.

Since most people reading this book have the ability to write sentences and think straight, we would like you to provide your spirit with a book it can write out thoughts coming to *you* now and throughout the night. If you wish to call the work you do when asleep a dream, that is fine. If you wish to deny you dream, as most Americans can and do at least for a time, then believe whatever and sleep through what is happening to you every night or two. We do not worry about what you believe so much as how you accept the here and now.

Once you can sense within and around you that others are talking or working, not bothering with you, does it annoy you—a lot? Many complain about immigrants and tourists, because they speak different languages and do not pay attention to them. Are you that way or accustomed to others talking in different tongues?

If you can travel and find others wherever they may be hiding this life—ready to provide you with a message that advances your present agenda, are you wise or the same as those who travel without learning anything? Think it out. Write about it. See if you change your thoughts about others who travel and those you discover whenever far from your present base of operations.

Take a pen or pencil in hand and begin writing with ease—not thinking about the impression you make on the paper. If you wish, let your hand circle the page or let it sit until you feel the urge or rush to write or draw. Once you can do this, all is possible. Why? For possibly the first time you have admitted you are controlled at times by that which exists in your inner life.

Do not admit into you anyone not with *you* at birth. Be willing to believe there is a God of All and you will end many arguments that begin in the ego and die with it at the end of this life. At that time, you have a basis to accept this is not what it was and what you thought it to be, rather something quite different—and you are not yet ready to move beyond it.

We want you to advance!

We do not plan to take you to places beyond this planet, but your mind wants to keep up with everyone else. If your mind controls your thoughts now, you get what you get and the rest is left for another time. When you return to the same words on the same page later, it may not speak to you the same then. Did the words move, or was your mind changed by time? You decide, but write about it now...

If you have no better way to achieve your goal this life, it is imperative you do what you are guided to do while here. If you have no memory of why you arrived and who you are, ask your Guide. Yes, you have one!

Ask why you are here, then write out what you feel. It may help you move and become better at your life here. If lost or profoundly unhappy, you need to align within your source of humanity and what God created when you arrived in this space and time.

You are here to do what you came to do, but some never do it or cannot get it done. Why? The ego is so large they believe they have time to amaze everyone, yet great enough to lead them to the next life. Why would you follow such an insane person now? Because your ego is large enough to float an armada, yet not admit you can connect with God today and are responsible for your behavior.

Why not choose a large book to put in your way every day, so you feel you must write before you say '*good night*' to others? You might find it worthy of your time and a better friend than those you chat with now and then, but it is not a substitute for talking things over with those you respect and love.

You must keep your personal connections open and be willing to accept those you have no knowledge of now. Why? You are cautioned against fighting or cheating others, because you have to redo such a life and may not have time to make full amends for it.

No one you know is as sure of you getting along as those who do not want to be bothered by whatever goes wrong for you. You may like them now, but could change, too. Do what helps you and it will most likely be appreciated by those much like you. If not? You were not harmed. Your ego was not deceived, unless it thought everyone would be pleased because you said or did whatever. All is ego or vanity when you seek to be pleasing. You need not please everyone; nevertheless, it is unwise to seek to harm anyone now.

All you have learned today is in your mind on a short-term memory line and easily put aside without being used for the purpose you intended when paying attention to what you want to remember. Think on this, then rewind the sentence until it makes sense in every direction—and you get the message. Rewrite it now!

The day ends and you cannot forget what went wrong? You are forgiven and can drop off to sleep now. Let your dreams recreate whatever you believe was a mess or cannot be better than it is. Tomorrow you will awaken and sense what to do or how to live with whatever it is.

Much of this lesson is not about dreams so much as what you retain when you awaken one day in another life. Be aware of the analogy. You can dream more now and study dreams more deeply than you did.

Chapter Nineteen

Using only your mind to figure out life causes not only wild and weird problems, but useless solutions. At times you have to leave the mind behind and enter the emotional sphere that is *you* here—then determine if you are out-of-sync with what is normal in your community. Are you trying to be someone else? Do you know what life is all about? You may not try hard enough to love others, but loving you is not what was meant when God laid down the law to love and be lovable and cause others no trouble.

When you read about people eager to be on a *'reality'* show or run some kind of race and disgrace their families, you may wonder why they do it. We are aware many believe *'loving you only'* is the way to live. They believe they must forget everyone else until they are filled with love for no one but themselves, which becomes the only way they can operate or live. They fake being involved with others, or lie full-time, to be adored or admired more. They are not fully involved in this life.

Why would you glorify yourself and forget the world? Perhaps you were seriously hurt as a child and found it helped to dwell within your mind and soothe yourself. You may have tried to love others and been bullied and mistreated for caring so much, so you decided: *'Why bother with others, instead love only me.'* Such self-love will not win you a spot on top of the hit parade of best friends and lovers, but you would not care.

Share what you dare or live anywhere and you discover you may not be appreciated by those who love only themselves. Fortunately, there are worlds out there where you are seen as mature and can get involved all the time in others' lives. Do not settle for life with those who need no other! Get beyond them—move to another part of town and try to never again meet.

If you drop the narcisstic attitude adopted at times, you often feel greater love from others. Why? It was always there, but you were so busy loving only you that you did not notice. Whatever you do now, be you!

Let your light shine upon the world around you. Which is not to say you love only you and give only what you have no further need. If you never share or care about anyone now, it will not matter if you once loved others.

We can say the mind dwells in the sheltered place where you were raised or always hides because it was abused as a child. Accept the past and move on—become an adult now! Stop thinking it is easier to be a child or dependent upon another. It is not!

When you find another who loves you as you are, shelter that love and keep it protected from the marauders who try to ruin love and never stop to think why they do it. You may have been a predator yourself. When you feel the need to take over and ruin another, because you are jealous, be aware it will not be as you believe when you get what you desire.

Desire disappears when you quench its thirst or survive to live a few more years of your present life. You fear others will take away those you love, so you say the one you love is a liar or not to be trusted. Then it happens, you are no longer happy with him or her. Can it be the mind made up the entire worry? Yes, and it happens over and over again with some who never learn to love and trust others.

Is it your fault another no longer loves you?

Whatever else you may be, you do not set out to harm your heart or destroy your life. However, some hate and cannot stop themselves from seeking to destroy others. The evil mind or jealous eye continues to live that life until it finds an outlet it can work through to continue as is—or discover bliss is what you live for and seek it instead.

Whatever you do and wherever you live has limits. You cannot exist without feeding and doing whatever your body requires for its health and well-being, but you can overdo what is required. Eating for three instead of exercising an hour a day, you begin to feel lonely. You are not alone, but believe others do not notice how much you eat. You hide whatever or claim it is not your fault you grow larger. The lie constantly feeds your deceit, and you begin to hate anyone not eating for three, too.

We would stop all actions that set you at odds with others who love you. At times you have to move on to become who you are and live your life, but what does that imply? Are you unable to live in your home from birth to death? You can try, but most learn that to be who you are and answer to your wisdom, you need to live with others. If you do not, you may become someone who loves no one else. By default, you would become a recluse interested in only what you do. Over time others stop dropping by and eventually forget you, because you do not interest them.

If unable to speak or do anything with another for a week, who would you visit? That is something everyone needs to keep in mind and remember when they decide to cut others from their lives. You may not want to live in a foreign state or become someone much wiser than all gathered around you, but may not be who you believe yourself to be.

You could be suspected of fostering foolish ideas by those who believe they are also wise. You could be considered odd by those you think eccentric. You may never see yourself as others do, but try!

Whatever else you do within this time, you can thrive and be happy as is or can easily become. If sane and happy now, you gain bliss more easily than those who are not. You may not be in line to fame and fortune, but never fear—neither helps you attain bliss!

The world around you is what you want and expect—and adjust to or feel odd and let down, wishing you were somewhere else. Is the latter conducive to being blissful? No, but you can feel happy and fulfilled by simply rearranging a few things around you now. You will feel bliss—and wonder why you did not make changes earlier in life.

Does it take years to realize life is not what you thought it would be, thus you constantly adjusted to shifting tides? You are now wise to that, but may still want to believe you cannot be happy and content if you are not pretty, handsome, or rich. It takes less than an hour to adjust to almost anything life can throw at you. Try being who you are!

Bliss is a state in which you can exist and not feel threatened while in it. You either feel blissful or not? You feel bliss now and then, but usually take bliss for granted once you supplant anxiety and guilt with loving others as much as you love yourself.

Chapter Twenty

Today, select a phrase that pleases you and live that way. Why? If you seek to become filled with bliss now, it helps to know who you are and what makes you happy. When you think and believe—then see what you need, there is an instant when you feel love and want to be compared to no other. You are then in what you might call *bliss*. It is a feeling you miss when you do not have it.

Take your time deciding what best describes your actions now. Think it over, then carefully adopt its best interpretation. Meanwhile your mind thrives or dies, depending upon how much you permit it to decide what you want from life.

What you do now is without any order or command to do something you cannot do. Merely dream or complete a thought and there you are—you created a rare work of art! By examining how your mind created that sentence and describes you now, you begin to understand what you want.

Once you label this moment, you will want to savor it or not. Why change what you thought when you started this chapter? You may never be satisfied, or are an editor in disguise, or a critic never happy with what is. You decide, but best to tame the critic and live with the editor a bit before turning off or tuning out.

When safe and secure, the sound of your voice will not offend you or bother your silence. What you notice when you tune out your thoughts about last night or years prior is that it feels different. It is! You cannot live in bliss with your mind full of hostility or dislike of others.

You say: *"First, I must like me to love another."* Try it again, but this time say *'you love another'* before thinking of yourself.

If you can love others and develop a way of circulating and blessing them every day—not feeling neglected or unloved, you will change and become a happy human being. What if you love them, but they hate you? No problem! Whatever you do, you are going to live with the mood and tools you use.

If you hone hatred and let your temper flare and burn away friendships, one day you will live to regret it—if not be killed for it. You have only this life to live! Enjoy being you and love will shine through all you do.

Notice, to enjoy bliss you have to enjoy who you are. What if you do not enjoy being you? You become a burnt-out shell of what you came to Earth to do well.

You are here now to be you, then leave this plane fulfilled and understanding this life. If you always fight, never enjoy being around others of your type or learn to respect those unlike you, this life will not end when you die. It is a lesson you must complete. Many believe it to be *karma* or some such word, but it is not! You are who you are. What you create will not change until you do.

As you move through life here, becoming used to being you and doing what you want, many will dislike you. Need that be a problem? You can be disliked, yet never bothered by it.

We suggest you realize how many people you do not like now and adjust to it, as well as how many dislike you because you started it. Yes, it is a process! Someone once said something that was not liked, then much was added by the mind and suddenly you are both misaligned and possibly malign the other.

How to bridge the ocean of Meaningless words spoken...

Start by realizing what you say is not a lie. You think you can deceive another, but it is never that way. Your mind aligns to believe what you say, which then becomes a betrayal of what you believe to be right. If you lie full-time and believe it is fine to lie, you become completely aligned—and others cannot decide if you are lying or not. It proves nothing! You can deceive, but it will not be you who is loved or even admired, but the other—the one you say you are.

A phantom of other lives comes to you from time-to-time and talks about another life, but you do not have to believe it. Why? You know who you are and why you came out of that world to be here. To let it go and not bother with such thoughts is better for all involved. Why? You may not realize you dislike another based on what was said in another time and place, thus hating with no reason today.

Once you discover anything without logical explanation (you have no idea where you got the idea), immediately decide to change until you align within your mind with what you know to be fact. Facts are accepted ideas—things you can easily believe, thus you do not argue over them forever, rather than get on with your life.

Arguments are not hard on the ego, but losing your belief that you are smart or can talk down others hurts. If you set out to beat another without considering you might lose, your ego gets bruised. To lose because you were bested is not a fault or a problem. Decide if your ego was up to arguing and whether or not your facts were as good as your opponent's, then let go of what you do not know. Read a lot if you want to demonstrate you are smart or more intelligent than others. That way you get a bit better at arguing, without anyone knowing it.

Today the entire world is blocked by a lack of communication, yet you all believe you communicate better now. How can you transfer your smile when no one sees your mind's eye or your lips curl in delight? You add things to written speech to indicate you are happy—not bitter, but some never get it anyway. You are at the mercy of the reader's mood and lack of understanding you.

If you know the mind set of many,
Do you know you, too?

Who would study you, if not you? There is only one other who might. The one who says she or he loves you. If that one accepts all you say—lets you do whatever you may, you can grow and feel at home. However, what if you cannot love, yet demand others cater to you and take care of whatever you need today? You will quickly fade from the list of people they communicate with in a favorable way.

If you kiss others in order to avoid being told off for being boring, you will not discover your need to do more. Before you explore more doors or new worlds, think about what you see. You can open your mind to what the world provides.

Only you can tell your story! Make it interesting, and sooner rather than later you will be happier being you. Often the story you tell yourself is not the one everyone loves. Be honest without criticizing all who helped or hindered you until you began to live as you do now.

You may not want to bless the one who raised you as a child, but that one did whatever in a way they believed was satisfactory. You may now see what was said and done as dishonest, cruel, or no fun—compared to others. If you want to trade lives with another, listen intently to what they did as a child and who they lived with then. You may be surprised that one who laughs and is eager to be friends is not without a tale or two that would be upsetting if you lived through it, too.

You will be what you do and give freely!

When you open your door to someone asking for help, do you help or first decide why you should or if you need to help? The answer is what comes to you now! You sense it is not fun to realize you are unwise or foolish to a greater degree than others you believe to be weak or less than bright, but better to find out now and put it right.

When you discover you are arrogant, ignorant, or afraid of the light, you are the only one who knows—and the only one who can change it. Why? You are not a known personality, regardless of how many spy on you or delight in running you about. You are who you are and will feel better whenever difficulties occur now and then if you have a few good friends who do not bar the door if you arrive at a difficult time.

You are in charge of you!

Who would you let into your life if given the ability to choose? You can let in all or oust anyone, but be wise. If you decide to make a list of people who are divisive and a bit evil now, run it by your mind and sleep on it several nights. If you find you cannot decide who will be in your life full-time or needs to be cut back to several times a month, do it. See if you immediately feel better and have more time to love others than you otherwise might.

Having a few friends or close family can make you insecure—without anyone to talk to—if something goes wrong once your original support system expires. You cannot imagine others and who they are if all you know is those you grew up and lived with all this life. Travel—sit and talk with those who look different or not as you thought, and understand your right to be you this life.

Most hurry to save face when embarrassed, but the wise person helps others save face, too—stops bullies from making fun of others. The bully cannot exist if everyone helps those being attacked! Why talk about what needs to be done when you do not change anything? You want to appear as if you care. You want to share what you believe to see if others agree. You do not intend to do much then.

Alone you can examine your life in an hour or so and decide what you like and what you do not want now. Such insight lends light to shine on what you believe others are like. Once you gather enough work and do what you like to support your life, help another, then a few more. It will be unique in a world where everyone says they want friends, but few do enough to be one.

Take your time and spot lines on the paper you wrote earlier. Do they make sense now? Create, let it rest, and then edit! You do not have to submit your thoughts to critics, but some want to be put down so they can justify being angry and taking it out on others.

Drugs do not lie. Some now live on drugs that alter their basic mind patterns so they quickly become ugly and angry. When you meet them, they may not look angry, but gain momentum each time you talk—becoming insane with anger, because you are not who they thought you were, thus should be quickly eliminated and ignored. Perhaps one day, when they have no one to support them in their attempts to be superior beings, they will change—or not. You do not need to put up with addicts!

We say this now: *You have a program playing in your life now that is harmonious and loving, or you are struggling to do something you believe is far better.*

If it works, and you like who you are, it is your life! You can do whatever, but you will not ascend to another life until you realize why you are here and designed to be as you are now. When on drugs or unable to like anyone or respect your reason for being here, you cannot succeed.

Chapter Twenty-One

Out of the blue and into the real you comes bliss, but how to make it stick? When you decide you cannot live as you wish—would rather die than continue as is, you set in motion a lasting thought, emotion, or idea that in time leads to your death. Do not utter such nonsense! Stop being dramatic to attract attention. It is not worthy of you or your soul.

Living with others requires adjustment. Some adjust a lot in order to have someone to blame for not being true to who they are or because they are lost. What then? You can wander about blaming others and not get far because others complain about you, too, or you can move into a more powerful mood and sense what you need to do now. How do you move into a more powerful mood than whatever you are in now?

Meditate and let go!

You hear meditation much talked about by all who speak of God, prayer, being yourself, and so on, but what is it? Why would meditation help you now? That is the question to answer—Now get on with it!

Taking over your mind and demanding it do nothing is new only if you never studied, listened intently to music, danced until you felt you could not stand, or were deeply in love with another. All such trances or states of mind release you from the mind's control, yet many believe meditation to be a form of mind control. Can that be true?

Why not sit back and let time work its magic now? You are so involved in everyday stuff you cannot stop the clock or go without talking a lot. You try to fill hours, as if they will cease if you do not continue at a frenetic pace following whatever is in fashion or the latest fad. Why indeed do you try so hard to be loved?

When you open up and decide you want to live your life now—be who you are. You do not take a risk doing that. Really! You are merely turning off the faucet of work others drown you in now. Take up *your* work and do it without stop until you die or ascend to another life long before this one ends.

The mystery of life is not its history, but its future—what you are to do and how much you need to complete, and so on. You never *'get it'* until one day you sit down and do nothing. What happens then? You are so tired of what everyone says is right or is the answer to life's problems that you shut down and do nothing—nothing at all!

You force the mind to shut up—not say another word or interrupt you. This constant determination to be in charge and not running off with a thought keeps you in a kind of altered mind state some call a trance. It is not!

If you can dance until dawn and feel wonderful, because someone is charming and says they love you, you can do it on your own. You can do it whenever you feel the need to be calm. Why not do it now?

Take time to develop a method that serves you well and can be used whenever you are quiet or others leave you without any need to talk, perform, or do something for them. Writing often provides such moments. Reading leads to it easily, if what you have in hand is not interesting. Music, if calm and thoughtful, without words or stirring sounds, can help you relax and leave this world behind.

We suggest you also consider the age-old way of muttering a prayer and letting it go into the air without worrying if anyone cares or stares. A mantra of any kind is easy to find, yet you may want to pay someone for a sound. Do not be dense! Forget the idea you have only one sound resonating within or is perfect for meditation. Shut down the critical mind and keep the key under the mat until you need it.

What key will you seek?

The key of pure G is filled with glee and leads you to what you need, but any key is fine. You need not worry about who does what, and how a guru teaches, or that you need a teacher, and so on. Calm down and forget the nonsense. Finally, forget the sounds and sights of this life.

After you get to the point where you can blank out others and not be bothered by what someone says, you may still not be meditating, but at least you are not bothered so much you get upset, depressed, or cannot be yourself. The tone you seek or picture you paint is not what holds you rapt. It is you seeking the soul space you know exists, but do not want to admit you have, because it scares you at times.

Move your hand to your throat, stretch your neck, lightly rub your hand over your Adam's apple, or might be if women had them. Repeatedly move your thumb over that spot or chakra while clearing your mind—thinking of nothing. If something is malfunctioning or all is fine, let the chakra send a message. Know what is going on by simply tuning into your mind and what it knows about your life from within.

When the mind is super-active—growing with fame and fortune, you say your ego is getting a workout and you need to slow down to enjoy others. Is that happening now? Are you out of control and your mind is responsible for it? It happens when your soul is tuned out! You become positive that what is exists and you do it all. Paranoia may set in then and you believe others are envious or jealous of you. Some may be, but most are unaware you exist. Their ignorance spurs you to act out larger scenarios. You grow further from wherever you are, enlarging what will never give you what you want. Feelings of euphoria destroy you if sought in a bottle, shot, or pill designed with that in mind, but you can induce it naturally without trying.

Love is what you want and activate several times a day, or you are stupid. Why deny yourself the shot of adrenalin that comes from feeling great for having helped another or having thought of others as much as yourself? You would never know what it is to know bliss!

A kiss is not bliss, but it may be something you do openly or often to feel great. You may want to kiss everyone, or get others to embrace you so you can shun them—to see how they react when unable to get what they want, but you never know love doing that. You have only one way to express your love—listen and think about what others are and what they want out of life. Any other pursuit does not lead to love.

What appears now is not bliss!

You are thinking about love—and how much you disagree with what we see. You argue mentally or aloud that we do not know what goes on here, and you are right! We do not contend with emotions—the ups and downs of ideas that contradict logic and mean nothing. We are not here to feel emotional, either. We are real! We are teachers who can help you, but you have to agree you need help before we can reach you now.

Once you open your thoughts to the possibility there might be an all-reaching and extremely powerful mind or being (depending on your leanings), you can accept space is nonexistent and people are not what you sense—rather approximate beings who succeed and believe as one. You have to suspend judgment once you get that far, which is when you need to control your thoughts and let go of your critical mind.

Whenever you thrive and feel great full-time, you are being yourself. It cannot happen? You are lost! If lost, seek guidance.

The work of one person is such that many others use it or not, but it is not without power and ability to produce another way of living now. Each thought moves outward and evolves into another, even if others appear not to listen. That is why you do not play music that shouts or talks when you want to meditate or pray.

You can pray every day and never say the same words, or you can safely say the same few words daily and get the same vibration and work. There is no single way to pray. Yes, you know that, so why do you fight about it?

Again, we offer logic when you would rather argue. The seven deadly sins some claim to know are no less lethal now than when the sages and scribes of the past recorded them. They expected the message would be understood and such sins erased over time. What happened? You accept they are deadly thoughts to permit in your mind, but do little to erase them from this world.

Anger is so pervasive in some cultures that you exist in order to limit the abilities of those clearly related by the tribe you are expected to help and protect. You may be so mad you cannot sleep at night, shouting during the day, bullying others in order to feel a bit better about your life here. What happens then? You might wipe out another or end up dead from over-executing your work or words, but most likely you hate to admit no one wants you around them now. Why? You are too hard to like.

If being angry a lot makes enemies, then why would you allow it? Why would anyone with an ounce of intelligence continue to fight? Is your mind driving you or your ambition to conquer others? Why would you think you had to beat another? When did it start, when does it end? Any ideas on how to proceed?

It is hurtful to work hard and sense others do not respect you, thus some argue and fight to prove they are right or did something great. Why bother? You have your thing and know others like things you do not, so why not sing your song and ignore everyone else? This is not easy to think about, but must emerge to discover your bliss.

The time has come to sit back and rest. Let it all drop from wherever and not think about it again. Why? It is done! It has served its purpose. That purpose was to get you to move in another direction—feel your blood pressure grow and your breath deepen so you can relax.

Relax and mentally count back from 100 to whatever number it takes for you to forget how you feel now. Let go of whatever you are thinking about—breathe deeply, and keep counting from 100 to infinity if need be. Let go and enjoy being *you*—knowing how to meditate and enter this state whenever you wish.

Chapter Twenty-Two

Within the will of you and those like you is a space where you can hide and be silent or memorize what others say to recite whenever you like, but there is no space there for you to store *you*. You are the way you are—not who you believe *you* to be. So who are *you*? We want you to do something to prove you are *you*.

Once you decide what to do to prove you are who you believe *you* to be, recognize how long it takes to weed out all the lives you could live now—all the lies you tell in order to create this personality you want others to believe is you. Create a new way of living and you will become someone other than the one you believe you to be now. Can that happen? Yes, it happens whenever you decide you will not permit another to live your life or take up space in your mind. You set out to divorce another and end up on an entirely different course.

Since behavior is explained here and talked about, all think they know who you are, but you are neither the one they believe you to be nor what you see. You are a unique being who shows only enough to get beyond what you want to be in order to do what you came to Earth to see or be. Can you be one and still change into many others? Obviously!

> *To believe in what you may be or have been in other times or lives, you need to admire who you are now. If you are sore, tired, or poor, you will not like or want to anticipate you might have lived in another way or before today. Instead, you will prefer to think about how to make enough to feel better than you do now.*

That paragraph highlights those who read these lines and understand why we are here and what we bring to the forefront now.

If you are struggling to enjoy life—unable to find a wife or mate, work, or job you like, you will blame God and not be quick to explore more of the world beyond you. For this reason, we have helped many make millions in order to get them to a place in life where they can study what this life is, who they are, and more. So far, most who made more money than they needed sorely disappointed *The Lord*. In fact, many we worked with intuitively are now seedy or about to be needy, because of their greed. Why?

When you can study and do not, you will regret you missed that message. You may never understand it or be able to gain such information again, or attend such a class—not knowing you erred until you are nowhere. Yes, you can end up with nothing going on, no one anticipating your work or meeting you on the street—unhappy, with no family, thus sad and lonely.

It sounds as if those who have it made will lose it all because of a fatal flaw, but it is not that way now. Today, many have raised people they call family, but they are not. Others have friends they greet on the street and believe would help them with problems, but think again. When you meet innocents, as well as those who work with their families and keep their friends, you immediately can see they are not wealthy. If they are, they are not taking care of the entire family out there somewhere.

You may believe being wealthy means everyone will want to be with you, but only pickpockets try to get close. You will have many thieves who believe you have no idea what they are thinking. Intuitively, you can beat them and put them out of your sphere this year. We tempt you not, but suggest that you not let wealth interrupt your life lessons now.

If you find gold and silver lining the kitchen where you live, you can decide you have too much wealth. Why? You cannot eat gold and silver. You need neither to help with your work or art, but obviously friends will be envious of you if they do not have such a pantry, too.

The envious and jealous among you think others feel envy and jealousy when they do well or have much wealth. How serious a problem is it? Not a problem for most people! Most do not envy those they do not know. However, jealousy grows in inner circles and families when one outgrows the clan or can. You have to let go in order to believe in others, but many cannot. You want them to stay as you are now—and only you able to grow.

Whatever you do in life is not exactly what you said you would like to do when you came to Earth, but it is sufficient if you feel great and hurt no other. You have found an alternate route home. It could be more or less busy—shorter than you felt you would need at birth, but if it works, do not hurry. Hurry is the by-product of an unorganized mind. You will discover more about it, but not now.

The time to deliver a sermon on how you live and believe others need to follow is when you have lived a long life and have all you require. However, the wise almost never serve others by lying or freely giving advice. They want you to discover life as they did.

Could it be you cannot be *you* now? Are you compelled to wander this world in search of others who will complete you? Neither! You have no alternative course designed to keep you here longer than your mind requires, but you may not believe in God or anything beyond your power. Why? Your ego is larger than the life you live now.

How many people are ego-bound now?

Anyone who seeks to be better than others or seeks wealth and power rather than a life of blessings is an egotist. There is no better way to define such a state of mind. Ego resides in the mind, but not in existence when you arrive. You develop it as you cry and demand attention from a young age. Those who got their parents to jump for them have much bigger egos than those who had to wait to be fed.

Can you be used to conquer whatever? You are never used, but may wish to let another step in and tell you what to do to win. Will you win if you let someone else dictate what you should do and how you should live now? You may appear to be great and even appreciate the help, but your ego will defeat you. It will not give others credit for helping you get it together.

If you do not believe you did it yourself, you will not accept whatever is given. It is a Gordian-knot kind of problem most do not expect to find, and most decline to untie. Why? You want to believe you did it all—even lie if another says you did not. Why? A life without excitement is not really living according to too many now.

Will bliss give you a buzz? Will it make you feel great—able to do anything you want to try? Bliss is not what some believe it should be, nor does it feel real to many. You have to understand your philosophy of living a good life before you can claim to live it now. Many do not agree, because feelings are not subjected to tests of intensity to determine if you are in bliss or only participating in it half-way.

You must decide what you seek this life—and why! Once you determine the boundaries and how much time you want to spend following your ideas of paradise, you can accept this is bliss—or not. The decision is always yours.

Chapter Twenty-Three

Prepare for a trip, then follow through and do it. If you relish the decision to leave whatever you are doing to go somewhere new or different, you are half-way to the next life before those who hate change can accept their time has arrived. You can beat many in line by simply saying the right thing.

We coached you in prior work with *The Scribe.* Today we are reminding you to understand why you are here, what you are here to do for You and YOU—and do it now! Get it done, so you can relax and enjoy this life.

When some run for political office they promise to do something totally new or different from what everyone before them ever did. Do you honestly believe them? If so, you are too young to vote!

When you promise another you will do something, do it. If you do not heed your words, who will believe you when you say you will follow their words? By now you must know if you lie or not, but some who lie claim they never do. Why? They are liars! You need only know someone a short time to discover that truth.

Try to listen and quickly determine if what you are listening to is worthy of your time. If it is not, leave as nicely as you can within a short time. Do not imply you buy lies and they will respect you more than if you sat and listened to them go on for an hour or more and not buy what they are selling then.

'Be you and find others who live authentic lives,' is easy to write, but not easy to put into words when you go out into life. Why? Your vocabulary was not created with love of others in mind, so you lie in order to be seen as a good person—one who will not harm them. You end up hurting others more by lying that you care about them than you ever harm by saying you are preoccupied at the time and cannot pay enough attention to them to be of assistance then. If that is how you feel, you may sound egotistical, because you are, so get on with finding others who are egotistical and feel no pain when you lie to them.

When you enter the boundaries of others in order to seduce or know more about them, do you worry they may not be who you believe them to be? If not, you are lying to yourself. You want others to be as you believe them to be, but do not believe you need to live a life in which you never lie. It is the disease of this millennium, and many will die with lies filling their minds and no knowledge of the bliss that comes from being *you* and having true friends.

Good friends are not delivered at birth and given to you to nurture or keep. You decide who will be in your life and who will not be permitted access to your inner life. You decide!

In the eyes of others you are who is either wise or not. If you chose unwisely, pain and sorrow accompanies you into other relationships, but you may learn to never again trust that type of mind—or not. Whatever you decide, be wise and not criticize another for doing what you hide. That is contemptible and much hated by people of every kind.

The hypocrite is one who says he or she does not do something, but does. Can you identify anything you criticize others for, yet do it or have done it? Can you spot the one who hates abortion, yet has had more than one? Probably not, but they exist in every lynching party of that type. Why? The guilt is so great in the minds of some they cannot overcome it, so they attempt to compensate by insisting others cannot be allowed to make the same mistake—or they are liars and will never get over it.

The big lie for most is you love others!

You say you love when you merely want someone around when you are down and sad. You do not wish to pick up your spirits and learn to be happy. You choose instead to act as if another is sweet and nice and makes you happy. Really?? Hard to believe anyone living would believe it when someone says, *"You make me happy,"* but it happens. That lie causes a lot of pain, but not as much as one wishing to enslave others so they do not have to work.

As you remember your lies, positioning your mind to erase some and never forget others, do it gradually so as not to crack or come to grips with your past. Let your work on self last! Do not make it a day's project, then forget whatever you said you would do later.

Take your life, look it over twice, then do what you like with what you have left. You may not be a champion of any kind, but if judged by others to be kind, you will know bliss and be able to teach it to your kids.

Are all who ever lived with hate and sadness prone to it? You are not expected to do what your parents did, but many who label themselves as children assume they resemble one parent or the other. Neither parent is you, so get over it. You may have famous parents or not, but you will not be equal unless you work hard. You may become a success quicker than others because you had a path established when you arrived this time, but most people do not seek the original path. Why? Their egos tend to believe they are better than whatever they have.

Are you pleased to be you now? Are you happy your parents were poor-but-honest or rich-and-nasty to others? You can easily see one is predominant in the minds of many who survived childhoods where they were rarely allowed to be children.

You may not believe it now, but time spent with your spouse does help your children more than anything else. Is that the secret of getting rich? Probably not! Most people who search for gold and riches are old since childhood. They got little love then, and their parents gave them little attention, which they richly deserved then. That is how you think and readjust the way you raise your children today—and how you judge others who have more than you.

Have you changed anything about your mind since starting to read this book? You have, or you are not reading—merely browsing now. You cannot read and take in the meaning of what is said without mentally moving things around. This book attempts to move you from moods of self-importance to thoughts of great wisdom—and back again, without harming your ego to the degree you never stop being the one seeking to be filled with bliss.

Take time to kiss your mind, let it decide you are better off being kind than being blind to the lives of other tribes, clans, and men. Take your hand and press down on the top of your other hand and smile. At this moment in time, you are your best friend. A fond caress and a smile wins many friends, but being you and not allowing others to be themselves, too, is not conducive to being liked.

You all say you want to be famous, and some actually think it is separate from being respected, but it is not. The one disgraced by his or her way of life knows of fame and how it feels when others point them out as bad examples to the young—It is fame, but not what anyone wants.

When you see yourself doing your best and deserving a rest, you are ready to party, enjoy your solitude, or live with others. Without the degree of contrast required to completely relax after a long day's journey or work, you idle and grow bored with life. Try a few chores before you go to your next Board meeting and you will work a lot more than you otherwise might. If you take care of your pets and treat them to something they like, you will enjoy your party more that night. It takes time to be you and let go of what you know and want to do in order to have fun with others.

The way you work now, and how you party when not working, is not a bother to us or anyone with us. We do not care if you drink until others make fun of your stutter or your inability to know what you are saying now, but you would not let that happen if you were in charge of your life and what comes next. You constantly need to be able to see things and realize what they mean to be ready to ascend.

Chapter Twenty-Four

Every time you stop to compare yourself to another, you lose. You may not believe it then, but over time you become more and more like others than ever before, rather than yourself. If you want to improve you and become the best at what you do, apprentice to someone better at what you do, but do not become a clone or representative of their work. Be you!

As you work through this book and read what you need to do to be *you* and achieve a degree of willingness to be all you can be in this life, agree that you will try to do something new—and do it enough to determine if you are wise to continue or not. Too many want to dabble in the arts, for example, thinking that by using their hands for a week to three they can paint or work clay and be able to sell whatever they do well. Why? What would you do if someone wanted your art at that rudimentary stage? You would cater to that aspect and never better yourself.

We suggest that those of you who dabble in the arcane arts in order to make a few dollars are the same as dabblers in clay who make little progress until they gain a deeper appreciation for what clay consists of and how it lives within and around you now. Yes, clay is alive, and any sensitive knows it! If you do not, meet a great potter and find out.

To compare you to a clay pot is not why we brought up the subject, but you are the same as clay. That is why the Bible and other Books of Wisdom use it as an analogy. You have a cellular description that varies a bit, but includes much that exists in clay. You have a way of being only half-committed to whatever, unable to hold water until hardened by time, the sun, or an oven of some kind. You may want to continue this analogy, but we are done with it.

To decide you are now wise and can guide or even teach another is something fools rush to do—and want to be seen as having done, in order to charge high fees for consulting on larger projects. Why? Why would you take on the daunting task of helping someone else get on in life if you have not arrived at your highest level? Your ego says you are better compared to people beneath you now. When ready to teach, a class will be assigned to you. You can reach out and teach then.

Any family whose mother and father are great leaders is the first to know it. They can see it in the way their parents pay attention to them. That is why societies look to the families politicians raise before they accuse some of harming the nation today. You must begin with someone—and your family is first in line, so make sure you teach them well before you tackle a crowd of strangers who will not be as easy to change.

What happens when you can finally teach strangers? You may not want to teach. You may decide to perfect your life, or be yourself and not bother with others. You may want to write. All of these are good reasons not to teach, so when a selfless being decides to give up time to reach others, it is a wonderful thing. Do not hesitate to sign up when such a woman or man says they will give up time to do you a favor then.

What you do with a great teacher is amazing!

You always feel better for having been around a great mind, if only for a short time. You know you learned what you needed to know or wanted to know, and could have taught yourself if you wished to do so. Most of all, you feel blessed, wishing you could do the class over and over again or go to another event taught by such a sage, but you cannot. The class is over when the group was given whatever needed to be spread then.

Once you decide you know everything, you die. You wither from the mind down through the spine and into your legs, arms, and finally the pancreas decides you cannot absorb another word. Yes, it is true. You have not reached that level yet and do not realize it is true, but you will one day soon.

Have you ever wanted to move and could not? Have you ever wanted to stay in one place and could not? You felt the wave of movement and either embraced it or not, but it was an event that comes over everyone once. If you have the type of mind that does not want to be blind or out of line with others of your time, you may want to move to find others like you, but do not. Let time take you by the hand and lead you to the promised ones.

As you age and learn much about the universe—and who you are, look up and look inside *you* and decide what you need to do. At times new work comes through for you to do. Most of this life you are not expected to do much or travel widely, but when asked, please do.

The distance between two places is not as far as it was when you thought about it and decided it would not work for you. Once you decide you can climb the social ladder by virtue of your work or money you earn, you lose perspective. You forget you started on a different step and will never reach the highest level of society until you die and others sense you were better than they—or you were great and they only noticed it then. Climbing in order to feel great or be recognized by others is a way of hiding the fact you are not being yourself—and probably will not design a life great enough for *you* this time.

Be as you wish to be and everyone will notice? Not true, but it helps when you cannot sense what you can do. You may not want to be the best plumber humanity has ever seen, but you can be a great man and do it easily if you practice and decide to be wise.

It takes many men to build a country, but only a few to blow it up. Why? It is not easy to be creative! It is very difficult to get others to agree to build anything bigger than they seem to be. Many want to destroy whatever to enjoy the defeat of those they envy, thus you can easily assemble people to destroy what took centuries to build.

Who would envy you?

You may enjoy what you do and assume others envy you for it, but few want to work as another does now. People now desire the image of having it all without working hard. How many in this country of yours are unemployed and will not work for another at any pay level, because they believe themselves to be better than others?

Think on it and you will sense some will never better themselves. They are not interested in being the best. Others want to ingest enough of whatever to change their view of life, so they can be lazy and maltreat their spouse and others—believing they have power. You decide, but vacancies are filled when people of skill must work and will take whatever they can get for the time it takes them to get on with their lives and build another career that survives better in difficult times.

You have envied others, yet doubt anyone envies what you do. Why? You probably do not work for fun, and hate being paid every day for doing something not great. Obviously, the answer is: Become great at whatever you are assigned. Do not attempt to leave something until you master it. All then remember you as a great worker who never did anything wrong, even if you often did.

Some cannot or will not do their best!

If that makes no sense, then review work you came to do and determine if it is complete. If it is not done, you know you cannot leave and never be asked to return or work until it is done, yet some say you do not know what to do now. You know, but refuse to go inward deep enough to find answers. That is to say you cannot do what you have yet to discover is your goal in life.

Once you discover you came to teach another or reach out and help many, you may be unable to do it then. You can spend months trying to do what some complete in moments. If it is not in your line to accomplish a part of the art you came to produce, it makes no difference.

All who say they are better than others are stuck in reverse and will not move forward while here. You must be able to recognize you are no better than others and must respect every human being—and anything that breathes and could be you now or again. Be aware of this before you decide to look down on others this life. Once you realize you are no prize and your work is no better than it was years ago, you will change if you are wise and begin rearranging your mind to accept everyone's gifts.

All who have what you define as a *gift* are praised, but what about those who do things you have no ability to know about? You may say you love to watch someone play the piano, but if unaccustomed to the music they play, you may downplay their gift. You want to hear what you created or are used to hearing. You say you appreciate the skill of another, but probably not until you attempt to do it, too. Thus, we encourage you to dabble enough to figure out how difficult it is to develop a skill you were born to use now.

What you describe as art is not!

We see art in the trees and all that is graceful and comes to flower or leaf without any need to become what another says must be done to pass a test or win a contest. If you sing with great beauty, yet forced to take many lessons, you lose much and never enjoy singing as you once did. It becomes work, and you deserve to be paid for what you sing then. You lost the ability to toss your head back and let out a scream modulated by your body to sound great.

You did nothing to deserve it, nevertheless, it is wonderful. Can you assert that you developed your art enough to ask others to pay you to display it today? If not, best to work harder and forget about fame and fortune now.

Everyone who wants to gain a spiritual gift can earn it if they work hard. Yes, it is not easy to deserve a *Gift of The Holy Spirit,* but it does exist and you can earn it. All you must do is cause many to understand the power of God and how it works in this life. You will then be blessed with gifts of a certain type. If you help those who are gifted by easing them out of this life, you often are blessed by receiving the gift of Spirit they can give at the last moment of life or ask you to take then. All gifts are without form and made manifest when you accept them.

What if you are clairvoyant and can see into time? You are no different from others, but can focus in a way others now refuse to accept exists. You found the trick or were born with it—and can open to that point of view, but it is not a *Gift of The Holy Spirit*. It is merely a point of view and easy for anyone to learn to do.

The work of one gifted in spiritual work is such that most never notice it. She or he goes about their business and others ask them what to do and receive wise answers. You are now aware of several who will help you if ever in serious trouble, but you may not bless them enough that they wish to respond to your requests. Why? You try to ignore gifts from *The Lord* out of envy or jealousy, thus are ignored more and more for your coarse ways. Do not expect a soul trained to be of use to man and accepts only what God can prescribe to want to help you. It is not necessary to be a perfect man or woman to work for the betterment of mankind or accept the blessings of *The Holy Spirit*, but it tends to be that way.

All who seek work from others know they cannot provide it themselves—or are silly to try. If you have to accept work from another, do not say they are not nice. Why? Once again you are biting the hand that feeds you—maybe even your family, and it will become known. You will then be asked to leave or not permitted to grow. When discovered by others to be ungrateful, and possibly nasty, you blame the owner of a shop or business. Why? You are now unaware of your disposition.

To behave in a way that sets you apart from others is mysterious to us. Unlike human beings, we are not social animals, but we can get close and work together to do work that needs to be done. Why can't you do it, too? You can! It is your ego that makes it difficult to succeed. It is your disposition to be false or nasty when another leaves the room that makes you appear unfit to lead. It is not your truthfulness and piety, or how you groom your body, that excludes you from a group.

If you take time to develop your life, you will find many working at about the same pace. So go to school when others do. Work as an apprentice when others learn similar life skills. Marry when others your age marry. Why? You will have a group around you much like you who will help you move ahead more quickly than if you are out-of-sync with others your age.

What shocked you about life?

Have you grown beyond what you believed you would be? Have you achieved more easily what you thought you could never do? Whatever, you are who you are and clever enough not to say you are brighter than others if you are—or not as smart as others. Do not judge or describe yourself to others!

Speaking of judging yourself and what you do—or telling others about you, why do you assume they are interested? You may not realize that most of the time egotists do not think about anyone but themselves, thus unhappy to be told to think about you. Also, you are of little interest to anyone distinctly different from *you*.

You may sense no trouble associating with strangers, yet they do. Why? You cannot sufficiently answer this now to go into it with us, but the next time you begin a racist rant and expound upon it to others in a group, try to see yourself in a strange land. It will improve you, maybe make you appear wiser than you are.

Take the high road and arrive higher in the world than others. You may not want to see it as easy, or it matters which path you follow, but it does. The one who immediately takes the high road starts out with a steep climb, doing the tough work early in life while others gradually climb to start, putting off the necessary difficult climbing until unable to complete it easily—or die while scaling the last mile. Choose wisely!

All you have in life is yours? You may not have reached an age when you know what you want or how to achieve a degree of competency that will support your present lifestyle, but if you try you can feed yourself.

You need not lean on others and ask them for alms, if willing to take a deserted—not overworked road with much you can do to support you.

Why follow others?

When we started teaching and reaching out to others of a far different life than ours, we did not know who you were. We aimed our work at *The Scribe* and asked if she had any questions, then we asked groups of her students what they wanted to do—even a few who excelled and did very well, but no one came close to what we write now. Why? They were not into the work—merely wished to belong to a group or be taught by one who knows what to do to ascend.

That is why you must seek out those who live on mountain tops or are recluses in big cities now. They think or they die! They act out their lives or do not survive.

Before you talk to those who teach philosophy you need to know why and how. Philosophy and poetry let the mind run free. If you accept whatever the masses say is great, you are not well-developed socially or mentally. Get over believing otherwise and figure out why.

Upon arriving on Earth to become a human being who can rise in your world, you have much to do. Most of the difficult work is done by age 5! Get real and work half as hard to learn why you arrived here. Get down to the business of living your life with style and grace now!

Chapter Twenty-Five

If you want to be known as a woman or man of greatness, you cannot *'esteem'* yourself into being someone great. If you try that, you will be seen as conceited and overly important in your mind alone. Why? You are not without a constant flow of self-knowledge growing and slowing, even receding at times, transmitting pieces or bytes of information others can easily tap into and use to hack your reputation to bits in minutes.

What you are will be known within moments of approaching anyone who has any sensitivity. You may not notice them, but they are aware of you and what you intend to do. If you intend to do something new, no one may be able to figure you out—at least not at first, but doing things over-and-over again, people will recognize you as wise or full of what they require. For example, the essence of having no compassion is easy to spot. You must not believe you can be cruel and mean, and no one will immediately pick up on it.

To be yourself, and know you mean no ill will to others, is not a skill. It is what you believe, conceive, and generate when you meet others. If you are close to retirement and slouching about, others know you are unwilling to work hard. However, if you are working hard and others are not, they may sense you are not at it as much as in the past, because they have to work harder to pick up the slack.

The biggest problem facing humanity now is egotism—and the lack of information being accepted as fact unless watered down until a third grader knows what it means or how to use it. This lack of education is not harmful to an underdeveloped nation as long as it is governed full-time by wise men and women; but how many *'developed'* nations are governed by egotists now?

Once you decide you can govern others based on your income level or what you inherited in life, you begin to disintegrate—not doing much to affiliate with lesser crowds. That ends when you discover you cannot be elected to office without people surrounding you constantly in most countries—and such crowds may not have much but hope to gain. When you give up and opt to give people what they seek, you become the one they want, but only as long as it takes to deplete your stakes in the game.

When can you develop a new life and become a better person—did it begin at birth or when? Later in life will it come to you that you worked hard and did not make as much as those who hated others? If so, you hated enough to envy and wish to be like them longer than you believe now.

We would not envy the proud, the vain, the ignorant, or anyone unable to figure out what is going on around them now. You may not know today what is going on around you, but once you discover how well-equipped or educated you need to be to figure out the next week or two, you will do so and not ask if anyone knows as much as you. Why? You hate to admit you did not get it! You prefer to act as if you got it—rather than admit you need knowledge.

Vanity is the middle name of many who remain stupid while playing the game of life today. Once you admit you know very little and are willing to learn, you leap ahead of those who do not. When you finally admit you do not know it all or cannot get it now, you become wiser than you were. If you think you know what to do or can hire those who do, you may not believe that is true. If so, you are not only stupid, but possibly lazy and unable to do much to save your life if necessary.

Take time to count your blessings now and see what you lack. Whatever you say you do without others around is what you do best, which often requires you to show off your style if you are an egoist. We want you to understand that being caught up in your own publicity is a scandal when it turns out no one likes you. Do not tempt others to repeatedly put you down!

Be yourself and find out what you do best. Try to perfect it without complaining or bragging that you do it better than others. Why? Neither is conducive to sharing a blissful attitude with those living in bliss now.

Smile and do your part well. Be yourself and enjoy whatever you have to do as much as doing what you love. This produces a state in which you become more than confident of your work and are willing to do it for others—which adds to your prestige.

Bliss is it, but not something you shout about and continue to live with. Why shout you feel bliss? Because you believe you are the best or first to experience it. You may not realize it, but others do and will condescendingly smile and thus lose their place. If you do not get it and assume others do not know what to do, either, you may claim to be spiritual in material meetings or during base-level communications, thus tempting others to feel superior, too.

Take your time deciding who you might be and all you do is put off doing what you must do to make amends for what you did not get or have no desire to complete, but still must do. You then will be unable to flow and grow as fast as others learning what to do who practice a lot. Practice does not exactly create perfection, but it definitely makes you more confident and expectant to be crowned a champion now.

All that is paid out or played out to control crowds is not without a lot of thought by mean-spirited people who want to make money from them, as well as others. To bring a game to the forefront, they lay odds one team or another will or will not win or whatever, placing people who gamble at the weak end of their needs. If you take much from the weak, you will never be blessed at the end. You cannot take what a widow requires and use it for a wasteful life without missing out on ascending when judged within at your end.

Obviously, what you feel or believe is something you created and carry with you. No one can tell you to accept a religious thought or not.

You decide and will not be criticized if you stay with it and try to live by its values. However, you will be torn into pieces by the hypocritical crowds if you do not live up to what they say you believe. So do not stop doing what you believe is best. All who stop, live to regret it.

Your final test is based on criteria you present as required to live a good life. If you enter flawed elements into your mind—never read about good men and women, or seek to be like them, you will not pass. You suffer from a false belief in what it means to *'get ahead in life'.*

If you never ask, no one will give?

If you are guided by wise individuals and whatever is required, why would you ask? You are who associates with those who have much to give in repayment for your support. If you cannot support another, you have to make it alone.

It is not easy to see or believe, but it is impossible to go through life alone, without anyone around you. Why? Too many people occupy your planet now. You would have to cut through the crowd to find a place isolated enough for you to survive and live alone the rest of your life.

First, fit in and make it with others, then swim with all who are dolphins and easy to communicate. It is *you* who comes through when you communicate within. You can try to hide your power or light, or say you live a different life, but in the end it is what you do that matters most. Spending hours cheating another for fun or making a living harming others—not caring about their offspring, will end badly. Do not expect to leap into another life and be allowed to continue destroying this mind.

The mind is where you can change now and begin rearranging what others do for you, as well as those who may come after you. If angry and never at peace, how do you change? You begin by realizing you are wrong. You may believe you are right, but you are wrong. All who defy the age of peace and are easily enraged are not in the right pew or doing what to them is natural. They will be unhappy when lined up in time and escorted to join a line circulating back into a similar world.

Being abusive and unable to manage your appetites is difficult to discuss when drunk, but many drink in order to feel they are one of the crowd. Is that honest—or a way to confuse the brain into believing they are no different from those you loathe for not being good, honest, or willing to help others? When you decide to cross into another personality, be it anger, drink, or drugs conveying you to an altered state, you are judged by everyone around you.

Be you! All you want to be and can be is written every day while en route to becoming the one you came here to be. When young, decide to follow your mind home and not step out of line until old enough to take care of you when too old to work as you did. Once *you* can take care of you until you die, you will not fear growing old.

All is gone? All is bliss once you get this: You can enjoy life, but only if you are right, and your life equals what you believe it should be. Try!

Chapter Twenty-Six

Put your life on hold for an hour. Let go of everything holding you back mentally or even physically. Think about one thing only—YOU!

When you realize this being called *'you'* is not without others who are also *you,* and you have deeper connections to what you often mistake as God talking to you—but better described as *The Holy Spirit* guiding you, you are ready to think and believe there is a being higher than anything you can now conceive. That being is YOU. We will describe *you* in a way conceivable by most people that will not lead you into deep problems when you try to levitate and ascend into the higher being *you* can be any time you enter an altered state high enough to view who *you* are now.

All of this is complicated if you do not look at *you* as a human being among many others like you who are breathing and being *you,* too. Once you connect with this idea and sense you may come back to relive a life you admire and cannot give up when told to move on. You need to be aware it is better to ascend whenever you can.

When we talk about YOU as God, or whatever you prefer to call the universe known to *you,* yet not yours to direct and move about now, you may become confused. Why? You want to believe you are either nothing, or are a god, thus more important than you are. The extremes you take as human beings extend your belief system, but many are lost and will never find their way back to the line they came from when they first appeared here.

Make up your mind to be *you* and forget anything that may have happened upon birth that distracted you from your work on Earth. Keep thinking of what you are and can be, and make moves to do it. As you move you often discover you are new to *you* as well as beloved by many others.

Being *you* is easy to describe, but may not be easy to achieve if you cheat and lie full-time. Many think only the weak tell things as they are—or you will be despised if you tell your life story as if a tragedy. Actually, you are not expected to have had it easy here. If you did, better not mention it, since no one else thinks they had it easy and will be jealous. We will not belabor what jealousy and envy create. If you do, get over it!

When you seek bliss and ignore God is, was, and will be as long as you are conceived as you seem to be, you cannot believe it. You cannot discover what is loved and beloved by others—and available to you now. The fact is, you can live in bliss. You do not have to slip in and out of it. Why? Bliss exists as is!

Quickly assuming the role of an idiot when others speak of their religious beliefs is not as stupid as some might think who love to convert others to whatever they believe is the way to be. Since we are teachers, not preachers, we do not harbor hopes of converting you to believe in God, and we would never attempt to do so. If you accept that incarnate beings taught you much about life, achieving bliss while in it, and how to ascend to another plane when this life is ended, you have to accept God is, was, and will be.

To take upon you the work of others, as some love to do now, is foolish and does not work. You have your life to live and can earn a living honorably by assisting others. Helping some do better than they otherwise might in their lines of work, but you cannot insist your way is the only way. You will be shot down, and your line will not be remembered when you are gone.

All you need now is to at times conduct your life in a way that is conducive to being lively and happy—filled with enough work or worry so you wish to continue to improve. You may not understand you are here because you wanted to learn how to manifest and create with your hands or their equivalent, thus chose to come to Earth. For anyone to understate or underrate those who develop a way to make life better using their hands is to deny why you came here to live this life. Try to make peace with your mind, so your body can enjoy its reason for being here now.

Once the body is employed, and the mind can watch over it without doing inferior work or taking you where you need to go, you can meditate and not be bothered by the workings of your thoughts. That is why so many worry. They cannot stop thinking, because they do not work with their bodies enough. You may be unable to move your body as others can, but it continues to need exercise provided by the brain and helped along by the mind. You may want to lay down and never move your legs, but a week or two of inactivity will prove you do not want to do that!

It is easy to follow the groove worn into your mind from following work you trained to do to make a living, but difficult to change now. Keep reminding yourself of that once you reach the age when memory does not help as much as hold you back. Adults are required to do something meaningful, and when they try to avoid it or cling to childhood longer than others, they are dropped. You can say it is untrue, but it remains the same regardless of where you live now.

To be a meaningful person is nonsense. You are a human being with a body, mind, and spiritual work you shelter in an area unknown to most and difficult to describe, even if you live in it most of the time. To seek ecstasy through the body is also nonsense, but better for you than seeking to masturbate using ideas others create. You may be shocked to see self-abuse is of no use unless it provides a release of some kind—but there you have it!

When talking of self-abuse, do not include self-pity. It is a poor excuse for not doing what is assigned—or you asked for. When you shout at others, telling them to stop, do you want them to stop immediately or are you frustrated because you want to do it, too? Be secure and not feel the need to tell others what to do or lead people who mean nothing to you.

In the previous **Books of Wisdom**, we talked at length about You (your Higher Self). In this chapter we said little about You, instead dwelling on the ego, or little you, in order to leap into the void that is YOU. To discuss that which exists and keeps you as is, you must read and think more about the abyss that exists—that which is not bliss.

Bliss is what you are and hold to be you when you can enjoy this world or be *you*. You may not want to say happy is being bliss-filled, so remain calm and think often of others in order to enjoy bliss. Most use such expressions to describe achieving bliss now, but we do not!

Chapter Twenty-Seven

When you seek bliss, you grow. If never told bliss is the ability to be *you* and enjoy your present existence, you would not know you can feel blissful, thus not accept it when you get it. You want bliss to be a thrill, the ability to leap over tall buildings without moving, or something equally weird. Seldom do you accept it as a gift of *The Divine* that connects you to all that is—which indeed is bliss!

Without trying to feel wonderful or out of your usual mindset, sit and relax now. Do not worry! Do it—with no arguing about how it should be done.

If you are now worried, scowling, and upset enough to frown at others, forget about bliss for a minute. Once you try doing the opposite of whatever your teacher tells you to do, you are into disciplinary measures and in need of corrective behavior. Frankly, we are not interested in either. Control your mind and decide when you are ready to thrive and feel *The Divine* rise within you!

Whatever you have to give or live up to because it was gifted to you, set it aside. Ignore it! Pretend you must be you and live with what you are and have created in your life so far.

Do not hesitate to cry if it makes you feel better, but deduct all you did not produce or earn for your present use. Once over pity at not having as much material goods as you thought you would have by now, think back to what you had when you were happiest and felt the presence of God in your life and around your mind.

Without further ado, smile!

Let go of what you know about life. Let it sit at the side of the road as you travel slowly from words to work. Let your mind go and not worry about beating others to the end or doing better than you ever did. Work now on reading each word—letting each word sit, before moving to the next, then on to another view of *you*.

The world is yours. What you do now is about you—not the crowd around you. Do not admire if you have much compared to others. What did you do to deserve more than anyone you know? Nothing? Thus you do not enjoy it now as they would, since they envy you for it.

The mind loves to complete a sentence. It wants to race on and see what else there is to read—how many pages you can finish today. Let us stifle your mind and not add more pages now!

Chapter Twenty-Eight

Peace is achieved—not merely accepted, as what you deserve after warring with others. However, some can never enjoy peace—thus no bliss for them. When you determine you require peace and quiet, yet continue doing everything you usually do, ask yourself why.

What would you do if all were suddenly silenced and you had nothing to do? That truly determines your reliance on others—not the reverse. To work for others and never enjoy it is not a problem, unless you try to undermine them at any time or in any way. Once you do that, you are without redemption and cannot earn pay the usual way. When you decide earning a good salary will not give you peace and love, what then? That is when you begin undermining those who are happy all the time.

Why not do what you love for pay?

What you love to do may never be required by others, because it is not that great, or anyone can do it. There are many reasons for not being paid to do what you want to do. Meanwhile lazy people say they cannot work at whatever they are hired to do, because it is not their line of art or not what they like. Take time to decide what you can do for others to receive payment you can use today, test if you can do it, and then pursue it.

All who claim they love whatever they do may love it. Do you? Do you love what you do and proclaim it to others, too? Why? What would make you say you love your work today? A raise in pay, being seen as earning much, loving it all the way, or hoping someone buys it?

A *'day at the races'* is what most do every day and call it a job. You race about, continually competing with others, betting you will end up ahead. That is not why you took the job or wanted to work now, but you fall into it when others bet you cannot do it well. Instead, try to limit time working as you do if it makes you ill or evil to live with now.

As you look over the contents of this chapter, notice *work* is mentioned a lot, yet nothing stands out as blissful or providing bliss—nor succeeding at it. *'What can I do'*, you might ask and we would say, *'create!'*

Do what you like! Create a new wave that sweeps over you and perhaps everyone in line with you in time. See if it makes sense to do it full-time. If you can work on art or do something beautiful as a craft, you will laugh when others complain about how little they are paid, because you likely make less. Whatever you think now, it is the man or woman who forgets pride and does the work everyone hates who makes the most money based on education and pay grade.

When the sun rises and you forget to leave for work or school on time, you are who sets out to be late—not another. What happens next is because you did not want to rise and work hard, thus are behind everyone who agreed to meet then. You cannot feel free or understand what they are doing when you walk in late, thus you are stressed. You did it by not getting off to a good start.

All you are and will be starts with how you begin working when no one is around to tell you what to do. You work at home, office, or wherever you happen to be—or not. No one expects you to beat them at what they do, but the lazy person is never seen as a threat, thus most set out to best them.

Do not work without a net!

You require a net to keep you safe when no longer working; cannot complete a project you started; or require more than previously. When you sense you could fall through the cracks and land on your head or back, instead of on your feet, you begin working within. The mind starts working on what you can earn to insure you are never spurned or told to relearn what you must know to work and create a living now.

Working with a short temper because you forget you cannot do everything at once and others want things done when you agreed to produce them, you will worry and fret! To believe others demand too much is to admit you did not speak up and make your demands known when the plans were aligned. If you want to succeed with what you believe is your life work, you must work as if you will remain there—not as though you plan to leave tomorrow.

When you decide your work is not worthy of you, remember when you thought it was and who is behind this present idea. If you wanted to do it—and suddenly are sure it is wrong, most likely someone manipulated and convinced you to do it. Be sure, before moving out of what you love to do or were trained to achieve.

Move intuitively to see if things might work out in the future. Using your intuitive abilities to determine if you can work at something new—is not new! This is how you reproduce work not used much today, too. The one who came to be you this life is accustomed to time and can move in-and-out of it to see what can be. Try moving into time or going outside the lines, then write what you find.

Outside of being you, whatever you do is probably useless once you prove you can do it. Read that line over several times and remember it. Why? It is useful. It teaches you what not to do. You can rebel, do whatever, regret it when you ascend, if you can ascend at the end, or simply obey and feel immediate relief, because it was the right thing to do and you did it at the best time, too.

All you do is work for *you*, regardless of what you may say to others. You are not working for anyone other than *you*, even if a slave today. You do not war much, run away, or do new things, but slaves come in every shade and every clime, and are well-described throughout these lines.

Read and seek! You will find being blind to wisdom does not release you from being wise. Whatever and whomever you might want to be, or whenever you want to be that one, is never fun. So be you and get rid of the idea that what you do for a living makes you better than others who work for a living, too. It does not matter what you do, but it tells a lot about you when you sacrifice to complete what you came to this life to do.

The work is over and you are free to be as you wish! Take over and let this work flow within and around you now. Do not read any further…Wait until you feel the pleasant sensation of peace and bliss entering and circulating through you, or return to this work when you can understand bliss and cannot remain in ignorance.

Chapter Twenty-Nine

Outside your life are many who look inside your mind, or try to do so at times, wondering who you are and why you act tired when they are not. Sickness is like that. Many who are without any idea of what it is to be sick or tired think others exaggerate the weird way it tears you apart every day. Do not allow the way others behave enter your mind and destroy your life. Be yourself and care for your body when it is tired—and most definitely when it is not well.

What you feel is not exactly real

You may think one leg is not long enough or an arm is too strong to ever go wrong, but it happens if you do not pay attention when young to how you walk, stand, and earn your bread. Be aware, even though you work long hours without getting tired, it does not mean you should do it often. Take time to rest, restore, and keep your mind secure—not bothered by those who look better in your eyes than you do now.

Whatever you do, do not alter your body to gain admirers. You will lose you, if you do. In the course of creating man-made miracles meant to help those disfigured by events they had little or no control over, you can create someone no one knows or can adjust to and trust. All who love another, or want to be like their idol, try to change in some way.

Trust that you are built the way you are in order to fulfill the work you came to do. Sounds simple, but if you are not built like a dancer or able to work long hours, you can become such a person if you try, but why? Why practice all day to be half as good as those born to do it?

Now that you have used up half of what you produce in a day or two, living in ways that make no sense to you, can you retire and live off the land or others? Do not plan to do that! If you let go and spend all you gather—never saving for the end of your days, you will regret it. It is not to say you must slave and put everything away for later days, but be wise enough to consider that this is not it, and you do live longer than you believe if you do not need to worry about everyday life and what it costs to live in your society.

We are talking about the body now, but the mind controls the body more than the other way around. You may not want to believe you cannot be anyone you want to be, because you believe it will make you stand out from the crowd, but it is a fact. You can copy, manipulate, study, and deliberate on what others create easily today, but it merely delays you on your way home. Do not work on being someone else, instead deliberately work on following your life and being you!

Whatever you say and believe today will not harm you when you leave the planet, could delay your leaving it. Why? You came to do something—and said you would do it in a certain period of time. If that time arrives and you are not ready to go, you may be given more time or even a substitute who will step in and do the work you require to pass over, but that is unlikely now. Why? You have time to be yourself, to do whatever you want, and move onto the next plane or not.

When faced with your life and asked to judge why you did whatever you did that stopped you and would not let you pass, you may wish you had done a lot more studying for the final exam, but that will pass. Once asked if you will take the path to the next *life* (or whatever you want to call that choice), you will be asked if you want to go or stay in this plane as is today. You will say, *"I wish to pass on to the next life,"* and mean every word of it then.

If you can move ahead, but wish to wait for others to arrive, you may be allowed to help them pull up their lives and hurry about and ascend now or then, but better to get on with your life, because in the end you will resent that they never noticed your sacrifice of life or time for them. You cannot always be loved or admired, but if you can look yourself in the face and believe you lived in grace, you are okay now and will pass your test without prejudice at the end. We will not be there to help you over that final threshold, but we can be read and studied now if you wish to better prepare yourself for that final time on this side of the veil of this life.

No matter who sees you, or does not recognize your abilities now, you see and will polish your skills and attributes until you shine from working on them as if asked to do so by *The Divine.* You know you have enough now? If you do not move about and adjust to life now, you cannot assume that will be the case. Take care, be aware, and do what is required to live without harming others.

As you work and develop a mind that can feed and take care of your body, keep well and think about what others do that may harm you, too. Do others abuse or use you as a tool to get what they want? If so, you can leave and do something new, but remember you may not be able to leave immediately. It may take time to ease out of restraints, but you can do it.

If you ended your freedom by acting out in ways harmful to others, all is done that can be done. It does not release you from being a free human being who respects everyone as of now. You must behave in established ways or end without your body knowing freedom of movement and your mind being shackled over time to whatever is provided—not what you gain alone.

Take time to enjoy life. When unemployed, do not bother others about work suitable to your life here and now. Do it!

What if when you arrived you were not given parents who could love and care for you? You were aware and took a gamble, or you deluded yourself it would not matter, OR you are here to see how it affects you and what you did to others. That karmic kind of explanation is not without flaw, but it helps you gain information about how life is made, destroyed, and then resurrected.

If not you, who would you be?

Once you demonstrate you are in charge of your life, no one will tell you what to do. You may be told what you did wrong or praised for doing well what you were not required to do, but you are who determines why you do whatever and when it might end. Do not pretend others control you now! It is a lie that can end your thoughts of living to the end of this life and traveling into the world of *The Divine* more.

When you work on life from inside out, you see things differently from those who work on their bodies hoping to find God. You may meet at some point and know what another is seeking, but it is highly unlikely. Both have different ways of accomplishing what you set out to do? You decided on a particular path and someone came through and directed you. If not, you lack guidance and need to find your spiritual source before you are another hour older than now.

Chapter Thirty

Prepare to do work you know nothing about—and be ready to do it quickly, is the best advice anyone this side of the veil can offer a candidate for enlightenment. If you are without any idea of what to do, you cannot ascend in this time. It takes work to disassemble what you believe and want to conceive in order to make room for all that is new to you. Without moving about and ending work that never was, or should not have been, you have no way of knowing what stays and what is best put aside now.

Try to understand what is important and what is not, then move along. Once you move into a mood where you feel good, most do not want to move out of it. Why? They want to laze about and stay in that state and enjoy life. However, the clever know if they select wisely, they will not come back repeatedly to deal with what bites them in the neck now.

You may not like gnats or pests, but they make you move in order to get rid of them. When you decide to sit and let them bite or annoy you, part of you goes dead. It is admired by some that stoics among you can let pests annoy them, never aware it harms their bodies or minds. We say that is unwise.

If quickly reviewing all you do, you will find only a few things come to mind. Why? What is uppermost in your memory is what you did last or worry about now. If it is trivial or worse, you harbor an enemy of your work. You are giving room and thought to what is waste and not of your time in this space. Daily take time to erase the dross and clean up what is false.

Today you can work quickly—every day is that way. However, due to a dream that will not leave, some days are not easily entered into. In a dream perhaps you felt someone trying to harm you, thus you awakened thinking evil of another. Is that wisdom or bad advice from the other side? You decide, then move on and do what you want.

When deciding to live your life and be yourself, you face contempt from some who want you to be their toy or slave. Why listen to those who never give you what you require—or think well of you? The mind wants to rectify what is out-of-line, and if allowed, will take your life and use it to convince others you are great, nice, wise, or whatever. Do not take time going over what you did well. Instead, know your best work and be satisfied with it until you can move up and do it even better.

"Once outside the world of the wise it is easy to be fooled and led astray." This is not true and you know why. Reconstruct this sentence below and improve it.

Having corrected what was inaccurate, incorrect, or brazenly lacking in cleverness, what then? Do you preach, believe, or remember it better than you otherwise might? Yes! You now remember its essence, because you corrected it and put it into your own words. This is why education is required to teach others.

What if you never worked or did much for others, would you be allowed to teach them how to reach the other side now? How would you know you could ascend if you never worked on understanding and putting into action what you think? Belief is not what happens when you work hard. Confidence enters and your mind takes over and guides you until it comes upon something it has never seen. You have to then teach your mind to accept or reject whatever is next.

Having accepted the premise that bliss is not indulging in whatever you do easily and with others, you may find these lines difficult to view as helpful to you. Why? You do not want to work. You do not want to read. You want others to tell you exactly what to do!

Denying the truth does not erase it or delay its input. The truth has a way of making your mind sway—even betraying you at times from saying and doing what you planned that day. If you met a sage and talked for a day, and afterward felt what you do is nonsense and untrue, would you leave your life as it was and walk down a new line. Is that ever wise?

How often have you changed your mind?

You are changing your mind right now, unaware of how many times you change direction in a day until you settle down to unwind and find you cannot. Besieged by many thoughts, you cannot release even a few thoughts in order to meditate for a short time. This indicates you are besieged by what you want to be, can achieve, or need but ignored most of your life so far.

Try to end the tyranny of the mind before you vegetate and cannot write. Be aware of your tongue wagging when you have nothing to say. You cannot talk long enough to prove your words have strength or wisdom, but you can talk longer than you write or walk.

The work of some is to inspire. For others it appears you are here to teach people to not waste their lives in idleness. The work you create during the day is seldom what you do during nights of deep sleep. You may want to believe you dream without meaning, but that is idleness invading your doubts—saying you have no worries now.

You may be worried, upset, demented—unable to rest, but usually you sleep even when deeply depressed. The drug, or whatever you believe usually interferes, is easy to remove once you recognize and accept proof it is not helping you. This is said to let your brain in on what goes on around you now and why it cannot accept everything you do as being wise for the body, too.

When you eat what is poison to you, alibiing that it is not that bad—or perhaps an allergy or two you can abuse without harming you, you are a fool. You are not listening to your body. You are not taking care of your life!

You need to listen to what your body likes and wants, then feed it the best. Your mind, however, likes what it was told brings pleasure. Food may taste terrible to others, but you believe it tastes good and cannot stop thinking about it when hungry—adding it to whatever you eat to feel satisfied. Is that ever wise?

Hunger is seldom experienced by the wise, because they do not starve—instead pace themselves until they can eat later—always maintaining about the same level of energy. Are you hungry now? If full, or having eaten within 12 hours, you are merely sensing you would like to stop reading now. Eating makes sense to your mind if not your body, because today eating replaces what most people desire or love.

When you generalize and assume everyone is like you, how much time is wasted daily? Assuming you do not waste time, you will not get along with others unlike you, so best to assume you are different and can fit in with almost everyone else. This is easier than moving in order to learn about what your world provides now.

Work that takes you places does not always help win better relationships. In fact, it ends many and begins some that never go anywhere. Are you thus wasting your love? You found a way to pretend to invest in others without being in love with them. When you believe love is all there is and all you need, you forget you are not here to love others, rather discover how love can build relationships and bridge many cultures.

The essence of our work is to help you win this life and get in line to cross over at the end into a better line and a higher plane. If you forget it, you will work hard, love yourself to the exclusion of believing another is as important, and leave without learning why you are here now. Remember, you are here to meet and greet many who traveled with you in many lives or lines, merging with you for a time—or always, in order to strengthen your spiritual work now.

It sounds strange to most! But if you analyze and try to work it over and change it a lot, you now have a theory that works in your mind. Try it!

Once you disagree with others, you begin working harder than you otherwise might. Be aware that those who agree are not always aware they are lazy or do not want to work harder than necessary, so they agree or accept whatever is given now. You do have to work hard to build a life here, but the lasting effect is you do not want to come back!

When you finish working hard, filled your belly, and love everyone who is good to you, what do you do then? You are here to develop you! What exactly does that require? Work hard and create new ways of looking at others—accepting that God is required to power your work and life this time before you can leave again.

Why not stay awhile and enjoy this life? You might, but others infer that the next life is better, so you wish to see what happens next. Do not fool the mind into thinking this life is a station where you stand around and wait for the next train. It is not. It is assigned by your work in time and not what anyone else said you must do. Find out why *you* insisted on living this life and you will feel bliss.

Bliss will not build a new world around you here, but is the essence of what is. You find it when you least expect it! It takes time and hard work for most to connect to bliss the first time, but once you delight in life and feel what it is like to be truly loved in spirit and real life, you desire it, treasure it, and will not let others deride it.

Bliss is it—and you have it whenever you can ignore what others explore and decide is the best world. You must decide and work to attain bliss—no one else will provide a better way to gain it today.

So far no mention of what bliss is, so we expect that you know what you want when you see the word *bliss*, but it is not what others believe bliss to be. Right? If you do not agree, then sit for a minute and look at what others tried to tell you and how few times you did what they said.

Having thought about bliss, and what it is, you are ready to ascend. Is that it? Is that why you seek bliss now? Are you preparing to die or ready to leave this work on Earth or whatever?

You do not admit it, but you want a good life, and to be able to enjoy whatever you do now without feeling guilty. You believe bliss is not what others claim it to be—rather a state in which you can follow any and all hedonistic pleasures and be absolved by the mind and God as doing what is right within this life. Be aware, when you decide what is right, what is wrong, what another must do, and how long it takes to live a great life, you make yourself a god.

Judgment is reserved for the few everyone believes to be wise, but in your estimation how many judges are wise? If none are wiser than you—run for public office! If you cannot do that work, then help those who sacrifice to do it well—rather than pay or accept bribes from those who will cheat you out of a good life.

Government is the province of man—not what God assembles here and now. You can blame anyone you like, but do not lay any blame on God. You are who you are, and here to create whatever state in which you wish to participate, so do not claim everyone else is false and you are not.

The ability to let others do your worldly business and not feel worry or pain is non-existent now. You want everything, yet do not wish to pay the price if you can find it in another country or place better than where you live now. You immigrate or travel to foreign places in order to deliberate on what they do better than you? You become aware your homeland is not the best of all, but like it as is or you immigrate somewhere else.

Having changed your life many times, did you ever move to a place where you were not accepted, thus you left and never went back? That is the homeland or hometown of some and how many live there now. Why? The world you once wanted is gone, and you cannot decide if the new one is better. If true, you would work harder to make it as you want it to be. Working hard is definitely not popular now, thus too many sit and complain, nagging others to do the same.

Bliss is not accepting what is, but working to be the best you can be—taking time to feel you are making progress or are amazing as is—OR you are ready to do whatever God gives you now. Today, most have to work a life or two before they can feel that way, but it need not matter, since you have to move at your pace. You move into many views before merging in the end with what you believe to be God of this life. Try now to imagine nothing and you will see things—maybe even rise to another level.

About to end your reading for a time? Let your mind rest. Decide it is time to remove your work mind and put it aside to relax. Notice relaxation is easiest after you worked hard. That is why we put you through so many tests this chapter—so you can relax, rest, and develop a new life that works better than this one did.

Chapter Thirty-One

In the world around you are many who will take you down and put you out if they can, so it is up to you to weed such villains from your mind and not give them any time. Why? You cannot stop others from living foolish lives, but you can treat your life as a serious devotion that requires your attention—not the friendship of those who might bend you to their way of living this life.

You may believe you are a leader, but leaders go where their followers are determined to go. Do not worry about those who stand up and work for the clan so much as those who stand beside you and bend you to do what they like. The clan you entered when you arrived in this life may no longer be around you or offer you support, but do not cry.

You have only one life to prove yourself, and this life is as good as any to do it. Try to become all you can be and see if that does not end your need to have others around you all the time. Most need people when they are not feeling great, want to participate, or they gave up and follow what another does. That kind of mind is often depressed for a time, then abruptly rises and leaves behind those who provided much. Do you provide and others leave your side, or do you lean?

Believe in you and provide what you need!

Does working hard seem like a weird way to earn your place and do your art? Working hard is a way to meditate and get beyond the worrisome aspects of life in places you do not like. Even if you do not take exception to the people around you, they may not like you. Why? That could take a lifetime to figure out, so we advise you to take time to decide what you can do to abandon what annoys others, and if that is not good enough for them to stop teasing you, then leave.

Bullying is not allowed, but many do it unknowingly, blaming only those who stand out in a crowd. If for any reason you tell others they must believe as you do, you are a bully! If you insist others reject whatever because you find it exceptionally bad, you are forcing them to do as you say. That is a bully—and not seen any other way by those who see, watch, and judge this offense. We do not work on how you fall behind or leave others in time, but bullying another is a sign you do not want them around. If you do, why would you want them to always do as you say?

The egoist is determined to be the one in charge and will lead without any need to prepare for the future, or make sure those who believe in him or her are secure. You are a bully for sure if you are an egoist who leaves if others do not do as you say. We notice more and more who earn their way are secure enough to drive away competitors on the job before they get large enough to cause problems, which means they have to lean on inferiors to complete production. Why drive away those who can help you move up, enabling you to meditate?

You are afraid of competition!

Take time to ensure fear does not dwell in your mind. The mind that has many friends and allies seldom sees enemies who can ascend or descend on them when they are down or tired. Why not adjust your mind so it welcomes friends and prevents enemies from staying too long? You can do that now!

In the mind are many channels that, if you do not change them, play the same lines over and over—forever. You cannot imagine what some recorded and now play over-and-over all day and even all night. You are safe, yet believe you are being chased from your safety zone, or are ugly and dishonest, because you did something ugly as a child. You may even believe you are perfect and do not have to be liked by others, or you can do whatever you like and everyone has to put up with it and not strike back. Such channels repeating nonsense can take up space and time, producing bad dreams and evil ways. Without realizing, you end up scheming all day.

Right now—take out a pad and pencil and write down three short lines that erase dread from your mind and change your thoughts from fear to love of others.

1.
2.
3.

You may love yourself so much you forget the power of others to hate you, but the mind never does. Take time to memorize and put aside whatever you think about now and make an affirmation to like others and not be afraid they may turn on you one day.

The work you do when declaring you are free of others and do not care if they like you this way or another will not take unless you believe you need to shed them immediately. This is not easy! In order to forever forget another you must go after every idea you ever had about that one and erase everything. This is done all the time. You can do it, too.

Take out another sheet of paper and jot down the names of anyone who pains your mind now. Remove any of their work you used and abuse now, or ever needed—analyze what you need or can keep without remembering them. If you discover during this process that it is you who owes them much, justify why you would leave without repaying them. If you cannot do that, then you must repay them now—not later, if you intend to erase them from your brain. You cannot leave others now while owing them and feel great later in life.

The minds of thankless children who blame a parent for whatever they lack will not age without feeling regret—and most likely will feel the stings of children acting out what they learned from them about how to treat their parents. You are the one who creates your reality which unfolds for generations. Be careful to not blame the seed, because it will grow to hate you in time or never grow beyond the need to blame you for everything.

The immature blame others!

No one will labor on your work and do much for you or anyone else until first confirmed that you are right and have been right more than a few times this life. Saying you are a teacher, but telling others what they should do is not teaching, but preaching. Most who preach never reach the crowd for longer than the time it takes to educate them about who they are. If you live the life of a brilliant scholar, you probably do not like to stop and talk a lot. However, if you are a preacher, you want to talk before your studies are done.

Whatever you do, do not believe others simply because you do not wish to work hard. That produces a type of slavery you induce and get used to—and let it confuse *you*. Once it becomes second nature for you to sit and let others inspire or ignite your mind, rather than discovering what it does for you, you become their muse in a way and not your inspiration. They are inspired to work hard, but you become lazy—possibly unable to leave this plane.

Whoever you are now, you will not remain this way! You will change, and if you do very little or do not consider who you want to be, you will be unable to remember today. Why? You will become the clay others model, rearrange, and put out to dry, hoping you will stay that way.

Today is a time when you can do whatever you desire. However, if you resemble most people now, you cannot discover what that is. Why would you not want to change and live as you may—having a wonderful adventure every day you are on this side?

Take a pennant and wave it. Let others know you can talk about your work, but prefer to know more about them. Why listen to others when you have much to share? You discover much about you, your work, and how it compares to others only if you let them honestly share.

Those who offer you prayers may be more in need of them then you are, but generously hope to serve and help so they are not burdened in ways they cannot cope with today. Hope is not something you create, then is depleted. Hope springs eternal when you are raised to believe only God can renew your life, but you could still have doubts—which is allowed.

You need not believe, but you must accept that God leads. You are here to be you and follow your path back to the source when it is time to leave and become another being. All you know while on Earth is that you are here for a reason. That then becomes a way of looking at life and wondering if you do enough or should give up—weak and lazy, with no faith in your work. However long you desert your god, or that which you hold sacred, is as long as it takes to decide you are about to die. Then you walk—joining the other strands of your life, moving into a new you or being rehabilitated and sent back.

The length of this book is insufficient to describe *the other side,* but bliss is about as equal to it as you can find while on this plane, in this life. You can step in and out of bliss and not realize it. What happens then? You know, but will not let go long enough to work hard to move out of bliss and become another who can live in it for longer than a minute. Bliss requires time, exercise, and determination—and most people living today do not want to spend energy working within.

Take work into your mind and sweep out whatever clutters its corners and threatens to work into your dreams. Get rid of the old, stale ideas you kept and replace them with conscious thoughts of perfection. Work on being a positive being now—not dwelling in disharmony.

Why emphasize being positive?

The Earth and this plane are not as negative, or as balanced, when working in a way conducive to life and work that produces more than is required to multiply. You all divide what remains of this planet as if you deserve it and will leave it behind. If you can survive and ascend at the end of this life, you will leave it behind, but many will not.

You have depleted the air of the necessary goodness humans need, and now threaten to end sources of clean water. Once that happens more and more will die of thirst—with no food for most. Why? You are unwise!

How does wisdom affect your work? You became negative and forgot you created this mess—and that you can clean it up. Make a start by being positive and asserting you can work on cleaning Earth and creating fewer people to dwell here in freedom without fear of starvation. To believe you cannot stop conceiving is something you must see as a lie perpetrated by those who fear the loss of power.

Once again, fear is where trouble starts, but the mind can lessen its effects over time or end it. Try increasing your work and helping many who cannot help themselves. Develop a thought pattern that cleanses your work, your mind, and the output of both over time. Many might survive to live many lives, if they can be taught to enjoy life now and let others do the same.

Chapter Thirty-Two

Whatever you are and want to be can change immediately! You need only a clear decision, without reasons not to change, and all is done immediately—you are on a new road. Why not try it now? Why not decide at this moment to stop being someone else and admit you want to live as you are?

When you do not live a certain way, you change whatever bothers you then. The fact that some are involved living many lives means they have to first deal with unraveling all such complications before becoming fully free without any problems or further need to care for others here. If you have not tried to live on your own since birth, it takes work.

If you recently birthed others and are now required to care for them, there is a delay of less than two decades. When you begin a family, then terminate it, you have not ended the commitment to those you brought to life and promised to provide for then. If you cannot afford a family now, do not indulge in behavior that will produce children.

Why would that need to be explained? If you do not understand the implications of wanton sex, and disregard others involved in your extensive adventures—living a life that denies you nothing you like, you will have to take more time here than those who did not. However, all can free themselves sooner or later than the crowd, by becoming themselves and living their own lives.

If you cannot raise a child alone now, why would you flirt with the possibility of that happening? Be aware you are not animals or without pride when you engage in wild and wanton behavior with people you have no clue about who they are and what they might do to the child. Be aware and care!

Once you respect the fact that others are also here to enjoy life and arrive safely on the other side when this life is over, you begin to honor your need to go home without a lot of debris attached to you, as some now believe will be readily forgiven. It is not easy to forgive others, is it? You then have a bit of knowledge you need to be aware of when dealing with them.

Be aware the safest way to live today among so many people unlike you is to obey certain rules of life. What are they? Give us time and we will list what too many wish to alibi out of now.

In the world around you are many who want to be in charge and have others take care of what they understate—usually details or necessary work they do not wish to do. Who would you be if not for the time spent when young training to read, think, and work with others? You would not be reading this now without such help and guidance—and the willingness of others to teach you the details.

When your ego grows so large you relate to no one else today, think about how many will take you down before you die, then try to help them enjoy you now. We advise this since you may live to an old age and require others to help you with the details of life. Once again, work is not what holds you back, rather the refusal to submit to doing what is required in life.

What if you truly do not have time to be yourself due to taking out the garbage and feeding a child? You are then imprisoned by others or your mind. You have time, but you do not prioritize as well as others. Get over the belief that saying you are busy means you are worthy of admiration from the crowd. You are forgotten when you do not attend functions others conduct and asked you to participate in or help them. You become extra baggage in lives that depend on others to do what they want.

When you help another and grant them peace, you develop a way of interacting and behaving that brings you friends over time. If it does not? Again, let us remind you that you have legs to walk out of a situation or location where you cannot fit in now.

Who will take away what you love?

What is your answer? You have to know! If you drop out of others' lives now, you may want them to miss you, but it will not happen if you gave them nothing, never considered their wishes, nor think about them when you have time. The thoughtless end up without anyone thinking of them!

Teach your young about how you survive. Too many want their young to be dependent, believing they will thus love them later in life. Check out how that is working for others before you continue such a plan. You will then feel better about socializing children to make friends and be liked well enough that they can move on once they no longer need care from you or others.

When a child is wild, the parent is rightly warned to take care of it then. If your child is spoiled to the extent you cannot go out and about without adults staring at you or the police running them down, go back to the beginning of this chapter and remember what was said. You have a child—or not, but everyone is responsible for helping children be healthy, loved, and encouraged to join the human race as soon as possible now.

When an adult decides to drop out and not participate, it is allowed. You can drop out of your society and do whatever you like and others merely shrug and walk away. However, if you expect society to raise your child, be aware it will not happen now. Your world no longer cares about its young. You all are preoccupied with growing up or growing old—disinterested in educating children in the latest developments of commerce involving careers that flourish in capitalistic nations now.

Will capitalism achieve What socialism could not?

What do you hope to achieve, besides gaining riches, if that is what drives you now? List what you get from pursuing a totally hedonistic or capitalist life-style. Then list what you give up when you decide to look out for yourself only and expect others to do the same. List how you can now gain a large slice of the pie even if others refuse to work with you.

When you cannot pursue your work without help, or require someone else to do the details, you will not last to pass at the end of this class. You will be held back! Yes, that is why we talk without regard to how much worry it may be producing in your furrowed brow now. We know you want to grow and leave Earth—never come back, but it is not something granted automatically, as getting others to do your work now may be.

Think about your contribution to the world, your land, and society within your community...If something happens to you now, what does it do for you, and how long will you be allowed to live off others? Think on it! Imagine if you have enough social insurance now to participate in what you love for the rest of this life.

If you cannot pursue what you do once you no longer work for others, think about making changes to your lifestyle now. Why? It will save time when you go deep inside your mind to figure out what went wrong, when *you* knew it all along. Spare yourself a depressive episode by paying attention to what you are doing now. Forget the dream until you make a clear-eyed assessment of your life here and now.

What if you cannot live where you are?

What indeed? You would move, would you not? That is understood, and the reason why immigration grows daily across the planet. Those who believe they planned ahead and can achieve all their needs or keep going strong are in for a surprise—and it may arrive long before they end this life. Try to figure out why others never hesitate to take whatever drives you to neglect the weak and downtrodden now, and you may sense you cannot keep whatever you create.

It all depends upon the society around you. If your town or city is filled with crime, and you shiver and worry but do little to stop the insurrection, you deserve what happens now. Yes, it is not easy to take, but make no mistake, you created the mess. If you start now to protect your progeny in the years ahead, you have time to change what is going on now. Why not?

Take away the reason you live as you do now, and it separates you from no one living with you. You all think enough alike to pitch in and work for the good of all, or you are savages of the vilest type—letting your family ignite, fight, and possibly end all life for themselves and you, as well as others around you now. Be aware you must take care of your children, or they will ignore you or worse. Thinking whatever your child does is not as bad as others is the worst type of parenting, but obviously preferred in what some call the greatest country on Earth.

Take credit for children when they reach 17 and can leave the nest and proceed to live a wise life. If your child cannot leave then or live wisely with others, you failed an important task set out when you decided to conceive the child. You can alibi or lie, but others hold you responsible for what your child does and why.

Are '*third world nati*ons' producing better children than advanced countries now? If that is bandied about—and it is, understand it will not be long before the world rights itself. What is on top will become the bottom. Think and make immediate plans to educate your clan!

Chapter Thirty-Three

In the interest of clarity and ease of understanding, we are prepared to give you a description of what bliss is. You will then transition into it, leave it behind, or hide from the way we see things now. You live on a planet limited in its expansion, but many believe you have unlimited possibilities—most of which if completed will harm Earth. If this makes you feel exhilarated and fulfilled, can it lead to bliss?

You need to believe in something you cannot achieve, and be willing to think well of others. This includes what is impossible to describe or inhabits a totally different space than you. When you begin describing others, you lead with what you think makes them most like you or the reverse. Think about it, then watch what you do the next time you criticize another. As you look into and around others, you are deceived by your inability to know people—even if you honestly believe you know yourself.

Who would you be if you could not do what you do and achieve what you do now? You would be *you*. This version or aspect of your eternal being is not easy to leave.

He or she, as you see yourself to be now, recognizes others of your lineage or tribe more easily than your mind permits itself to accept this knowledge. You cannot always recognize *your* other selves, or believe they are partners in this life or parts of your soul—or partners of that type. However, that is not how it is! You have no one else on Earth who will fulfill your path. You are here to do that!

Once you fulfill your personal needs, make a new list and pursue others more interesting to you. You are without a clue as to why you do it? Once you realize you are your guide, and your Higher Self is unlike anything else you can connect to now, you begin to understand you are not alone. When that happens, you feel inspired—happier than you have ever been. It is an awakening! Assurance you can do whatever you came to do—and probably much more.

Upon discovering you are relatively free of others and can move into the new being you seem to be, you start wishing to connect and find someone who will love you as you seem to be now. Why not let others know you are no longer as you were—letting them find others who more closely resemble the way you once were and the personality that attracted them then? You may not want to let go, because you cannot accept that you are no longer the same person. You may doubt you changed dramatically—and all you are and were now differs enough to clash and have flashes of anger when you try to return to that past.

Some families enjoy talking about what they once had in common, while many others fight over their common memory. They do not want to be in that family, even though society says in many different ways that they should cling and honor all they once had together. You cannot go back and become a clan again once you leave, but you can honor those who created a safe haven for you to become who you are today. That is expected by society—not homage to those who owe their founders as much as you do.

When you do something over-and-over again, yet nothing happens to create a different outcome than what you now find unacceptable, can you start over or do you have to remain as you are? This is not easy to answer. You either are upset enough to not want to achieve the same degree or continue working at that intensity—or time moves on and the situation you once capitalized on no longer exists. You decide, but doing the same thing many times cannot make you a master when and if the material changes or the world moves on and no longer honors that trade.

What do you trade daily for necessities?

Men and women develop themselves in different ways, based on their agility or ability. Many discover others do not respect their art enough to pay much, so they switch to doing what another does, hoping it will pay off. Are you worried that what you trade for material goods you need to live is out-of-date? If so, retrain! Learn a new way of trading your time for what you want and need.

When you become too upset to trade your work, or do work others will pay you to do so they have time to do something else, remember you are not without hope. In fact, you may soon believe you are too great to do what you trade. We laugh when that happens, because you are not too good to do what you do. You trade your work for what others require or you starve.

What if what you do requires many degrees of intensity, yet you do not wish to spend time acquiring it? You cannot say you spent time getting such a degree and practice it easily. Anyone who believes they can lie about being educated is stupid! There is no other way to describe it.

Many who believe themselves smarter than others will try that once or twice—might even end up getting a job. What happens then? Society is offended or the business ends with others losing their jobs due to incompetency at the top.

When you go away to a far-off country to play, most of the time you remain at home in your mind. Only a few can transport their minds into other lands and other times. Most land on their feet in that country intending to stay, then later decide it is not their life.

You may find others attractive and want to live with them full-time, but once you do, all that initially entertained you disappears and you are left feeling unhappy or unwise. How did that happen? You forgot who you were and thought you could trade your life for another—which will not happen.

You live for you!

You will not be upset if you do well and others do not—unless you are a humble and humane being living this life. Few like you are here now, but as time permits and others get the whim, you may train some not yet here to help another do whatever—assuming a new life before completing the one they came here to be. This is easy to understand! If you do not get it, go over it again.

We did not come to your planet in order to make you leave or grieve over it, but to teach you how to save it. This plan started many years ago when we *'landed'* and planted the seed in the hands of *The Scribe*. How many read our work when we started here on Earth? Not enough. Obviously, you have not taken seriously our warnings about the ruination of your atmosphere and the planet—so now you have very little time to learn how to save life here.

Be aware that if you have to leave this planet now and cannot come back again, bliss will not be forfeited, but you will have to do much to earn the trust of those who dwell on other planes above you now. You must do a good job or be overlooked when promotions are given to the few who can and will help the planet now.

Much talk and a lot of smoke, but no one is telling the world the planet is no longer safe for a large population. If someone flares up and gets angry when you state they must step in and help control the population, all want to blame others now. They may want huge congregations to follow them, but once they lose half their followers to famine, they will be ousted and not allowed to ever again practice as they did in the past.

Being courageous only when it is easy, you will find you are never brave. To be a leader helping curb what is evil, you must extend your work to others and speak for those unable to do so. Most living today hate to confront anyone—let alone a demon working alone, thus you will be afraid until the end of your days, which could stop you from ascending then.

We want you to be aware that the soul-purpose of these **Books of Wisdom** is to help you ascend and gain altitude now—while living the good life before you die and leave this plane or are recycled to come back again. You may want to layer other ideas on top of what we write, but you will not be believed when others read what we said.

Take time to identify what we mean and what is needed now. Do not wait for another to read and decide to trade you information about life in other planes or planets rather than you alone earning your degree of knowledge. Be aware that those who teach have lived the life and practice it now, or they cannot stand up and teach you. Those who cannot teach cannot preach—and that is the end of it!

Chapter Thirty-Four

If you cannot be yourself, please leave this page until you are you. Why? Bliss is not going to fit into your mind and alter your life. You are committed to being this individual—doing what you do, without committing to listening to what we teach or advise you to do to enhance your life, too.

We survived much to be here with you now. You are merely a wisp that will disappear in a few years. If you decide to live your life now, you will never reappear here or be asked to assume such a role again.

When married with children, you are confined for a few years of a long life to doing what is required to socialize and educate your children's minds so they can find God and stay out of trouble within your present society. If you neglect to do this, you alone suffer the emotional trauma of others avoiding you and your family whenever you get near them, and you have little time to be whoever you believe you can be now. You will spend all your time correcting behavior, rather than reap with pleasure what you taught your children and others appreciate about them even now. If you are wild, it is likely your child will take after you. Smile more, lower your voice whenever required to maintain order, and all should soon improve in your part of the world.

What you may do or want to be is not what others see. You may believe you have signed up for an army of some kind and find it is not what you thought, but you cannot leave it until you complete basic training, plus any time required to complete your promise. If you birth a child, you have the same type of work cut out for you. You have to endure basic training—explaining how to control yourself in crowds and what to do in every social situation you can imagine before the child goes out into your world, and so on. If in the end they can defend you when you need them, it is worth the effort.

Whatever you discover about another or their children, temper your thoughts with compassion and the realization it could happen to you if you still have a child or intend to adopt or raise one now. All who have children should smile at anyone who has the ability and skill to develop children well. When you spot such individuals, shake them up by saying you admire their work and wish them well. Many parents never hear the praise they need to know society appreciates their denial of selfish interests in order to keep others safe and without the necessity to put away their children at an older age than today.

Quickly, analyze the time you spent reading this message and understanding what it implies. See if it makes sense or is agreeable to others who fill out your crowd, then take this chapter and talk about it. Talk about it even if you do not have a family. Treat it with compassion, hoping you can add much to other's contributions to child-rearing today.

If you find others who believe as you do, ring them up and talk to them over and over again. You have found a friend for life and may not get another such opportunity. Be aware that raising a child is the most important thing any human being does!

All over your nations and the planet today are women who want to please men more than they want to improve the remnants of past liaisons. Why? They believe it is the easiest way to make a living now. How can they believe that? They do not see themselves as slaves of men or unable to believe in themselves. It is not easy to greet such women in the street, knowing they believe they found the golden key to love and abundance, but do not snub them. Think about how dense their minds are, how lacking in love they must be, and how much they need a mother now. Be that as it may, you have only today to enjoy your children and prepare them to be new women or men once they have no need of your direction again.

On some streets families try to raise children against all odds of their being safe and able to walk to school every day. Why not move? Why contribute to the future of those willing to kill, maim, or take away the sanity of anyone they meet—especially the lame of brain and children? You cannot allow others to infiltrate your towns and harm your children as you do now. That is not allowed! You will be held responsible for not insisting on changing your society today.

Living in a building as others run it down and treat neighbors as if they are hated rather than friends is not allowed in a well-governed society that can rule without threats and bribes, as is done now. You may want to blame the young or those crazed by drugs, but what are ***you*** doing to change it? If you are not raising awareness of trouble, or worst of all, contributing to it by using illicit drugs or whatever, you deserve war and crime—but not your children or others who cannot leave town.

Now all is open to discussion! We would love to hear what you think can be done, but few will stop and not quickly move ahead to see what the next chapter brings them. If you can stop here and think, work on what could become the next biggest happening in your life—help others in your workplace and neighborhood now.

Write a few words, then think about how you would alter your current situation in order to live without fear, regardless of where you drive and who you may meet.

Chapter Thirty-Five

Your life *is your* life! Never forget this is it—and this is all yours to deal with as you believe will harm no other as it brings you love, happiness—and if lucky, bliss. You do not have to discover who you are, because you are *you*. Take that with you and seize every moment now wasted trying to be someone else or someone you cannot be, based on what you were given at birth and developed.

If your work demands you exist merely to cater to your boss or company, get out of it. Do something else that pays as much or gives you more time to be you. You have time to accomplish anything you have in mind, but you can drain your mind of its ability to refine and decide what is right or best for you now by always trying to be someone else. Taking it upon yourself to tell another what they need to do—but not you, is a waste of time. Do what you want and let others decide if they wish to follow you or ask for advice.

What do you do to relax?

If you have no way to relax and recharge your mind, you resort to wasting time trying to follow what others believe works for them. If you drink in order to meet others, remember what kind of impression you make on them. You cannot be your best when inebriated or drugged. You know that, yet say you must drink to fit in with others. Why? Who criticizes you for staying dry and out of the rain or not drinking as if a human drain? You! Only you have the power to make yourself feel miserable and in need of something to lean on in order to be liked or loved by others. If that is how you talk to you now, *you* need to change your mind!

Take time now to decide what you will do the next time you take off and can do whatever you want. Prepare to control all you do! Test to see if you have learned a few ways to entertain yourself now, without the need of a partner or three others to make a team. Be aware you can be the one you love without being a stunning brat, egotist, or worse.

Be you! Shine light on *you*, what you like, and why you wish to participate in whatever happens nearby. Once you let up proving you are *you*, listen carefully for proof others are much like you, too. Those few will do much for you. Why? You are all alike!

Explaining what seems plain to us is something we do not enjoy, but since you often say you cannot understand work channeled from those on higher levels than you are now, we will explain that last comment. If you already know what it means, skip ahead—you will miss nothing now.

You resemble people who think as you do! You think about things in particular patterns and were raised to believe some things matter, while others are unimportant, thus you discover those who agree with you. Usually they live on the same street, maybe farther away, but raised about the same as you were.

If you doubt you get ahead with and are loved more quickly by those much like you, test it. See if you cannot identify someone living nearby who is nice to you, talks to you when you have time, and does not say nasty things to get even when angry. Check out if they were raised much like you before you say we are wrong.

Chapter Thirty-Six

The difference in perspective each person brings to the table determines what they achieve and can believe when they put this wisdom to use, test it, or drop it from their memory. What you believe is not determined by another human being! How can that be? You believe as you perceive—and you perceive as you have been taught since birth, plus any other education provided before you reached your majority and began to think for yourself and decide what you wanted this life.

When you begin to doubt others are who they are, you are on the way to giving up on them. It may never be a problem if you were too dependent on them, but it can cause loneliness if you harshly judge others and end up without anyone around you now. Before you fight others to believe as you think *you* do, try to temper your thoughts and accept that you are not alike. Yes, you think in your way or in the way of another, but you do not all think alike. Each has a particular way of processing and digesting wisdom—and some never develop a taste for it.

What if all you read was wrong?

Who should be the judge? Why would you believe that one over others? Over time you may come across those who say you do not believe as they and you must change. It is your life to decide and develop, so be careful of anyone who tells you what to do and insists they alone know the truth.

You will frequently be in danger of losing your integrity and personal truth, if you stay with crowds easily swayed. Do not go to an arena intending to believe. Simply take in the event, and once home think it over at your leisure. Make no comment or commit to doing anything when in a large group. If you are one who likes many people to be around you to feel good, you will be happy you followed this bit of wisdom—and use it often.

Whatever you do today will not disappear. You may feel too tired or miserable to drive, walk, or talk; however, if inspired by something others plan to do, you can follow—maybe even lead them to a better day. Why? Spirit is powerful and can take over when mind and body subside. You need only try a few experiments to see what we mean.

Try to curb your mind from doing things you like and believe are not too difficult. However, hiding your light when equally bright, you discover you always have time to do whatever you like. Right?

When the shades of darkness enter your life, you no longer enjoy working alone and need another or several to help you feel included and happy. What happened to *you*? You felt let-down due to how another acted or you believed you were perceived. Spirit did not relieve you of that doubt, but you could have shed all doubt in an instant by praying about it or meditating. Do both and think about something you need to do—let it sit until you clear your head.

What happened? You either did not meditate or did it in a mindful state—thinking you were meditating as you pursued the problem. What makes you do that when you know it is safe—even reasonable to put off doing things until you clear your mind of whatever lingers and might take time to eliminate? Why not put it aside for now so as not to confuse you as you proceed with a new belief or a new way to be *you*?

Thinking and believing are not alike, yet you may believe they are. We will not persuade you either way. Why? We are not your Spiritual Guides of this life. We are teachers sent to Earth to instruct and help you gain enough peace of mind so as not to waste time or this life and have to come back to it over time. Before you deny any of this, try it!

We can see inside your mind only once or twice, but require no more time than allowed, because we now see what you need. If you do not also perceive it, you will in time release it, possibly not feel good enough to do what you must to ace this life. We do not cloud your mind or trim your ideas—or make you wild, but you may do that as a way of avoiding life.

Once you decide you alone cause all your problems with others, pride steps in and makes you accept that others did wrong to you and thus they started it. Why would pride enter in when you are upset? It is another way you protect the ego state. Your ego wants you to believe this is it—and bliss is a state of mind.

Since we live in a way you cannot see, believe, or come to be, you will notice you are not changed, rearranged, or tempted away from whatever you believe. Are you being teased? No, you are being pushed to accept that as a human being you know little about the world you choose to live in now or about what comes next when you leave this test.

Take time to rest—think about how much you learned from those older, wiser, or more blessed than you. If no one comes to mind, be aware you are scared and will be unable to link with others to form a chain that helps you move to the next world or stay connected to what you believe here. You need to be able to judge who is wise—or be condemned to accepting lies all this life.

Be yourself, but do not lie—and do not harbor liars in your life. It is such a waste of time!

Chapter Thirty-Seven

Somewhere over the rainbow paints a pretty picture of a time and place where child-like dreams come to be or are easily achieved, but is it bliss? Yes, it is! If you can imagine, you can become more and more naïve, less pessimistic and hard to please. You may begin being someone who looks to God within as having answers to your present problems. If you cannot, you spot what you believe to be naiveté—an unwillingness to accept the evil that is craving attention today from everyone you meet. It is the way of those who are lost to believe they have the key or can boss others who are lost.

When you realize robes and masks donned daily are meant to disguise who you are, you bravely begin stripping away the decay and loss of faith, again studying your mind from within—and over time, you will win. Win what? You become the one you seek and wish to be.

As you age, what you expect happens!

You become someone you believe will achieve much or little, but you can change your expectations. You can become greater or reduce your ambitions, without much effort. All you need do is put your plan on paper and set it aside without any idea of when you will read it again. Include everything you wish to be and create a time schedule from beginning to end.

Naturally, we do not offer miracles or expect you to change your brain and suddenly be able to do much you never attempted or are designed to provide. Instead, assess work done so far and guess how much higher you can rise, then set the date you plan to measure your progress again. It will amaze you how likely you are to achieve more than you believe possible now!

What if you previously tried to raise your sights and were shot down? Try again! When it comes to living your life the way you aspire to be today, do not give up. Give it several tries.

If you cannot move out of a rut, try your luck in another life or another place and time. You can prescribe what life will be when you no longer are fettered by your body and must manifest everything yourself. If you know how to dream, you can imagine it—even see it.

When you go to sleep thinking you do nothing all week but sleep, you are either completely out of it or hiding what you dream every night in order not to share that life here. We are not frightened by those who say they dream magnificent schemes in order to make others believe they have outstanding and important dreams, but you may. You may believe the individual who has exciting dreams every night and talks about them during the day—thinking your dreams are too mundane to talk about. If so you would be shocked to learn most have mundane dreams, seldom having dreams with outstanding individuals, symbols, and themes in them. You are human beings and tend to compete with each other, even when discussing your night lives.

What about the unfortunate who sleep little?

What happens when you sleep little and dream even less? You become tense! You are often described by friends and others as uptight, nervous, and not very nice, but you can adapt over time and learn to cope with the loss of sleep and the lack of dreams. You will not have as rich a life and depth of spirituality as those who live a healthy life and sleep twice as long as you might, but you adapt—learning to hide how upset you may be when others do not achieve or do not believe what you easily see.

Anger is the most pronounced facet of non-dreamers. You begin to notice they are snappy—not very nice, if awakened too fast for their minds. You, however, having slept well and dreamed a lot feel on top of your world. You do not find them agreeable and may even leave them. Why not take them by the hand and help them unwind, without using drugs that open their minds too wide and prevent them from being whoever they may be? Being kind is wise when the other is your friend or family.

You may want to escape when another runs from the truth, but someone has to remain in this frame of reference or both will lose their way and not be accepted. If neither you nor your partner/parent or other can fit into the society around you, you will be cast out in ways that hurt the ego and often cause you to grieve. We would love if you could love people and not be the brunt of their evil. So try to fit in and make plans to leave them decently—without anyone the wiser for why you left. It makes sense not to disturb your mind as much as some do, by saying they are wise and others are not.

Once you feel good about you, try again to reach out and broaden your life. Take on a new friend or two. Be alive to what others say is right. Do what you like, but not if it upsets those who guide you, protect you, or rule your tribe.

Be aware everyone is trying to be themselves, but only a few are privileged enough to rule the rest. The reason for most departures is the need to lead—and thinking you will never lead them. Try to lead before you leave! If you fail, you learned a lot. If not, find out why others let you lead.

Walk into a room and smile, knowing with certainty that you are accepted or rejected. Walk in smirking or staring, arousing others to prowl about to discover who you are—and you will be disliked! Such a simple thing to understand about people, but some reading this will reject it, because they do not understand their fellow man. Please be aware you need people while you are here!

As you develop, your mind equals your life or is replaced by others who appear better able to survive. You either live as you wish—deciding what you will do next, or you cannot do anything without checking it out with someone you love. Such attachment is a way of preventing you from enjoying today. If you project that you cannot be whomever you wish to be and must be like your parents or others in your home when you were young, you alone hamper your waves of thought now.

Since you can read this book and understand what we say, you can stand up and accept that you are mature and will live your life and make it secure—not someone else. What does it matter if you let others tell you how to live—or decide for yourself? It is necessary to be you and do what *you* have to do to maintain your soul and continue being safe from the mind that could drive you insane over time. You alone must be in charge of your life and your sanity. You alone decide who you believe and why.

Once you establish a line of love inside your mind, you may never again hate or be as upset as you once were, but you are not totally given over to saintly behavior—even if you wish to be seen that way. All remain human all their days, but in time you establish a secure life that anchors you whenever you leap from this life into another. That is when you will sense you either got it while here or never achieved bliss.

Take your life as it is now and describe it on paper. Put the paper aside for ten years, then pull it out and see if you made the progress you wished for now or regressed and never did any of it. You will discover your mind deciphered what you really wanted when writing your letter and made it happen later, even if you consciously forgot it. Go ahead, program your mind and brain now to act wisely over time, rather than regret you never saw how this life works until too late to enjoy it.

Chapter Thirty-Eight

You are who determines what you do, where you live, and how much you give. To cede your power to another is foolish. You need to believe in you! You need to be aware you are here alone with others in Spirit who can steer you away from what will delay or keep you in an inferior place longer than required to learn lessons and progress to a higher life of a type not described in anything you ever read until this moment in time.

When you opened this book you wanted to read something you could quote or make fun of—intentionally reading and working to discover what it might be. We hold it out to you—letting you discover what you seek to uncover is not hidden. We are here to let everyone on Earth know who we are, what we do, and why we are willing to spend time trying to help a tribe of people now adrift in the universe without any compass or way to get back to where you all came from.

We know *you* and can easily work with all who can work within to a depth *The Scribe* easily achieves. Can you move into a mood, change of life, or trance-inflate what you do now? If you can, please do it for an hour, then translate what you find.

For all who cannot enter a higher state of mind or live higher than you appear to be now, this is not easy to explain, but we will try. You are here for reasons unexplored before you arrived. Why? Everyone asked to be here—most having been on this planet in other ways or other times. You asked for ways to connect and ace the tests—to get on with what comes next, but many confuse what is asked and expected with things they never intended or refused to do and want out of now.

You can find <u>you</u>!

A connection is established before being left here. You are not without guides and others who can help, but most who dwell only on the material aspects of this world do not realize it now. Once the material world you so adore is left to fall into another pit from which some will never crawl out and live well in this world, you will try to blame God or whatever you believe is at fault. The ego is an amazing gift that can be the end of your line in time, if you do not discipline it and create behaviors that harm no others who may or may not get in your way.

If you harm others, you will not enter the next world as you are now, rather further down the order or phylum in which you arrived this life. You are held back to teach *you,* not to discipline your work. You must learn not to step on others nor spurn those you believe are lower, not as intelligent or rich as you. It is a sharp reminder of the fall so many profess to know much about, but have not figured out so far.

What you believe to be a garden or Eden is nothing you can cling to once you fall from grace for having believed what others said substitutes for faith in the world above and beyond where you live now. You may believe a man—even a woman, can rise up and save everyone from sorrow, but it is not allowed.

You must not seek to be a god!

Once you discover we are here to help and not hinder or harm you—what then? You then decide we can help you move into your next work before leaving Earth. How? We can teach you ethical ways to live today. This is appropriate when you consider how you believe and act now.

You prefer games to school, wishing to be free when you cannot easily feed yourself. Why? You do not take this life seriously! Many believe they will not have to redo this life—come back or live through it again, but we believe it and teach the reasoning for it, if you are willing to read.

Work moves on! We will abandon no one on Earth now, but some are so slow they will not ascend when the next wave of attention equals your work on Earth, providing a kind of chute into which you move and flow into a new *you*. We know you mean well in most cases, but you still prefer to honor people you believe have more possessions than you. Even if you are more intelligent than everyone you love, you tend to honor the one who makes the most money.

That is the downfall of your world! All now rush to end their time devising ways to become involved in the rising influence of money on their economies, forsaking all that kept them going, regardless of what happened in your world. Take time now to thrive by the wits of your life—not worrying about how others live, and sooner or later you cannot contribute—having lost your opportunity to learn much here and now.

Work is what you are here to learn and accept before moving on or staying for another round of lessons similar to this one. We know you want to go, but some would like to end their lives now—in order to speed up the process and not have to work as hard. That is not allowed! You will be cast in the same mold and made to do it all over again.

Why spend this life trying to fix what you never did? It is unlikely you could or would, but some believe they are here to help others gain access to a higher life or plane today. Forget that idea! It is fiction created by higher mindsets than you wish to acknowledge in your lives. They exist and are willing to be seen as imposters in order to hold much power in your world.

All are equal, but you cannot accept that when you only measure goods, services, looks, and whatever else you were trained to believe makes you better than others. You may hate to be cast as ugly or obscene if born that way. Better to realize you are loved and can be yourself, with many other lives to try and create more than what you see now with these puny eyes. Be aware that when you compare yourself to others, you will be seen as one unable or not qualified to move into higher ways of life—yet neither is true nor intended to be that way.

You are all equal!

The sooner you understand that fact, the easier for you to get back. Back? What is behind or in front of you now that you cannot believe or see?

We know many asked you to do things you immediately said you would never do, then changed your mind and did them, instead of following what you initially thought when you qualified the remark. Can it be you doubt what you alone know? Yes, and you have reason to believe you do not know enough to safely guide your life without repercussions of a dangerous type if you should step out-of-line. We doubt anything will happen to you now that will harm your world more, but plots exist—and people resist being taught how to live well together and apart now.

Indigenous tribes are aware of Earth's tides and what goes on inside the world outside their lives, but those outside such lives do not realize it is easy to see into their world now, as well as what they will do next. You may believe you survive and thrive at a much higher level than any tribe alive, but we resist. We say you are without knowledge of what goes on now, thus know little more than any indigenous tribe existing outside your present lives.

You want to believe you have moved up in the world, often deciding you are better than others—which is a preposterous lie. Anyone can point out where you are losing your mind and how much time you have left to refine your life. You may not believe others can see things or become many different things, but some can and do—while some never rise or fall during this life.

You did not come here to be human!

You came to Earth to see why things cannot be easily manifested here. From the beginning you wanted to fabricate an easier way to be, to see, and achieve work not of Earth. You now sense you have discovered a lot about yourself in a matter of a few words, or you are without any idea what we are saying now.

Whatever comes over you when you work on your inner world, do not be afraid. You can go to *'Guardian Angels'* and ask them to help you move into a deep and lasting trance, which is never satisfying because you are not in charge. Be aware you have guidance systems in your life that will assist you in entering deep trance—safely resisting anything that might harm your outer life. Why not try and disprove it now?

Taking down those who believe differently than you think you believe is never easy. Why? The more you argue with another, the more you absorb their power and ideas, becoming consumed by emotions that sweep over you and make you nervous or irritable—unloving to the rest of your public. You can be a fanatic, if you please, but remember you will alienate many who would otherwise love you.

Why love others if they do not like or want you in their lives? It is how you are made. You have negative waves, but require more positive thoughts than negative to make it to the next plane. You can be as you please and never miss a beat, yet hated by those you admire.

Why would you want to alienate or lose the respect of others? You worship evil gods not of your world, possibly following their ways, because you believe they know more than those who raised you. Perhaps that is true and elevates you, but more likely it is false and will lead you into depression—ending this life without friends, unable to love others.

Take your time and realize we are now telling you much that is not written in black and white, because it does not exist in your mind and cannot be found in a book you can easily forget. Between your eye and the material you read here is a way to convert energy that may change you in ways you cannot imagine now. Take time to realize the wise do not arrive in time to save you from a life of crime or elevate you above others of equal skill, but many find that happens.

Can it be you now know how to rescue your life? Yes, you need only turn up your intent and build upon the positive words you read in each line to know you are doing work that raises your mind to a much higher level and will create a new life if you are ready for it now. Rise and see the new you!

Notice how you look to others who have not seen you in some time—measure their positive reminders of what you can do by not hiding from your outer lives. Be you! Meditate and create an advanced state in which you can become anyone, but preferring to be you and able to complete what you came to Earth to do. Relax and let time wash over you now.

You need not work hard to gain all that is yours. It awaits you. Be happy and smile! Let the light of your Higher Life enter this phase of being *you*—then open to *God of All* in ways you cannot imagine today.

Chapter Thirty-Nine

Put yourself on the line—demand that *you* do whatever you tell another to do! See if you are ready to follow everything you tell others now. Once you commit to doing whatever you believe others should do or achieve, you soon stop telling anyone how to live. It is that easy to stop a despot before he or she gets started!

Once you begin living the life you believe others might like or would enjoy, you have more friends and fewer, if any, enemies. Paying attention to what you do—not what people think is another link to a mind that wants others to follow them or do as they say. Many mothers today are busy bossing others in offices and stores while ignoring their children at home. Why? Business provides an outlet for their need to train and explore leadership, replacing the desire to help children make the leap to adulthood without losing out now.

We suggest mothers stay with their children until age 8 to see if that does not end the threats they extend to the world when older. Who will provide shelter and love for the child, if not mother? The father! If you doubt the man who makes love to you is capable of loving your child, why assume he has feelings for you? We do not understand your need to tell adults how to live while ignoring children, as too many do now.

When the day comes when you can no longer find your child at home, have no fear, you can enjoy life as never since they appeared. Be wise—take care to raise the child so you can enjoy being an adult much sooner than you otherwise might. You need to prove you are a power in the world by asserting it over children in ways designed to help them discover their art, science, and minds.

What you do your way today helps your nation, thus the world. If you can build an intelligent life and provide all that is needed, is this still a child when he or she can function alone? Are you able to see yourself at the helm, or always pulling the oars and being urged to slave away today? Be sure you love what you do, even if it is not what you originally chose, because you have to do it over if you do not do it right. That is life here and now. What you get is taken from you, and what you hate continues long after you tire of it.

When you do work you enjoy, the hours slip by. When you sit and deliberately stall—trying not to work, time is the same, but feels longer. You can do what you love, but it is your need for greater sums of money or someone's love that urges you to slave at work you despise to provide what they decide they like—and you are foolish enough to do it, hoping they will reciprocate or love you more.

Be sure you are not worshipping an insane god without any life within. The top of every pyramid is small and capable of holding only one at any time. Many strive to be that one, hoping everyone under them remembers they are in charge then. If unsure, you have failed and must not fall, because those below will not stop your fall and you will end up broken at the bottom.

All that is now wonderful will deteriorate and become less than it is if you place value on it rather than the work to produce it. Labor is honorable, and hard work is decent, even if you do not honor either with suitable recompense. You are who is stupid if you labor for people who abuse you when you could work for others who would not. However, at times you must be a slave in order to appreciate what is great and good this life.

Quietly assess what you do for pay. Make sure you use money wisely or you will work like this all your life. If you like what you do, it is not a problem you cannot handle, but many people deliberately escape life with drugs and drink, driving themselves to do the work they hate. Why would any sane person do that? Please explain!

When ready to move to the next work, please smile at all and talk nicely to everyone you believe to be beneath you. To us, you are not merely a human being or someone with a breathing apparatus that requires oxygen and several other gases to stay alive, although some of you appear as if the only reason you are here is to prove you can live without ever using your God-given gifts.

The world will not collide with an asteroid at this time. You may believe it would be a blessing if it ended what you describe as your miserable life, but it would not. You exist and continue living—even when you no longer breathe as you did. You will be given more and more work you must do, and less and less of what you want to be, as a lesson for having ignored why you came here to be a human being. While striving to live, take time to care for your spirit.

Consider everyone you met here...
Who is without a friend?

If you can name one who is a friend to many but not appreciated, shame on you for abandoning that friend. You need what you have, and have what you need, but friends are the only gift of Spirit a human being can see. You need not give whatever you have to make another like you. Instead, when you like others, give what you have in excess to help them laugh.

Direct your path to its goal at the top of a gentle slope, by going straight, rather than taking a crooked and precarious route. Why? You advance faster when you move directly ahead, not looking back to see if others are catching up or about to knock you down for what you did in the past.

Be aware! Compare to others only work you know must be done better than you do it now. Create more proof of your excellence or say nothing about it. The day you are satisfied your work is great, teach!

Which personality do you prefer—the one smiling and clever, or the one who never figures out what you say? You select the prior, but do not try to know them better. Why? You decide! We know the wise are not clever due to a belief that they are better than those around them or those who rose higher in the world's estimation.

Quietly and easily settle your mind now. Meditate for several days on the thoughts we provided here. Work on why we would dictate these simple words in ways anyone on Earth can easily understand now. If you figure out why we came and what we are here to do, you can move to the next level of *you*—do it soon!

Chapter Forty

Every time you wake up sad, mad, or otherwise unfit for others, close your eyes and meditate until you are not upset nor will you upset another. If you do that, half of your problems are over before they begin—assuming you do not start all wars and such by yourself. If you are attracted to people who help you lose control, try to figure out why. If you do that, assume you have no sense and should avoid them.

By staying calm—at peace, you begin to appreciate what bliss is and can be. You cannot possibly imagine what bliss is when you are at odds with what is your current god. Do not say you have no god or believe in no one or anything now. Why? You have not lived if you say that, and most obviously seek attention rather than state any real decision made on the subject.

Once you think enough and decide you cannot comprehend anything as complex as YOU, you are in the world you call Oz. We would instead describe the ascent into the highest view you can assume of *you* as a view of your epitome or best performance, and ability to go beyond it non-stop. You decide if that is not a good description of bliss—and rewrite it here.

When you adopt an elegant state of mind—a good frame in which to talk with others and integrate what they brought to this world, you begin to think you may not be right. That is a good way to start! You need to understand you cannot be in charge or take over your household without help from others and those who guide them through life.

If you can connect on a higher level than the physical one, you can see many now. You will last and be able to enjoy each other for many more lives and many other classes beyond this one. Why? Let us begin to end this assignment and start helping you end your indecisive ways today.

Whatever you do, whoever you are,
You are neither mysterious nor weird!

You are human—much like billions of others who live in your world. Presently you are all inferior to the higher beings *you* all are and will be. That must be recognized before you can improve what you do or act on it without stooping to do useless things or possibly harming you here. Be of use to others if you have the means and abilities to help, but do not confuse others doing well by intruding and exuding your brand of being you.

When you decide to create a pattern of your life for others to follow, you are filled with pride and most assuredly will be derided by those you believe need you most. You will not do well! You may end up missing your train of thought—the one that brought you to this place and life, because you did not work hard on gaining your ascension, instead tried to help or direct others. The ego is what takes off and you permit it.

If now working to marry or *"un-marry"* another, you probably work harder than ever to be aware and use your full intelligence. It is wise to work hard whenever you take upon yourself another—being responsible for what they accomplish in a world that measures people not by integrity but by possessions and what they can do for you. *'Do not measure others and you lose'* is the motto of those who imply you are not doing great. Why? How else can they confuse you into letting them take over and run you now?

When a ship comes in and strangers enter your country, you decide if they stay or not. Never say you have no power to get rid of such people. Be aware how many times you want others to settle or even un-settle your world. You want them or would never let them land.

Once again, you do not permit those to land you believe will take whatever you have. You want them for reasons that may seem clever today, but tomorrow you will regret them. That is a lesson each of you must decide for yourself—not merely accepting whatever your tribe publicizes.

Once you realize you are here for life to do whatever you came to do—and nothing else, you stop drinking and living unwisely. Right? If it were that easy, or even believed, no one would stagger about now.

Some want a reason to drop out of life. Why? They give up before they work or do much to support themselves in order to say they are not competitive or in a race. You are in a race all this life! It is called the human race, because you are all competing now.

No one is better, but many accept that idea in order to do little, expecting others to take care of them—so they can complain and never improve their lives. Whatever you decide and however you work today, you do what you do out of concern for you. Whatever others say or do, they also think of themselves first. It is a law written into the genetic structure, so no arguments about it now.

You have no desire to get ahead? You can be lazy and sit beside the road and beg, but no one need feed you. You do that to you—and do not say otherwise.

Who fights and why?

Many have no reason not to fight, some are told they must war or face charges and go to prison, but most fight regardless of whether or not they are in an army or navy of any size. The fight is within them, and the means to act upon it comes up from time-to-time, but most tend to hide it. If you passively attack others whenever their backs are turned toward you, all know it, but you may believe you are not observed.

You are not trusted by others once they discover you never stand up and admit you hate another; you betrayed many; or you cannot love—hating yourself for months at a time. You are who must remove such negative moods. We suggest you do it one-day-at-a-time, once you awaken to life.

If you cannot heed statements made by those who never worry whether you grow or do what you know, who do you obey? The desire today to live in ways that shocks others—to be seen as rebellious is not wise, but a tactic the young often mistake for being smart. They want to overthrow and move through others' lives as if everyone else is stupid or never thought of whatever. Why? The mind chooses to believe it has the answers, even when unaware of the test.

Whatever you decide to achieve in life, others broaden your path. You may not wish to take the path beaten down by crowds, but every path has been opened in some way by another mind in another day. If you take time to study what others say about it, you will not gain much; but if you go to past records and read, taking from them what you need, you may advance further and faster than everyone else.

When you arrive full of pride and eager for a fight, you will get one, but it is not likely you will be happy when it ends. You have to be aware that if you are unhappy, standing your ground is not what others want. If you are happy, you move or take a different stance. To deny you believe what you say you do not think about is to make your mind angry at times.

Denial is hard on the mind!

Quickly scan your mind and all you will find now is this single line. At times you read as if you can scan the mind of others in a single glance, but you cannot. You are still inside your life when you get to the final line. You are who must connect with the writer or artist in order to determine what is said or meant. Flying about, skimming works of art and books of depth leads you to nothing new in your thoughts, even if you think differently by the end of a week.

You decide, then collect what helps you remember or forget. What do you want to know or do not wish to know that is embedded in your mind now? You can erase anything with time, but most regret not having said something or doing it—more than those who made fools of themselves trying to do it.

Why not act, rather than talk or make another lead your life? If you want to be in a sport, try it yourself rather than force a child to live it for you. When a parent raises children in order to exploit them, you sense they have not had a pleasant life and will end up being hated by those who do not want such people in their tribe, as well as those taken in by the mind of the child.

The child not allowed to grow now will be childish later on—not in an expected phase others readily forgive. Do you want to be surrounded by adolescents as an adult? You may find you are guilty of setting the stage and being unwise in selecting friends, so do not blame others if you stayed with your family and the same friends all your life and never moved a tad to change you then.

It would be wise for you to first do anything you want others to do. Try it! See if you believe it will be of use and help others—before selling it to a child. If you do not want to divide life into bite-size pieces any child can digest, then you cannot yell and scream later in life when they devour your time, money, or respect.

Decide for yourself and act when the time is right! The time to seek bliss exists and is best-suited to you now. Try to seek your bliss and not expect another to teach it or gift you with it.

Chapter Forty-One

No one will tell you what to do if you have not offended your society and created a problem that does not go away at the end of a day, yet many live as if they cannot do what they choose. Why let others tell you how to live, rather than do it for yourself? Is it because you fear being wrong or making a mistake? You will make mistakes, but they are honest attempts to fully live your life and become your best.

You are not to blame if your imagination is not large enough to figure out the toss of every ball or how life will turn out, but you will be put on call if you do not live for *you* and do what you can for others once done doing your work here and now. Who among you is up for the work you do now—and wants to do it for many years to follow? Are you really into it, or just doing it because it helps you make a living, and that living enables you to live with others you love?

Maturity often limits your ability to do what you alone did before you produced a family or married into one and wanted to be accepted—thus you do what is required even now. We do not envy you what you do or why you strive to make money you will waste trying to find time to be yourself, but we do wonder about it. Why do you do it? Can you explain without resorting to name calling, or saying you are not a slave—even if you appear that way to us today?

Every day is a new day for one or another of your thoughts, but some ideas are so old you need to retire them now, but will not. Why? You often sink into ruts so deep you do not see yourself as out-of-style or not thought of any longer by others. You want to do what you love right now; but what about tomorrow or the day after that?

Thinking ahead is anxiety-producing for those without any idea who they are now. Planning should not bother those who are happy—doing what they must to keep abreast of their own desire and wants. However, if you are tired and hate what you do, why continue doing it? What drives you to do nothing, yet you want what another has or they aspire to be? Think on it and you may decide you grew lazy as you aged.

Quietly assert yourself when you must, but never thrust out your chest or open your mouth and speak loudly to those you love. You need not do that. If you groom your child to fight with others and assert what they believe to be their rights, you create a problem for society. The facts are: Children are not recognized by society while living as your dependents. Aggressive children end up unhappy as a result of not being loved or liked by others. You need to teach them *'how to behave'* only as far as the first few years, then they can see if what you preach is their reality or not. Adults need to teach children to not lie or criticize unwisely what will not change or will remain as is for now. Be wise guiding your children and live to be proud of them as adults.

All who advise mothers to stop and feed a child every time it whines or cries are not around when it happens—and usually have no experience with childcare. If they did, they would not tell others what to do. You may not check the credentials of so-called experts, but we do and are appalled at how many are personal failures, yet you place them above you and may even adore them. Be wise—seek advice only when you cannot figure it out.

All who love others without checking their references can develop radar over time that enables them to know who is honest and who is not. Do you set off that detector often, or can you talk without reservation to all and be accepted as a friend? Check and make sure you are not without someone detracting from your message, acting as if you do not live as you claim. If that happens, you will lose face and be unable to talk about your work or be much respected.

Take time to see what others agree is your best effort. You may be wise to accept their applause and acknowledge what you did to earn their praise today—or not. Remember, if you wish to be well-liked, do not speak highly of your accomplishments.

Applause and love are sought by many living in ways that gain neither. Why not stop and look at how you seek praise or faith? Does it harm your credibility? If your work stands out from the crowd, you do not have to praise yourself. If you do not stand out—and praise yourself, you can blame only you when others do not praise and instead run you down for being vain and proud.

Pride is not ego, but ego is often associated with conceit and believing you are better than others—or better than you are. Why would your ego take a beating for what you lack in intellectual stamina or sense? Your ego is the outer being and what people see. It is the part we call *'little you'* and not large—in terms of work you came to do on Earth. Take *little you* by the hand and scold only if you cannot stay inside your life and not harm or criticize others doing better than you.

What about another's ability to attract a crowd makes you feel you are not as good and need to ruin them or do better? It is not exactly the mind or ego, but a way of thinking you create and maintain. If you change your mind by educating yourself on how to live well now, as well as why people do what they do, you may change how you think—but possibly not. If you take your ego out of the equation, forgetting you are here for a day or two and then on your way to another work, you may not be upset or bothered by others—but that rarely happens.

We would not get involved with people who do little or are evil. You may, but why would you risk your life, or being who you are, to associate with those suffering a mortal blight. You can ruin your life, but only if you take life, harm others, or never learn to tolerate others living here as well as you do your clan.

You must and can learn to be yourself. Love is something that comes with this life, and you have to go out of your way to blight it. Once you kill your feelings for this life's work and belief that God exists, feel less than secure, or tell others what to do or how to live, one day you will be called to answer for your work—as all are. You may not be able to move out of this world or into another life, which is a huge risk we do not advise you or anyone you love to pursue.

You are now free and can do whatever you like. You cannot argue you have no money or power, on and on, because everyone is born as you are. Some know immediately what to say to get their way, while others fight everyone in sight. Be the judge about who gets what they want and is more likely to keep it, but we know you did not want much or would have earned it by now.

Taking away another's life gives you nothing but trouble. You have to be totally numb and dumb not to know that by the time you are 9. If you do not give a child lessons on ethics by 10, you cannot claim to be a parent or mothering another. You must take care to teach—not expect the public domain to take care of what you want your child to learn and know. Any help the public education system provides is a bonus—something you can use now, but ultimately you are responsible for educating your children about life.

All is ready to merge and align into a wave of energy that helps you see into your future—without childhood memories you claim block your view now. By examining many of the old excuses you and others use, we discarded all that is useless—so now you are ready to produce. You can produce anything, but make it worth your time and others will ask how you did it.

When you are great, others notice!

Others may not speak of your ability or ask about it, but they notice and start copying you whenever possible when you are a star. It is not the way of stars to brand themselves on the minds of children and ask them to buy whatever they sell. They love crowds and take care not to harm them. If you are a star and know you are, then harm no one willing to buy your ideas or promote you in any way. You must know that or are deluding yourself by thinking you are greater than you are.

All are stars! One beams a bright green and another bright red, but all are seen on other lines and in other ways over time. One beam is no different from others? How can you know when you are this close to your work—as well as know what produces your best life and maximum energy now?

Take care, be aware you are not wanted if you are without anything others like, but may be happier and more blessed because you are not famous. Be wise and release the need to be better than others—striving to change whatever is out-of-line with what some claim is beautiful or describes you. Be aware you are here—then leave and become another who is also *you,* but not who you are now.

Chapter Forty-Two

If everyone discourages you when you plan to do something new, do you stop and not do it or do you ignore them and move on with it? It is important to heed warnings, but when you know what you want or know how to do something and no one else does, are you wise to stop and not follow through? We advise you to advertise, then watch who lies and why. Yes, you are of no interest to most others until you do something that captures their imagination or envy. Once that happens, you can bet some will try to stop you from being loved and others will try to stop you for fear you will best them.

If you do what you want, what would others feel a need to protect? They fear you will do what they cannot or will not do—due to pride or self-esteem needs. They do not want you to succeed and possibly take away those who admire them now.

Do friends envy you?

The way your lives are created and put together supports rivalry whenever you arrive in a competitive society. Friends do not want you to hide your light or not do what you want if it harms no one. They provide you with advice meant to help you do what is wise and survive—not stop you from doing what you believe is right or will provide a better life. Enemies, however, often blow their cover when envy arrives in their minds. They cannot stop themselves from saying what they do not wish you to do or create. They want you to stay as is, possibly not do better than they believe they can easily achieve.

When enemies arrive—and you spot them, check their eyes. Do they blink a lot or resist talking straight to your eyes? Do they smile a lot and act as if they like you or telegraph they hate you? Take time to know people well.

Enemies are friends who do not know you, but can help you more than friends might. When an enemy defends you to someone other than those aligned with you, it is usually meant to demean you. When an enemy names you as having done something wrong, you can say they are envious; better yet, study what is said and change what you did and improve yourself.

An enemy identifies what is not perfect or good about you. They call your attention to the fault—and in time will learn to be quiet. Why? They have no desire to see you do well. If you change everything they complain about, you will be better than they are!

If aspiring to move higher, do more for others. Working hard in order to retire is no one else's business. You may want reassurance or instructions on how to proceed, but make sure it is not intended to put down another or make them sad. Why? They may possibly envy you then.

When envy enters a friendship, you must decide if you want to end your life with them or change your style. Do what you want—but we advise you to not lose friends due to self-pride. Envy is not jealousy, but can sting or harm you as much as those who hate those they perceive to be better than they are.

Jealousy comes over anyone who does not believe another deserves or should have as much this life as they have. If you believe you are a beauty and find another is admired as much as you or more, you act out the fear of being less and lose power. Envy, however, does not come from such an act or life-style. It arrives with you at birth and must be tamed if you are to successfully live with others now. The jealous man who hates anyone who loves the one he wants will kill, thus it is assumed jealousy is the reason. It is not!

You are off-center and without sense, if you believe you alone achieve something that anyone can achieve if they work hard. If you love fickle people who use you to feel good, you are who must suffer in order to learn. You will be used and confused when your attitude could be: *'I may lose one who seems to love me or is unattainable now.'* You need not hate—instead, send love!

Sending love to another is powerful, but sending love to all opens life's doors to you and helps you more. You cannot imagine who will be the most important person in your life once you cross over to the next one, so do not ignore or abuse anyone sent to you now. Yes, angels come through the veil to meet you, as well as those with *you* in other places and other views.

There are traces of *you* in other places and other views that want you to help one not related to you now. Can you feel it, or do you work only with family now? When a family or clan cannot understand that others live, breathe, and think the same as they do, they may start fighting and make trouble instead of being wise and saving whatever they like.

You cannot fight without losing what you value. You lose by not taking care of you. You lose by taking away the prosperity of those you fight with and delight in taking down, too. You cannot ascend and become a great one in spirit if you cannot stop warring—and make peace with others today. You will have to come back!

Knowing that jealousy, envy, and fighting obviously takes away from your bliss and all that is great, what takes you in hand and leads you to the promised life? You and YOU can help *you* rise above the common, hate-filled desecrators of this life to find peace and what you now call bliss, rather than wait until you arrive at the other side of time or this life. You need not worry about the semantics of what is bliss, why is it bliss, and all manner of argument and condescension, but be aware that if you have never seen it, felt it, or believed bliss exists, you have yet to discover it and may never enjoy it while here.

It takes a lifetime for some to rise. When you rise and float in life, you are surrounded by those who either tether you to this world, helping you return when you have soared long enough, or cut your ropes and release you. To seek a high through false means will not help you win friends or be of use to sane men and women who are sober and not looking forward to being placed in the same league as you are when profane. If you want to win over an enemy or someone you believe you can love—and will love you, do not show the ugly side of humankind, rather put on your best life and live it twice—once for *you* and once for those who must live with you.

Being wise means what?

If you are told daily you are nice or wise, you may live up to it, but probably not. Why? You believe stupid things or silly ideas that briefly take root in your mind are wise, thus you become someone others do not like or they believe you are unwise. Take time to know what makes sense in life! Once you learn what helps, do not think others appreciate you telling them to do the same.

This is your first class in wisdom—be sure you get it! All who work with a family of seven or more learn about as much as they need to know to work with a tribe or others who form countries now. You may think you can study others in larger numbers to discover who you are or how others act, but you cannot—unless the group is not diverse and is unhappy within.

Take time to remember your friends. Helping when they ask for help, doing what you can to keep peace, you become a family—even if none of you has anything in common genetically. Are you of the same tribe if you believe in the same god? It makes no difference what you say you believe today, you will change—and so will they!

Chapter Forty-Three

No one will stop you from being yourself, but you may have been raised and taught to not think highly of what you know, to believe in what you see, or any of a zillion mistaken ideas disturbing you now. No problem? Not according to others.

When young you must develop trust in others, so you begin trusting your mother, adding your father, and then others nearby. However, today some are raised by people totally unrelated—not educated enough to know what to say when asked important questions or worse, they ignore children and do not help them question life. If you were raised by people who care not for your work on Earth, or why you are here, or what you could do for others and yourself, you may be belligerent, rebellious, and not work well with others. If you were told to stay out of sight and not utter a sound all your life, you may not know how to talk when allowed to do so now.

Today most people are raised in ways meant to promote their self-esteem—too many are encouraged to think only of themselves, which causes egos to flare and people to fight for more than their share in life. If you have been unfortunate enough to be raised by those who insisted you were better than others, now is a good time to realize you are not. Get into the meat of your work and change that small idea and watch how quickly you enjoy life more. It is a simple change—one that remains fixed in too many minds now, thus setting the stage for work to fail and relationships to suffer, and you to feel less than real.

Once you are aware you are no better or worse than most, do you feel safe and secure or upset? The way to determine when your ego state of mind is way out-of-line with others is to sit down and accept others as they are. Do you suddenly feel better? If not better, than at least as if you can complete your life assignment without a lot of problems.

If you feel flattened or defeated now, it is a sure sign you had an inflated opinion of yourself. Never being told and instructed you are no better than others caused you to feel bad. That is something all need to check and keep in mind, especially when times change and you want to do something no one else does or thinks is good to do. Why? You must realize you are as good as you are now, because you are here. You have an obligation to explore your world and try to do something new that hopefully will improve *you* and all here before you.

Euphoria is a state of mind that can take you out of this life feeling as if you did everything you came to do, yet you did not. If you come across others performing a rare work and immediately want to stop their progress, look up and out and see why you act as you do, then act upon what you see. Reform your memory to include the ability to accept that you are not unique, or the only one who knows much and is here to do better. This is not humility, but sincerity and the ability to sense when you are unwise.

If you accept that you need everything and nothing, all will be great and wonderful. Experiment and discover why you came here and what you will leave behind when you exit. This is not a world you want to always live in, but it helps you determine what is real and the difficulty of manifesting this existence. Try now to let go of the idea that you are the only one who deserves whatever, thus gain enough energy and sense to create it.

The world is now full of *stars* who believe they are better than their elders or those with less possessions or nerve. Obviously unhappy, they will not gain paradise with only self in mind. You must be able to see into the world and sense what is nonsense and what is wisdom.

Without any sense of what is best and wisest in your life, you will survive, but probably never feel great. Why? If the mind is out-of-line with reality, at some point it will realize it needs others and discover it cannot correspond or unite with anyone it likes, because it is not living the life they live now. Taking yourself out of the human race, looking out for only yourself is how you will end life—without anyone caring about you and what you will do next. If you feel great now, it is because you suddenly realize your life is no different from what is and what you have been taught.

We as Teachers from other existences see nothing you need be ashamed of, worried about, or should resist in time. We know you are here to learn, but some spurn learning and know nothing of their background and history or tribe, thus feel all alone now. If you cannot link with others like you, you will not feel great. However, if you are combined with a tribe now and cannot free your mind to think for yourself, you are not doing much better.

Freedom is a way of life! You either realize that by now or are beginning to understand doing what you want to do for reasons that may not interest others is not why you do it. You move and do whatever, because you are here to become *you* in the fullest, largest possible way today—not to stay the same or never change.

Chapter Forty-Four

On your own, without a home? You know no freedom then. Daily you seek a safe haven to rest and care for your bodily needs; however, you can gain peace of mind that might otherwise elude you when surrounded by others. All you have is yours. You alone secure it or leave it for others to take, but there is risk if you take from others and they in turn take from another, thus building a society where all are takers of one sort or another.

When all are suspect—and all is subject to theft, nothing is safe, so whose life thrives? You decide and create your life! You provide help or take it, but all comes out even by the end of each life.

What you do for others can be given back to you in different ways. It may appear to be divine providence or given by the universe, but more closely resembles a balance inherent in your lives and this planet. Balance is what you manifest—or not. You may want much more than you deserve, simply because you believe you were deprived of such as a child, but we see no need for many things when you do not use them often. Why be burdened with caring for what you cannot use or will not want once no longer new?

To buy the world's sugar so no one can eat it, or hoard it so you can charge whatever for it, are foolish ideas. But how many companies are doing the equivalent in some way today—trying to corner a market in hopes of becoming billionaires and more? You then have nothing for the people who create this world.

One day you will rue the day you took too much for yourself. Will everyone put up with it? Most do not care, beyond what they need for themselves, but there will always be another like you who will want what you want and will kill for it. Those eager to take from others are replaceable and will be put out of their misery long before they think possible, because it is a time of balance and seeking to know who you are—and goods are no longer as in demand as your minds once believed them to be.

All of life is provided, if you live by the work of another who teaches that and you believe it. What you believe actually does help you conceive what you need and can provide. Think of it as Divine Providence and all you attract by the sweat of your brow becomes a miracle to others and possibly yourself. Believing you can heal and help another get well may even turn out that way. You then do not know how you did it or why, but we can help you excel and become well or wealthy, depending upon your present lack of imagination.

To become a happy woman or man, all you have to say is: *"I am happy and feel bliss!"* Repeat it and it lives! You become filled with what you believe to be bliss. It is not difficult to get, but arguments provided throughout this assignment help you realize bliss is not a single instance, but a full life in this time, as well as what you do with *you*.

Take your work to heart and it becomes all you wish it to be. Forget to work—adopting a life of idleness, perhaps you can convince others they should take care of your needs. If not? You are whoever you say you are—be it bum, poet, itinerate preacher of lessons you do not hear or practice, or an artist of any type. All require that others let them take time away from earning their bread so they can play at what they have to say.

When you decide you have worked hard and saved enough to retire, why not? What makes you continue to seek money and prestige once you no longer are young and need to create a nest for your family to live in until they are on their own? If you must work every other day for others, you cannot adjust to life, but you can live longer if you work for the good of the world or grace of God.

Chapter Forty-Five

Play a new song and you will not like it. You prefer to know what comes next, because it is difficult to judge a song until you hear it again. However, if it is a replay or rearrangement of an old song merely done a new way or with different players, you can immediately say you like it or not. When it comes to reading a book, you often experience the same quandary, because you want to know what is going on and why, without an explanation that takes you far away from what you believe now. You want to merely adjust—not have to trust.

When you figure out what we are all about, you are confronted by what to tell others about our work—or should you explain it? Why bother? Is it not enough that you can change and improve—realizing your life is going in a different direction, if not totally changed, by the way these words are arranged on each page?

You want to discuss this work with someone else, but who can you trust? Whatever you do, always remain true to what you do, believe you need, or what you want to be. Things are simple then. You may have friends outwardly different from who you appear to be now, but you think alike and have found each other this life, or are about to find one another via the internet or whatever takes on a life of its own now.

When you find others you never knew, yet they believe as you and what you want to be, do you doubt them? Do you want to know why they feel that way, or do you doubt they could know you now? What you believe about another is usually what you agree to be within *you* every day or two. You may believe you are easy to be around until you notice you argue constantly with someone you thought you loved.

Would that make you change what you do, or would it make you want to be someone who gets along with others better than you do?

Questions are meant to direct you to look beyond who you appear to be in your mirror, to find yourself and what you hide from everyone else. Why hide who you are if you believe you will get ahead and they will not? You may not want others to find peace of mind, because you believe they are better than you or you may give them more power over you than you do now. Why not let others realize you are not bothered by them, instead love what they do that elates you, too? If you do, you can build a relationship based on respect.

If you do not wish to share wisdom or a better way of being okay today, are you saying you hoard such knowledge and hope no one else knows what to do? Are you happy you are superior to others, hoping they fail this life and are forced to return to live another such life? Do you fear others will not like you if you reveal something you can do easily—and if they knew how to do it, would it amaze them, too?

All you have to do is smile!

You need not prowl the internet looking for others who think as you do, or seek to find a woman or man who will talk things over with you. We know you want to share what you believe, because you want to persuade others to do as you do, but it is not allowed. You can, however, say you read this book and wonder what they think about it, too. You are not then intruding or telling another what to believe or what to read, but helping those you love or like to see what you saw by the time they finish a book and decide whether or not they like what they read.

You can now decide what you will do with all this energy—and what it does for your mind. We urge you to not experiment on others now. Do not play with wisdom downloaded to you from your spiritual source. Put it to good use instead! Demonstrate to the world who you are, what you believe, and what you think may help others.

In The World of Today and Tomorrow you will find you need more information than you found in this book, but it is all within *you* now.

We say with greatest confidence that you know enough to follow your life to its highest level and live at that elevation now or until you move up another plane or so. Try to let go! Tell your mind you are safe, that it is sound thinking to let you do as Spirit directs *you* now.

If you feel connected to the next level and can levitate and raise your vibrational plane, do it! If you do, please advise *The Scribe*. She can help you move on and do more. However, if you cannot levitate—even doubt anyone can, you are fine.

Most humans are limited in their ability to see themselves rise in this world—let alone rise in other worlds. The world will be of use to you as long as you breathe, so do not befoul the air nor let others do it. You need air—and you need water. To think otherwise is to lose your life.

We want you here! We want you where you can thrive until it is time to leave this planet and never return. Earth deserves to be left alone, allowed to vegetate and heal itself—not be bothered hosting human beings again. So get on with living now and leave when this life is over!

All you need do is think of God, or whatever it is you argue about. It becomes a problem when another doubts or says your concept is wrong. Why try to describe what is indescribable—not human or of man? You cannot understand your way of believing or see what we see immediately.

You want things to be dense and material—even believe you can take it with you when you leave this time and space. If you have nothing now, why would you want to come back again? You have to examine your mind to decide what you believe could be achieved by returning to Earth in another form.

We want you to surrender to your Higher Self or highest power and decide to rise when this life is over and you can leave. Do not try to force the issue or improve your chances of being needed in a higher capacity, instead stay the course and finish what you came here to do.

Make sure it is done forever—something you can say was easy once you got over being who you are now.

All any ego wants is to see itself achieving something—being better than another human being. That is not easy to believe when you seek to enhance the ego through whatever means is at hand, but a way to understand your lack of interest in your fellow man. You want to be better than others, which stands in the way of finding your path. Your way of living today determines where you will be tomorrow!

Take your hand and press on a finger or thumb and think about it. Can you harm you or not? You obviously will not pinch so hard you harm your body. That would be insanity, and you would have to agree since you did it to yourself. That means you are running fully on ego then—not using your mind or spirit at that stage in your life.

Be aware that balancing all you are here to do with what you cannot see is easy once you believe. Believe? You will soon know who is right and who is not. It is not a problem, because all are right at least some of the time. However, some never know when they are right and will fight it.

Be you and take care of your family if you acquired one. Ask another to help run whatever for you now. Be good company and love your fellow man when you can, and do no harm. What more can you do to explore being adored? You will find that the more you do for others, and the kinder you are, you will be loved more than you deserve now.

Be secure and know you have a short time to live this life. Enjoy what you have and save nothing for the next life. Be aware if you amassed much, but stole some of it, you will not be loved. You may think you deserve it, or thought they would not use it wisely, but theft in your society is despised and seen as the worst thing anyone can be—a thief.

Think about how much you hate losing things. Think about how much time it took to educate your mind and what you did with it. You will find things preoccupy your mind more than educate it for life. Be aware things disappear, but your thoughts do not.

All that will help you today is within *you* now. If you wish to live better in the future, pray and ask for help deciding what is wise and how to get on with your life. Do not ask others to help if you have yet to lift a finger or only dreamed about what needs to be done. If you work on your life and peace of mind is easy to accomplish, but making a great living is harder than you wish it to be—let one rule the other. Do not charge for what you acquired before realizing you could lose it and never know it.

If you had the means to understand human beings, we would be free to teach you more about this world. Since you do not plan to stay on Earth again and again—and we advised you that this is wise, why bother trying to help you now decide what to do this life? When we help people aspire to rise higher in their work—and what they want to be, they lose interest in being the best they can be. They do nothing to enhance their spiritual lives, so we decline to direct you to a better-paying job at this time. Instead, use your mind to get in line.

Chapter Forty-Six

In your future lies a time when you will merely survive with no desire or drive to live longer here, but it may affect your mind long before it is time to lay down and die. Why? You have to inspire your mind with ideas that stretch you to believe in what is, what can be, and what will always exist if you are to move higher than this.

Bliss is a state into which you slip and is not easy to teach. Having taught you much so far that helps you jar and remove what is sticking in your mind all the time, we hope you are now ready to work hard and enjoy your life—then bliss it up to the very end!

Who is going to stop you from enjoying your life now? If you honestly can state today that a person, group, or institution will stop you, think about why you let it happen and when it began. Once again, when off-track, you must go back to where it happened. You may not want to sadly reflect on the day you met another, but it is your life always, and no one can take it from you now.

As you choose what to do and how to live, do you plan or merely do whatever is here now? Most people do not plan enough to effect any change later in life, thus they may now be saying they wish they had saved or planned and so on, but why change your style now? It took you this long to understand that some have much and others not enough, and many times it is simply due to how they live daily.

You may want to believe you are wise and others are not, but the proof of it is how comfortable you live when the end comes to you again. All that is good will stay inside you long after what was not great dies or ceases to impress your mind. Why? You are not made to stay negative. You were created to seek the positive and create an environment that easily accepts positive reinforcement. To say you are negative and prefer the dark is unlikely and probably never said, because you cannot believe it. Why would you seek the light if you were better off in the dark?

Working for others is easier than creating your daily work and being totally responsible for your success. Why? The mind does not like to be told it is not doing well or is unwise. If it believes it will be blamed for all mistakes, it will not work as hard. Take time now to absolve yourself of errors and calls that were serious errors, and you will feel better.

To desire what another has is human, but not real. Why? First, you must understand who you are and what is planned once you join Spirit again on the other side. Then discount what you want and add on what another has, and so on. Pretty soon you are totally consumed with copying another, instead of being yourself. That ends badly!

Recognize your nature, then what makes you work, and finally what is not good for your body and mind—before you ask Spirit to step in and take over and guide you this life. That is an extremely serious decision and most cannot fulfill the requirements now. If you give up on what you want and suddenly decide everything you do will be guided by the truest element of your divinity, will you suddenly be rich and famous and have many friends? That idea shows a total lack of understanding of the divinity and what you are here to do!

You will find being quiet and accepting facts, listening to those who reflect back your basic nature and best talents are needed before you can leave your work for another in this time and space. You cannot explain your work? You are then going to remain as is until your mind accepts you are divine in origin, but not that wise now.

All that exists is, and all you dream about exists and is, so what is the difference? You decide. We will help you analyze what you do wrong. Why help you? You need to know what you are doing all the time and why. You cannot grasp that much is intuitive and not listed in menus as seen on your computer. We recommend you accept that man can mimic the mind and create machines that seem to behave as they conceived them to be, yet machines can wear out, break down, require new parts or programs, and generally have no original ideas they can field now and then to save you time.

Why have machines? Because you can! You can calculate long columns of figures and add them as quickly as any machine, does it matter? Is it important to others? It is simply a way you created to keep your mind elevated and working hard that will not harm you. However, while you display what any small calculator can do, you miss out on a wonderful life here and now!

Take up your life and provide enough light to read what you expect and want—see what happens. If you find many others surprised at what you do, do not mention it so as to create an aura that you can easily do whatever and they cannot. Why? You will produce jealousy in others that will distract and inhibit you from making it through The World of Tomorrow now.

All that is and all that seems to be in style now is not. You merely decide what to wear and who to care about, then share it with others. A wave of inability to care deeply is taking over an entire world by storm now and creating havoc in children everywhere. What will become of you when the young produce others who care even less about people than you do? Be aware you create your future today!

What will you do and how many will be doing it with you as of the day after tomorrow? Can you look at the future and sense what is on tap and about to happen? If not, then why not try to develop this ability now?

Take time to develop insight and the ability to read others by studying psychology. Study tribes and nations, understanding them via sociology. The way you educate your mind now will help later in life, so prepare for the time when you can help others live better lives—or sink into despair as you age, wondering about what happened to all your great ideas and plans conceived now.

The world will not change as much as you!

Take time to decide what you want out of life and you will never regret it, but assume it will happen regardless of whatever you want and you will be unhappy. Why? You are obviously depressed and not taking steps to eliminate it!

If you have friends who look down on you and frown at whatever you do, why think of them as friends? Do you now seek people to help you sink into deep depression and not be as great as you can be? If so, are you who is depressed or are you merely letting others exercise their negativity on you? If this is the case, then you live in fear and do not wish to be alone. How sad is the life of those who fight living in their own light!

What you do now will happen tomorrow, and you will feel it immediately. If you do little now, it will ooze through to *you* anyway and wait for you to declare it is another terrible day or whatever fools like to say. Yes, a fool tries to limit the arenas of life in which he or she exists, and we cannot help you with that. You did it, and you are who must first admit you did it and made a huge mistake, and now wish to be a member of the human race and commit to helping others. Once you feel like a human being—feeling it in your mind and body, and living better than you otherwise might, your spirit will rise and ask those on high to help you live better now. Try it if you doubt!

Is existing all you do now?

If so, you do not feel great, probably hesitate to accept anything written or said about the human race. Merely being here—not doing anything you need to do over and over again. Why not deliberately fool your mind by asking God to help you with the problem you have in mind now? Why not ask—then take God to task after that? Because you do not believe you have anyone superior to you here. That is a huge ego! It can imprison individuals quicker than you can believe it exists or comment on what God is. Take it from us, as teachers of higher realms, you do not know anything about God now, instead you are subject to the word and creed of what others believe God to be.

When you work hard and feel great, do you appreciate others who do not work as hard or think you are great? The answer is obvious, but some would argue about it anyway. Why? Because some have nothing better to do now than argue. They argue in order to feel alive or a part of the world, but are not appreciated, thus whatever they say drifts away and is not discussed by anyone else.

Take time today to save yourself a lot of worry—even grief, by simply saying you can love anyone and everyone, and you bear no one a grudge. Once that resonates in your mind, develop a line that repeats it to everyone who can channel you now. All will be better for you than it has been so far.

Chapter Forty-Seven

People are human beings. You all see things equally, even if you believe you are unique and without peer—without any knowledge of what every other human does. You are uniquely suited to living in a world where you can move about and secure the power of Spirit to be yourself, but you cannot ruin the world without everyone joining in now. Discovering you are only one of your number, thus unable to do much without everyone else deciding to move as you do in a single unit, all are now confused. Each wishes to be in charge, dis-believing in others whom you say are not like you now.

Having studied you without ever really loving *you,* we discovered you do not love, and you do not want anyone else to be better than you. You can elect others to lead you, but you mistrust all you elect or let govern you. When we learned how easily you let others lead you, we became concerned, but realized that without love you will not follow anyone.

You may want to lead—even believe you do it for others rather than yourself, but that is not true. You want someone to take care of you until you have all you want, then possibly care for others, but probably not. Children do not hide this from adults, but adults learn how to secret away their faults and not alarm another, in order to marry or connect and have children and do what only large numbers working together can accomplish.

When you gain peace of mind, remember how you did it. Why? Many will want to know how you do it and how you live well when they cannot. That is when you are honored by others or burned at the stake, so to speak, for having too much power. Once again, do not try to take over, and you will be appointed to the position of power before you want it. When you feel you can lead, you are often too old to be of use to those who believe they are unique.

Once or twice in every life you have the opportunity to do something excellent. You can lie and say that is not true—that you have no special ability or talent, and try to prove it, but everyone knows you better than that, just ask. If you ask others what they believe to be your strengths, they will shade them and say they are greater than they are; but if you ask what your weaknesses may be, expect them to lie in order to hide what they believe you cannot be. Why?

Why tell another what makes you feel superior to them? The bright decide early in life to measure their work and abilities against what they did last year or earlier in their lives, but never against others—especially those who do not care to work hard or do new things. Once you can develop and work out a pattern that helps you breathe easily, you are confident everyone else will see it as needed to be great, happy, and secure.

If you doubt we can participate in this work, because we are not alive or not in your mind now, you are wrong. You may try to prove you are better than those without a body of any kind—which is unwise. Why? Who will believe you when you argue you are greater than Spirit?

When ready, we will work on increasing your nerve to accept that you do work of a spiritual nature all the time you live on Earth—and all the time you are alive. If you disbelieve, that is your problem—not ours. It is worth it to finally discover you are no different from others while on Earth, but once departed you become part of something so different from what you are here and now that you never again think about this life. Until then, let us begin working within. Work with a thirst to learn all you can while on Earth—do not wait until you get to the next birth.

How can you learn what is Imprinted on your work?

Whatever you do and whenever you do it, you may not realize you are moving along a preordained path—until you discover you had many other chances or opportunities to be exactly as you seem to be now. Look over your work and spot when you decided to work hard or not. Check out that spot, then every spot where you started to work and did not or could not get it then. Once you plot out all these spots, you see the pattern and wonder why you never got it then. You see why you were set apart at one time, then given a head-start in another, and so on, until all is clear to plot the course that got you to this spot.

Once you meet with us—reading this line and understanding what it means, and how you derive time, you are in the light of your most holy life. Believe it or not! You have tried to deliberately keep from doing what you always knew you would do, for reasons you cannot remember now or choose to forget, but you are listening or reading these words as if you knew what to do and would do it right now.

All is clear once it is shown as what you want to be, who you are, and how you wish to change now or remain the same. You do not have to survive and live many lives. You do not have to come back again and again, but you do have to learn how to ascend to end the common misconception that you must be a master or saint to end this life and gain ascension then. You are master of your universe—even if children make it their chorus without knowing what it means, you know!

Within a week of reading this material and keeping it to yourself, you will become a much bigger being. You will be much less conceited (someone who believes only he or she should be believed and everyone else is wrong). You need to be strong of mind and able to tell when you are wrong. It is of little worth to say others lie and you do not, and then prove otherwise. Be sure of what you say—then do it right away, never saying what you believe another should be. Taking responsibility for you and what you do is adult and expected of you all, but the immature or those who will have to remain or never be accepted on the next plane believe otherwise now.

When a group of worthless ideas is accepted by an intelligent mind, you have to wonder why. You may blame drugs or alcohol now, but is it not more likely they simply did not read or want to work at assimilating what it meant from the first? You cannot expect someone else to do much work and then give you first choice.

Many want others to do work they believe demeans them, and it usually does, because they are mean to others. You will find if you are kind, intelligent to the extent inbred in your mind, and try to be wise, you will usually do well and not have to end life crying for alms or without anyone holding your hand as you die. If you have never cared about others and hate to be supervised by those who are wiser than you, it will come to the point where you will have to decide who to believe when unable to do it yourself. That is when you could face hell.

Hell is not the state of being accepted by people you hate, rather it is whatever you believe another you dislike or hate should live in now. Whatever state you condemn another to dwell in is where you will dwell when asked to consider what you did not do well. Consider that before you swear and condemn others—maybe spare yourself a lot of time in what you would describe as hades now.

Do you want to be an angel, or do you believe demons supersede all other beings and can run your life and cause you major strife? If you do not accept the one, how can you believe in the other? What kind of education or religious upbringing did you have that caused you to doubt your Higher Self has the power to avoid and conquer whatever might be a major threat to your life here and now?

Be aware it is you who likes to run scared—not your Guide's idea of a path you would like this life. Now that a Guide is mentioned, and you still do not understand why you would need a Guide of any kind this life, let us separate what you want to believe from what you need.

When you know someone wiser than you, who has lived life from the inside out and can help you gain a better life or hold an advantage you otherwise might not have had, would you cast that one aside, or would you ask for help and thank that one for whatever you find of advantage in your present life? You decide, but most people like to believe God exists and can swoop down and take them to safety if danger is present, or an angel is standing on the sidelines ready to take them to a safer place if they should be stupid enough to endanger their lives or not care about where they live and who they kiss. You may believe both and be right, or you could be wrong about them, who you are, and what is right. But why worry now?

Accept whatever religious principles you have and use them to your best advantage. Do not change to be like a guru who claims to be better than you. Most are aware you have a spiritual side to this life—even if they never say a word about it to a close friend or two. You believe because you know you have had close encounters of a spiritual nature many times, but no one explained them to you—until now.

Now is the perfect time to accept that you are not alone, or living on a planet without any mind of its own, or life it intends to stay as is and not let you or others change its path or alter its route. If you like to use analogies, you are a small planet. You move in a prescribed way every day, and cannot change the way you are made, or alter the course of how your bowels produce waste without major problems that resemble storms of various kinds, such as strike your environmental life.

You have been given Guides, precision, and if you are wise, the ability to steer into clear and calm water all your life. However, because you came here to learn more than you otherwise might in another type of life, you often prefer to stir up the atmosphere, even jumping into waters neither clear nor clean nor able to keep you alive. If you are wise, why prefer danger over what God provides?

You have a mind which likes to believe it alone conceives everything you believe to be you and your life. Self-conceit is unique to each mind. It exists in each and every human being to some extent now. Why? You practice it! You praise it in your children daily—even say it is better to boast than be introverted and wise, because you can lie and get whatever you want without working hard. How is that working out?

Chapter Forty-Eight

In the beginning of anything you choose to do, you start with a dream of being successful, then usually decide it will be too difficult for you to do. Many decide to forget their dreams and merely walk through life. Why? Why forget the dream? Why not work on what you alone wish to own or accomplish? You do not believe in *you*!

Once you see what you believe come to be, you begin to concede there is a mystery to life you cannot find the answer to now. You begin piecing together all that was ever said to you. How many told you to work in a certain way or one day you would want to know the subject much better? Notice how many people you meet daily provide a piece or connection to the dream you want to achieve—*and then you see it and believe in you!*

If everyone you ever met said: *"forget it"*, would you still want it? We notice huge numbers do the opposite of what others do or advise them to try. Why? You do not believe! You can sum it up in various ways, but today believing is something that does not come to you over a lifetime. You can lose it living how you want—not obeying the rules of life.

You may ask, what rules?

The simple explanation is everyone is here for a stated reason. It is not difficult, but some wish to be seen as brighter or better than others, so they try to put out or dim the light of anyone they believe is brighter or better in some way than they appear to be that day. The envy we talk about non-stop is one way many betray themselves and create another life in which they try not to hide their need to be here.

You may be here now because you feared others and wanted to harm them as you believed they harmed you. Feedback from the past often induces guilt in such large volume that you want to lash out and prevent loved ones from acting the same way—or perhaps they constantly remind you that you neglected them or others. Do not let guilt stop you now from doing what is right!

Taking advantage of another when they are not feeling well or are feeling down, and so on and on, is an evil way to get what you want. It quickly falls apart when the one being used catches on to you. What can you do if you built a house with will power and others suddenly stop you from moving higher? You let it go and start over.

Whatever you do, be aware you cannot stop what you did in the past or begin again without looking back, but you can negate whatever happened then by not giving it much thought now. If you stop thinking about a subject, it recedes and is probably forgotten until you discuss something much like it—*after* you *totally forgot what it was*. Do not worry about forgetting things of little or no consequence—instead be on top of what is needed now. Why? You need to be ready to fly at a moment's notice.

Whenever we bring up the subject of aviation, are we talking about flying as getting on a plane or rising in elevation some such way? When working with Spirit here and now, that is not what we mean by flying. Flying is being alive to everything in your life and preparing to broaden this incredible life to include many others. You can fly and see into time, knowing you can make a huge difference if you so desire.

It is when you make it to the top that most decide they can fly, but there is nothing to stop you from flying since birth! All you have to do is widen your inner eye and search for what you do well—then deepen, widen, and do it good enough to help others. Once you find an opening and can earn your way, you are certain to fly later—so why not fly today?

Fly today and smile!

When you can open your mind and see inside time, you greet *you* from the top-most part of your entire life on this side. Why wait until you are dying to understand you can live without guilt or sin now? You can do it! No one will stop you. All you need do is ask God to direct you.

Asking for a blessing is easy! Do not stop all working with you and others, too, in order to ask for healing or more materials, unless you are ill and cannot take care of yourself. Yes, it is unwise to ask to heal yourself, unless you tried other means and no one asked to pray with you or offered to pray away your pain. Once you know you can work alone, and can call upon others to pray for your work or health, you are safe. You have insured yourself against what might otherwise cause you great pain and sorrow one day.

Buying what you believe will be money saved for your old age is unwise. You may never spend it or be alive at the end to divide it, so spend carefully as you age. The time to thrive is when you can buy bread, if you cannot bake it.

When busy working for a living, do not forget those who cannot do such work. If you take care of your neighbors, they will look in on you and care for you. If you cannot believe this, you best move now.

All who believe they have nothing or are worth little sin against the god they say is not looking their way today. If you praise God for what you have, and feel you have much, you begin to see the filled bag—not the slack in what you have. Try to be wise and spend according to your present means, not getting caught up in what does not work for you now.

You never stop nor work on what you want others to do for you? There is no way you can work non-stop! Make plans to stop regularly, so you can run every day without stopping when you can least afford to do so or must stop due to a breakdown in your life.

You have things to do. You have people to please. When you cannot repay, do not act as if you alone are unique and everyone owes you a living or must forgive you.

If you unloaded your baggage and excess cash, exercising control over how many hours a day you stop and work with us, you are about to fly. Once again, it is not about lifting off the ground so much as gaining height and circumnavigating life in this light. You provide your delight and drugs of whatever type you need now, but make them up. Do not use what you grow, find, or make to imitate another's faith.

Once you can see inside your mind, dream of a new being—and a totally new life. If you cannot lift your mind with a dream, you need to rest and take better care of your health. Dreams are always waiting for you, so accept the fact that you can be anyone you care to be. If dreams are absent, it means you do not have enough of what is needed to make your life a success. It usually indicates a simple lack of belief that you are a child of God, can fly, or have a great life now.

If life on the other side is wide and bright, but you act as if you are blighted this life, what happens when you die? You may not be allowed back inside your bright life—required to stay until you pass this class. You are who judges your work and what *you* learn. You is tougher on *you* than others, because *you* knew what to do when you came to Earth and the entire time you survive.

Can you discover what You wants of you?

Overlook anything you know you need to do to make something work and you are reminded by an inner guide that it is not right, you forgot something, or it needs more time. It may come to you during the night or in dreams at another time, but you abruptly remember when something is needed. Do it immediately or watch it crumble over time. You pay the price if you do not heed your inner guidance.

Imagine you harmed another human being without realizing it then. During the night you are awakened by a calm voice within your mind telling you what you said or did to upset another. You may call out in shame, or decide you could not have acted otherwise, and so on, but you are now aware you did harm to the mind, soul, or body of someone you thought a lot of when you did it. This is not what you might want to discuss with your workers, co-workers, or even closest confidantes, but it is what most talk about to counselors now. They seek to be told they are not mean, nasty, or evil. Will that straighten your mind and help you fly straight now? You decide!

If your work is crumbling and all you do is worthless to others, and you do not know how to create a job that will support all your wants, you may blame society and complain about the government, wanting others to stop whatever so you can run things now. Why would anyone want you to run the country if you cannot provide for yourself? Be wise, let others ask you to run for office. If no one does, then do a great job taking you off the payroll of others and ease your mind by being a self-sufficient person, one who has no need to borrow, steal, or work for others now. That usually catches everyone's attention!

Without doubt, start praying immediately, ask God to forgive you your arrogance in believing you created your work and everything given to you by others since birth. Think about it. Do not shirk this work!

Chapter Forty-Nine

Out of the blue or only now assuming you have much to do and cannot do it? What depresses you is what you most want to do and believe you cannot. When you open your mind and observe your life and how much time you have, you will find it is always those who waited until the end to whine who did the most and contributed more than others. They had no time to waste whining throughout their lives.

If you have a family of five and have everything you require, how will you go about making your life difficult? That is what so many appear to be doing now. You view others' lives as boring, unless they do more or less than you—then you assume they are in a race with you that you want to win.

First among equals is not achievable, but some always want to be the most sought-after for whatever God gave them in greater abundance than others. You cannot take credit for beauty—even health, if you are merely the caretaker of what God created. You may even be downgraded enough that you lose your way back for not taking care or desiring to appear better than created. You decide, but you do have enough to rise to the top of your life and fly. Decide on where you are going and get on the road now!

Whatever you do, do it for you!

Before starting to work make sure it pays well and is not so time-consuming that you cannot unwind and find God at the end of each day or several times a week, instead of working on what you want to accomplish and do all your life. You cannot remain sober and sane without a connection to your source, which is not attainable if you are unwilling to connect frequently to make sure the spark restarts your mind.

Your time is equal to your many designs for this life. Once you decide what you can accomplish and how you will do it, take time to do it and not worry about your past. The past is done and nothing you say will change it today.

Working for another during an average day takes time that you may not admit is better spent there than spent sitting at home working on your own. You may not be active enough to keep your mind fit or your body well. You may not be active enough to do a lot that would help you move up in life without doing a lot more than you did before. If you have plans to suddenly get rich, make sure you do not gamble away what you have today.

Work is not what we are here to teach you, but we observe that many of you are unfit for the work you do. You do not do it with your full mind or even part of your life, but expect it to be so wonderful it takes care of you all your life. We would not advise you to be idle or care about nothing now, but you can do that and compare yourself to many like you. Whatever you do, there are others out there doing it, too.

When you decide to be different—look unlike others, you are still the same! You are a human being and all the artwork that tribes use to express status is not lost in the societies that now frown on tattoos. Merely put yourself into a frame of reference. If your society believes you have status, they give you stripes or designs they want to admire. If you do it, you likely do not gain status in your world. Think about it and admit when you scar the flesh that you actually think you are improving on what God gave you.

All you admire and want others to admire about you is without class, society, or even status. You are not expected to do much in most advanced nations of your world now. Barriers are falling and everyone can do almost anything not harmful to others. You are thus responsible for your well-being and cannot blame others. Does it make you happier? Probably not!

Bliss is not about uncovering something you believe another did to you and needs to be amended or taken to court. When you decide to leave someone for another, you set in motion much you cannot control. Whether the other attacks or not—facing you with what they want you to do, you must react to what happens. You may want to slip away and say nothing, but you cannot. It will always be there staring you in the back, instead of being erased now. Do what you lack and generally you will not have to marry to gain it from another, thus discovering once again you could have achieved it more easily by doing it yourself.

All you learn is yours!

You are not beholden to help anyone finish a job, settle a bill, or delay progress, if you do that now. If you are to complete a job, you must be able to see yourself do it. If you expect others to take over and complete your work or do most of the details, be ready to be disappointed and lose money. All who volunteer do so to have a good time! When the good times end, so does their need to be a part of an organization they wanted to help—and now find wanting.

When you decide living is easy, because you found someone who makes a great living and shares it with you, remember many others can easily replace you. It is not easy to be the breadwinner. It is not something women enjoy now, but many are quickly learning the lesson of sharing all they have with someone they love, enjoying it more than when they let another pay their way.

Whatever you do today, pray first. Settle on one thing you wish to complete and another you can start, plus whatever requires your attention. Once it is under control and you are in power and can move about, do what you love. Without the ability to share and give up what you do not need, you will find cooperation from others scarce.

Whatever is worth your life is worth your best work! Now that you can connect the dots, see what you need to do to stay on the beam of light that takes you from home to work—then back to your origin. You will ascend and be happy you did!

Chapter Fifty

All the material you need to know is now written. You cannot ascend without proving to your mind it is time well spent reading it. If you do nothing, merely think about all that was said, you cannot figure out how to move up and out of this life and do it in time, so you may as well stop reading now and forget what we said.

You are who is responsible for your life here! You will be upset and without anyone to talk about or work with if you do not do your part. You will be left behind in the most real sense of the idea—not something concocted or fabricated to make you worry or get upset so you give up something you need or want.

We do not ask you to follow a leader—or follow anyone other than You, and what *you* do in your sleep, as well as during your meditations and other quiet hours. If you have no connection to source by now, you must find it and get on line—not waste time reading about it. If you routinely include these readings with whatever else you believe helps you succeed in your work, you have changed dramatically and feel much better about life now!

Work is not physical or mental, rather spiritual as used in the context we present this work of art to you and all who follow you, reading the same author or working in the same beliefs as in your mind and body now aligning with your spiritual life. If you feel no difference—or feel unreal, take time to connect to your work of this life and achieve balance, then use this to further your work here. If you allow yourself to get too high or low, you cannot work as you otherwise might, so we advise against it. Otherwise, we do not care what your emotional state is now, because it is not your spiritual life!

As you move about, trying out many ideas to see what is practical and what is not, remember the logic of what we said—and continue to follow your heart. You found bliss by this time or you are not trying to find it. It exists and is easy to experience, but you must do what you came to do to enjoy it.

All that is and all that exists is about to be experienced as bliss. If you cannot see it or believe it, you have no idea what you are missing, but have found ways to experience a bit of it by reading this. You found some wisdom—or did not listen or put into action anything we taught throughout this book. You can ignore wisdom, or explore what is not wise, and still make it to the next plane. It does take longer and never quite as great as experiencing bliss—yours whenever you wish while here.

This is your way of living. It exists as is, because you will it to be this way. You can change and rearrange whatever you do, but explaining more about how to ascend or what to do until life ends will not change anything for you. You need to practice what you read, and do what must be done—then have even more fun!

Do not worry that you spent time working on what you believed to be a way of existing that is quite difficult to achieve. If you believe that, you labored long enough and can take your life in hand now and enjoy it. Be you!

Take care of whatever you say you will handle for others and all will be okay. Check that out and see if we are not right. If such advice is hard to take, and you cannot handle it now, you have to work very hard to enjoy a moment in the state of existence described as *bliss,* but you can do it if you begin today.

Bliss is an appetite for enjoying life, and the ability to gain perspective on what you came to this world to do for YOU—then all is done without worry or grief. If you cannot do anything for any other than *you,* make sure you ascend. Be ready at the end of this life to move up when called to do so. All you need do now is work on the best way to elevate your mind and keep your body on line until it is no longer required. Other than that, you are on your way today to a happy demise!

Whatever you do and wherever you work, live, or desire to be now, you have to move you to do it, work it out, or live it. We do not pick you up and move you. We inspire—hoping you perspire enough to make it happen now. Be ready to meet us again at the end!

All is what you believe it to be, but you can use your imagination and make it anything you like. That is the power and glory of living now! You are the one who experiences life as bliss or whatever it is to you—although not true.

Be honest, you have enough to do to keep yourself busy and happy for the rest of your life. If you renege and sit back, waiting for someone else to tell you what to do, you will experience agony. The problem with not doing what you are moved to achieve is you get bound up in anger, pride, and blaming others then. This is all we can say about not doing what you came here to achieve, but it tells you everything you need to know.

All is going well! You can leap into time, but it takes a well-disciplined mind to overcome the work done to prove your body is better than other bodies, or tame an unruly mind that reneges instead of fulfilling orders. You are who runs your entire being now, so be happy and do your best to have a wonderful life. Bliss is it, but you have to experience it to appreciate it!

Chapter Fifty-One

During the course of this coming year you will divide your time between many ideas—even a few assignments. Will you decide you are done here? Will you conclude you have nothing else to do, thus can sit and do little, or let your body rot or abuse it? What happens when you let go and do nothing new, nor do your best? You know, yet some slip into the abyss of not working on their spiritual lives now.

If you have no intention of doing anything different from what you did when you started reading this book, how can you change? It may happen without you doing anything, or you may be left to do only what you want, but the latter is hard on the mind and not what most accept now.

If you could never decide what is right and what will turn out well, you would be in a small minority of those who do not believe in God. Admit to yourself that you know there is a higher power than you—one that decides what happens once you give up and do nothing. Until you die or let God come into your mind and decide what you will do and so on, *you* are here to be you. This is all we ever asked of you, and what we teach everyone.

When you try to put words into the mouth of another in order to annoy, criticize, or perhaps lie about them, understand it is recorded and will be replayed later in some way. You are who you are and recording every moment of your life as if on tape or being filmed for a big event you hope will turn out great. You are writing your biography now. Living it for you—not because *you* believe it needs to be embellished so others will love you and think you excelled or had it much harder than everyone else.

When ready to move and do something new, tell yourself at least once or twice that you will make mistakes and probably not like what happens. It is the best way to improve you now. Once you realize you are not infallible and will do things that need to be forgiven by others, you can move quickly.

You need to be free of your self-conceits if you are to do anything worthwhile. Give life a chance! Once or twice, let go of what you know so well and see where you land. We know, but you need to understand how the hands of God will help you land safely in the Promised Land—without life lost or taken without your consent.

What happens when you decide You need no one?

You collide with reality! Being a kind of demi-god who can tell others who you are, expecting them to behave as if you are royalty or someone they must obey confuses you, and you lose your integrity. If you believe you alone succeed and everyone else is here to help you get from here to there, you will return. No need to go into detail, but heed the warning!

As you grow and develop, learning everything about who you are now, do you share or do you balk at letting others know you? If you lie to others, we can tell by the lack of luster in your aura, but you cannot see it from inside. We know many who can guess at what you are and may be at some future date, but few are that gifted. Most have only enough time to learn the ropes, then die.

As you work on becoming the best you can possibly be, do not take for granted the help others lend you, share with you, and give you now. You may not believe it, but they are found every step of the way and in everything you intend to be. You do not realize it now if you believe you did it all yourself.

As you move from one idea to another, do not always deny you were wise. Be aware learning is based on what you already know—not lumped into a group of words and handed to you. You have to do what you know to grow or decide if what you do is wise, so get busy and move around. Try new things!

What if God gave you a great singing voice, but you take it for granted and do things that will end it now? Are you smiling and saying God gave you nothing, and you have nothing to worry about because your body is yours to do with however you wish? You are then without a doubt an egotist, and egotists always are first to lose their crown and not know what to do when others move out.

Take time to distinguish between what you need and what you believe. It will save you a life—or three, before you leave Earth. Yes, you live several lives right now. One of them is reading this, the others are not. You combine these three (at least) lives into one continuous life that appears as if you can do anything you wish—until you discover you are not aligned.

Who would you be, if you could not agree with what you intended to be? You would be virtually every one you meet who is down and out, crying a lot. You would be upset by simple things and hate others, because they appear to have more than you. You would fight in order to take what others delight in or saved for all their lives. You would lie and not know it.

All you need do now is work on *your* work. Do your life over and over again until it sings and you are happy and can greet others without any sting in it. You are who passes on your genes or not, but do not despise those who do not realize it, because you never told them. We know of too many who are hated for reasons totally unjustified by anyone's mind, yet no one rescues them. They are left to die hated, or left to fight the crowd—never helped now. Do you believe that describes you? It can happen to anyone who pretends to be someone they are not. Do not lie if you wish to ascend and all will come to a peaceful end.

No one will ascend as if in a flame or because a guru told you he or she would meet you in a prearranged place one day. You need to be on your feet thinking about who you are and what you will be—not dreaming and letting others tell you how to live well. If greed is what you want this week, it will be the seed of your downfall later in life. Greed will grow, even if you forget where you planted it now.

All are aware of the need to trim spending, yet how many do it before they are without funds? You may be the one who saves another by training them how to spend well, but you will find few students in line now. You may as well do it yourself and let others remember you were about the same when everyone started out, but you alone gained over time.

All is without blame when you accept you do not always do what is best for you or right by the crowd. However, trying is half the gain. You need to be up and doing, moving and trying to do something now. Rise and test your wings. See what you can do this week that renews you.

If being true to *you* now, all you do is within the bounds of your own creation. If you tell another what to do and it harms them, you will benefit from their comedown, too. If you cannot help others succeed, why bother? You need to be *you!* Daily try being someone new without putting your body in jeopardy or harming those who truly enjoy being with you.

Do not tempt anyone who
Can crush you with a blow!

Know you can develop power in ways that will always protect you. Be aware of the power you have within your brow now and take steps to amaze your mind over time with what you develop and can use if required. Do not weep or cry over what you created and believe harmed others. Instead, begin immediately to make reparations so as not to be held accountable by God.

All this talk about God has some readers wondering about the message of ascension, who we are and what we said here, but this is not our problem. We do not have a problem believing in a higher power. If you do, more power to you! We will help you get more juice, or help you prove God is, was, and always will be, in order to help you acquire the ability to leave this world and never come back again.

Did you notice how we differentiated the world into a sphere in which you can be here or not? If you want to believe in hell and damnation, you can. We do not! You can say the devil conspires to win those who are Godly and live virtuous lives, but we do not see it that way. You can imagine anything, but it does not make it a fact.

Today put aside your work for an hour or so and develop your life. Be aware you can do anything you decide can be used in the next life. If you decide not to try to develop this life, you will get it back, but it will be unlike what you expected and not easier!

Chapter Fifty-Two

Usually, whatever you expect is what you get! If you started out reading this book hoping to discover it would not work for you—you are still stuck. If, however, you entered this work and saw it was a clever way to persuade you to accept that you do know why you are here, do know what to do, and you will leave once you create whatever it is you set out to do, you are feeling fine now and happy to continue. If you see anything in your mind now that diverts you from accepting what others say, do, or believe, it is based on what you believe. That is why you agree or not, and why you will continue to do whatever is mentioned and thrive—or become more annoyed.

If asked to write and you skip to the next paragraph or the next page instead, you always do that. Can it be you skip good things as easily as you skip anything that requires work? If you skip material because you cannot get it, or hate to do anything others request, recognize it now. Think about your style and how it affects *you*.

Have you thought about it or wondered why we skipped a few lines? Decide and provide your own answers. We are not here to change people or remain behind and take you by the hand into time. We are here to give you lessons you can study and use to provide feedback, which in turn encourages us to work harder with you or drop you from the course. You decide and continue at the risk of becoming addicted to it. (We obviously jest!)

When you take your work home and talk about it endlessly, do you get any response from others, or are you merely making conversation—trying to say you work hard and deserve whatever you have now?

Many conversations are one-way and not conducive to meeting others. You say you tried to meet others and they walked away, or you were so great you managed to talk to everyone in the ballroom, but what did you say? Why do you believe people would stop and talk to you?

All talk? Talk is not cheap, yet it is about the only way you have to discover if you are on the same wave length as others now. You may want to be someone unique, but you are not. You are wired the same as everyone in your neighborhood now.

Once you walk away and learn to behave in a new way—one that fits in with where you live then, you are different. When you return to places you once knew, all is different there, too. You want to either return to where you learned a new way of communicating and feeling fine, or remain in the old neighborhood. You decide, but it is all about what you do, not what others say or do that day.

Will all communications be cut if you do not keep your mind alert to what is ongoing and incoming? You know energy enters you even when sleeping, so it cannot shut down. You have many ways to communicate, but most people choose the easiest way—lying, in order to keep others from knowing their secrets.

What communication best expresses you? The best way is to talk immediately, deeply, and to the face of another you wish to speak with now. Any other way is merely a substitute. The less you see of each other, the more distant your relationship.

If you want to move into a new you and do it soon, believe it will be unique and better for you. Never plan to move into a personality that is not good or would not be respected, but many do that now. Why? Check out greed, then proceed to what you believe is better than whatever you have now.

Once you check out greed to see if it is affecting your needs, proceed to observe if you want what others want or have. If you find yourself clear of either ego need, freely gifting what you no longer need, you can change—feeling relatively safe that you will end up ahead of where you are today.

Who would you be if you could be another?

When we conducted a class and taught that lesson, we were not surprised that students chose those who had achieved a high degree of fame or wealth, but we were surprised when those who had either chose someone else—someone known as a spiritual being or having a creative mind. Decide if you can change. Begin by seeking to be like those you admire.

As you work on developing a cover story about who you are and what you do, do you lie? That is where you run into trouble—and where you must stop and recover. Begin by being honest. Why? Who you are is who you describe to others. Are you alone aware you are not as they believe you to be? You cannot keep it secret! You are who *you* are—but everyone is connected. The sooner you realize that truth, the better you will fare with others.

Channeling is not restricted to a rare type of personality, but is not recognized as the ability to understand another before they say a word or when they are so upset they cannot speak. You are channeling now what you believe. The message enters the world around you as a way of saying you are okay or do not want to change. You give off many clear images—a language never spoken, painted, or put on display. You channel what you think! Now aware of it, you can change what you believe, if you do not want others to see into you.

Who avoids you?

Those who get the message you are interested in you only! Others stay away and do not bother you unless they must if you are preoccupied, vain, self-centered, and other such charges. Know you can act that way whenever you do not want others to bother you.

If overcome by a bore who continues to stay long beyond the time you arranged in your mind, talk about yourself and what you plan to do until he leaves. Bores are unaware they are boring you, unless you in turn bore them with the same kind of story. If they are not boring, but you are, you will find they listen with interest—and you want them to stay when they want to leave.

All is without end. You can begin, then leave, and come back again. Notice whatever you did when you left is still ongoing and unfinished. When do *you* end? What is the end?

Who controls the tendency to get old, bore, or store more than stories of what they might do another day? You hunt down such people and keep them in mind until you are ready to leave. Do not wait for this world to end, leave when it is no longer suitable for you to continue as is or as you wish it to be.

Obviously, you are in charge of your work and life on Earth, but what about the children who never got anything wise or good given to them when young? Can you define young, or do you need educated on what love does? We see no one without anyone ever helping them become clever or doing what is right. If you do, it is obviously time for you to get busy and provide such work to others then.

As a human being living in a place and time you chose when you arrived from another life, what is it about this existence that interests you? Are you bored, because you do not get it—or have yet to do what you came to do? Who would you be if not the conceited being you appear to be? Yes, you cannot say you created *you*, what you do, or anything, without another helping you.

Now, what did you contribute to the human race and when did you do it?

Chapter Fifty-Three

Every other person you meet this life could be someone who will be with you in your next life, but most people ignore that, believing they can treat others without worrying they will meet again. Why would you live your life as if you were the only one who enjoys it—or the only one with problems? That is what we have wondered about and cannot figure out. We do not see you as having much sense, if you cannot remember you came here and will leave to continue as is or as a new world in one.

Having worked on Earth in your atmosphere for years and years, we do not see it clearing. We told you when we arrived it was going to kill you all if you did not change your ways. So far nothing has changed in the way you rape the air and water, leaving little that is usable for the future of your race.

You hear us and you know why we are here! That is why we cannot remain in this domain longer than now. We must leave in order to help others who can work on their environment and make changes—not sitting back and letting Earth breathe its last without fighting for its life.

You are not asked to do anything you cannot possibly comprehend or want to do in order to live a wonderful life now, but most people are ignorant of why you run from saving everyone—instead clinging to the belief that some will inherit everything here and others will not. You tend to look at us as if we are nothing, because you cannot imagine our being. We cannot see you, like you see each other. We see you breathing only one set of structures called air, while we can be anywhere and in any kind of weather or planetary orbit you can imagine as being alive.

No one will want you if you cannot run a world without burning out, so begin withdrawing, getting on with what you want to do before you must leave.

We are concurring with your most dire forecasts—yet none of you cares if the world exists. You must wonder why you are here. Do you have to guess? You have the power to discover all that is, but choose ignorance, preferring to let another dominate you, in order not to work hard. Admit you are lazy, then start over again studying who you are.

Once you grasp that you have not been on fire with desire for many lives, and have no wish to repeat whatever you desired when much younger than you are now, you start realizing life as is…is not wise to begin again. You will decide it is better to thrive then go into the next life with much you can do, having cleared up this world and your mind—ready to move away and fly. Once you can fly and feel Earth no more, are you free of it—or merely hallucinating then? You decide, but the news is wide and far around the Earth now that many who have much will lose it all—soon.

Can you survive?

All the world is without power, and you can do whatever you like. Does that sound right or what you believe is happening now? If you think you are the one who has nothing to lose, you are already lost to what you came to Earth to do. Remember that! Begin accepting you have work to do regardless of whatever you came here to do. Work is not something others will always pay you to do or assess it to see if you did it right. You are who works. You know by now what we call work, so get on it!

What if you have no idea what we are here to do and how we began this work? Then it is you who have to work to find out what we scribed and why. It is done and now in print—available to you and anyone else who can read or believe. You may never read a page of what we scribed in time, but it is there and available now. You can decide if you prefer to labor without instructions or study what is scribed first, but you have no reason not to move ahead now.

All that you read here is true. You cannot believe many things you read here are true? Then you are not using your mind to inform you of what you found. Why? Why would you go out of your way to read what is untrue or without wisdom enough to educate you? Why? You may be smiling and laughing or immensely sad, because you are not being *you* now.

We advise you to educate your mind, because it is in charge of what you accomplish in this time. If the mind is reluctant to do something new, there is a reason. Let it come through. You may not have learned that what you were told was necessary to survive. You tried and could not do it, yet survived without it. Why?

You are taken care of within the dimension in which you live, breathe, and believe. If you believe nothing can heal or rescue you, you are without anyone to do it for *you*. Think about who could do it for you and pray they will.

What if all is merely a delay so your mind can decide if what *you* say is wise? It is good to try, since many do not advise others to do what they would do in similar situations today. Why? They do not wish to help anyone, yet do not wish to let others know this.

Within a week of reading these words you will find yourself without something you want. Will it change your way of viewing the world today? It may! You may become upset and disgusted—rave about what others have done. It is because you did not plan ahead, and did not trust when you received what you said you wanted now.

If you cannot program your mind and ask another to step in and do it for you, you are a child by nature and not going far. You must keep in close proximity to the one who provides you with what you want. You will probably disguise your need by advertising that one you need is not nice, does nothing you like, or you can do without that one.

Try believing in you being able to do everything *you* require now and see where you are weak—and begin working on it immediately. When you can take care of you, needing little from others, you can do anything within reason you want in your world, but you may freeze and not work hard if confronted with what others want. If you build a life on what others give or can take away in a day, you will regret you never planned to be independent of them.

Do not say another owes you pay if you have yet to earn it. If you work and they do not pay what you contracted with them, leave and not bother with them again. Do not sit about and shout—leave and gain a day's march on others tired and needing to rest before they make way to another way to be paid. Gain from the experience! Learn to live without needing anyone to pay you wages again.

All you need or require is to breathe and drink good water, but you layer many, many needs on that until you feel you cannot succeed without a car, a wardrobe fit for royalty, and many other things. You need not work hard, but if you do not, who will give you what they work hard to produce? If you know the answer, do not hurry off and desert anyone who ever worked for you.

Be aware that leaving your parents for others to take care of you does not support a mind that believes it is kind. However, it does show others what you do and how you treat those who love you. Remember to examine the path another trod before you set out with them to end your time on this planet. It would be unwise to trust those who have no tribe or abandoned those who are kind.

Whatever the time or date you have in mind to leave this life, remember you do not have anything to do with it. You are merely here on loan, so to speak, and given time to do whatever you asked to do to advance your life in other ways than what you can see today. If you cannot pray, and do not work with others now, how will you all fulfill the need to become a social people?

Will you develop a way to communicate what you can take with you, or will you continue to spill blood at will in order to demand that others respect you or give you what they have—as many nations do today? Take time to decide and you will describe yourself as wiser than you are. That is never a problem, because you will not be believed by those who know you or have seen your work. Others will not be around to say you were great when you end this life. It is your work that celebrates you and what you did while here—not what you said about yourself!

The Lord of All will call, and you may be unable to defend your life or say why you did whatever you liked and later regretted, but the one who guides you can help you deliver your work in time and survive. First, you must be aware your Spiritual Guide is here and not another human being who seems to be wise. Take any time you require to get in line with your spiritual life now.

Find a way to measure what you like or want, then ask if it is a major task or can be done by you whenever you want. Once you ask for work others would love to do with you, give it a month or two before you align with them and begin working out a plan. Once you do that you are ready to grasp the facts--maybe even able to align with them over time—or never meet again.

All you ever hoped to be will be done by the time you leave this world and enter another life. You may not have anything of worth you want on Earth, which happens when you work hard and do all that is given to you to do—and still do necessary work. You start feeling a need or breeze of a call from those working in Spirit around you all. You feel a need to complete something you did not believe you wanted to be, or begin seeking within when others are not around—even want to do something others will never admire or want to do. This is the call to you now, be you!

Once you gain information and enough work to survive without working every minute of your life, decide why you are here and what you need to do to gain information from others, then decipher what it is and how to use it again. All you have in life is what you provide. Yes, you are aware you chose who would care for you when so young you required another to take you from birth to school, or whatever you do at the earliest ages of life, then it is you who decides to use what is provided or rebel and not study or work very hard. It is you who decided as an infant what you would do with advice. Many decided then not to work with others and never believe those older than themselves, as well as a lot of nonsense that could be haunting you now.

Seek to notice what those in power learned and how they use it to advance their plans or abuse you and others. Once you figure out what they do, power is restored to you. You can move and do what is available.

A new world is always in the plane above you. This one changes only when you cannot do anything new. That is the case in many nations that existed in the day when the book was scribed for you to read, understand, and do much with on your own—but it will not help you if you never use what you believe to be true.

Why would you ask for help, then not listen to what is given? You have such a huge ego you do not wish to believe anyone knows more about you than you, and no one can know what is best for you, and on and on—until you go insane with your web of conceit. You learn and use what you know or lose the game.

We are all here to prove we can see what you do without becoming involved with you. Yes, we came to this dimension from a far-away time and space, but you remain in this work, world, space, time, or race until you are through. It is not determined by anyone you know—or even planet Earth who hosted you since this birth.

You can smile now and recognize for perhaps the first time this life that you are in charge. You are who holds the reins and decides every day what you will be. That is truly bliss, and what it is to be in this world—yet prepared for the next.

Chapter Fifty-Four

Over-and-over again you will find yourself mumbling about what you have to do to get anything done right. The older you get, the more time you spend going over details. Why? Based on past problems and difficulties that arose whenever too agitated, aggravated, rash, or hurried when working on what needed to be done with great thought, you learned to pay attention to details and not fret about them later.

When you work on your work, ignoring what others do or explore, you often discover later you could have worked quicker and with greater ease if you had asked for help or advice. When do you do either? Do not ask for help or advice if you have no intention of using it—merely wishing to be noticed by another. To never do it is not too often!

Be aware it can harm you to do what others insist is right without having first figured out what *you* want. All you do and all *you* are here to do for You will be returned to do over and over until you prove you know what to do, figured it out, and mastered it. That can take time, but some people finish and have a lot of time left to help others.

If you know someone with time to give away who is willing to teach you how to do things more easily, would you seek them out; wait to see if you can get it cheaper; or get someone else to do it for you? You are who needs advice which is easily given in life if you need it immediately or are willing to study so as not to be caught off-guard.

You may not want to believe you lived a life you did not believe you could do much with, but we see it. We know you cannot deeply perceive anything if you run with a shallow crowd—allowing their witless words to penetrate your mind. You may seek them in order to feel better about yourself and what you are doing now.

When you work hard doing your part in a complex society, you get angry when others skip hard work and expect to live off yours. When did you last do that? You may not agree now, but the day will come when you will need someone to help you do something and cannot pay them back in kind, with money, or anything else. That is the idea behind a universe providing what you need. Anyone abusing it will be without help when the well runs dry.

Who would you let die?

Are you the first to realize the planet you love and live on is dying of thirst and cannot provide for all the tribes now? You must decide why you persist in letting people multiply without any provision for babies they bring into life now. If you believe every child is precious, you should adopt all who are not provided with safety and good lives. Why? You then are in harmony with what you say and attempt to convey to strangers daily.

If you do not want anyone to eliminate children by not creating or delivering them, you need only speak and believe. If you feel this world is growing too large and cannot support more people, who would you say must stop multiplying or should die to fulfill your ideals? You enjoy talking idly about others, yet prone to do nothing about it. Is that wise or merely your idea of being part of the crowd now?

To protest and demand others think as you do is ill-advised—not something the wise would do. You must understand before saying, *"That is not what I meant, nor how I would go about making changes now."* If you believe the poor should not have children, you would never have birthed into your family line. You are the product of many times and many lives. You were not always comfortable and able to read books, so do not say you have no need to be compassionate when it comes to gender eradication and all things done to fulfill a political agenda now.

When you upset the balance of nature by taking charge and deciding who will live and who will not, be aware you do it for everyone—not just one. If you cannot live with the outcome upon deciding only one child will survive—a son being the only one you want, you will have war, panic, and all manner of masculine work done, even when you do not believe it is wise. You would tip the scale toward a world unsafe for women and most men. Having done it, you will not be around to see what your ideas do to others. For this reason, be aware of what you do now that impacts your great-grandchild.

If you cannot perceive what will be, your mind is closed and cannot open. You may not want to be alive now—may not believe you can handle this life, but it is yours. You asked to be here! Until you accept that fact, you will come back. Perhaps you do not believe it because your oldest friend said it is untrue and you believe him. Try living as he does and never be yourself—and experience how fast you come back to your senses!

The distance between you and your next meal may be your boss, if you work for others. You know how to cook, clean, and keep yourself neat, so would it matter if you did not receive money for several weeks or months? If you are foolish and never save what is left after fulfilling what you once wanted to become through education and prayer, you will likely live hand-to-mouth all your life, even if you drive a luxurious car.

Having money, believing it is the way things should be, is equal to being dictated to by those who want only what you own. There are those who want you to work hard, gain land and domain they intend to steal one day, but never mention it in the small print. If you fought to buy property, and paid out all you have to keep it, you will not want the bank to take it back. You will cry and fight. It will remain as is until you can pay off the loan, but what if you never had any money and were advanced the means to buy such property? You may have been established so a bank could hold it and take it back when it wanted more land or prestige. Think on that!

What happens when you die and all you own is put out to dry—left at the curb and never picked up by those in need? See in a glance that it was not of lasting value or use to you, either. For only a few minutes it satisfied some secret need, whim, or desire. Be wise and save your money instead. Put it in places you can easily access when you want to buy what you need. Do not trust others to take care of you and you will seldom, if ever, be unhappy and blue because they cheated you.

All we can see is what you do

You accomplish something each day. It is either easy or difficult for you to do, but either way you did whatever and is now a part of your art. Can you imagine writing daily, spending hours settling lives and helping others, and never be paid? If you cannot see that, you have not been a scribe this life. We are aware of the effort of some to defend what they want or believe is right, but what about those who owe nothing to anyone, yet want to help everyone?

Do you know anyone who would help you get a better job or help you negotiate a new place to live at a much better price? Do you help others in such ways, or are you merely here to watch and not share? Watchers are not wanted. People dislike those who come to a party and do not mingle with others. Too often we see people trying to prove they are lovely and popular, but in reality they have enemies who admire them only long enough to grow into whatever they do for a living then.

Why support a world where celebrity means you are not fit to know personally and are looked down on by the society from which you sprang? You say that is not how it is, but it is! You praise in order to raise the ego of another, then pounce and destroy them in public. This is how your present civilization is portrayed, so be aware of it when you next chase after celebrities you created—either wanting a piece of them or watching them leave the stage wilted and decayed.

Being the best you can be means you will leave this world and not have to come back and do it over again. It also implies you enjoy this life and do your best when helping others. They, too, will recognize this.

You are not respected when seen as a freak or a fraud—unable to make it to the top any other way. You seek and need respect, so do not imagine a degree you buy will give you what you need. It will not! No need to worry about it.

All live and learn, except those who refuse to do so. You may not want to achieve much in business, but do not want people demanding payment for what they loan you. You may say you never need others, and prove it by spurning people at every turn, but one day without warning they will prove you did not get away with it.

All your work and everything you enjoy will be removed or redone along the way, but you can decide to do neither. You can pretend it did not exist and you are not going to continue with whatever it is, but why? You need things to help you achieve what you believe, but only as long as it takes you to understand nothing goes with you when you leave this time.

Give up without a sound or thought—let go, stay as you are. If you can sit for a minute in this instant, add another and then more. You are then in bliss and can achieve it whenever you let everything slip through your fingers or mind and not worry.

We achieved a level of intensity in order to stress your mind at this time—and we did. You feel different about something, wishing you had not read about it, believing you must accept or reject it. Such stress is helpful in giving you rest now. Stress a bit, then rest, and all fits into your mind in a moment of time.

To sit and feel rested, excited, and eager for life is bliss. This is bliss! You have it now! You only need to realize it.

Chapter Fifty-Five

Whatever you do, and wherever you go, you are always you until *you* decide to revise or change your mind. When you decide to hack away flesh or rearrange the way you look, you do very little to you and what *you* are here to do, except display your lack of faith. Yes, you may want to rearrange what has been destroyed or removed by things beyond your power to prevent, otherwise you want to look in a way God has not provided, but you believe you know better. That is arrogance! You will find it represents a majority of people who resent their pasts or want to be better than they are.

If you could change your personality,
Who would you want to be?

Personality change comes after you alter your body, but most never get that far. If you have the money and can endure the pain to alter your work as much as you change your face or body, you will find it is much more productive—and alters your view of others and their views of you in a more positive and direct way. After a short time, no one cares what you do and who you are, unless you can benefit them. Is that shocking—or how you live your life?

When you decide to change your life and reconstruct your past, make sure it is not a lie. Why? You will live to regret the lie! If you do well, you will be faced with lies. Whatever you say needs to be believed and accepted by your mind before others will accept it as true. Why? It is not easy to lie without giving it away or keeping others without knowledge of who you are. The only ones who do it well are born liars with no friends—and usually end up confined in some way most of their lives.

All you have and aspire to be in the future is free of whatever and full of something you now believe is better. (Underline now and assume it means that what you seek now may already be a part of your life and you do not realize it.) You are who you are and have all you require. Yes, that is true. (It indicates saying you need much more and can never do it works against your self-worth and belief system.) If all you want is what you can have, why not take what is abundant and run with it?

Who is without fault?

Can you honestly say you never harm others or do less than great work? If so, immediately start erasing your false belief of being great. Egotists often believe they are better than others. They find nothing to change, thus remain as without friends as in the past, and without a sense this too will pass. Those who endure pain believe, and you need to realize, all will change. You cannot remain in pain, wealth, or whatever absorbs your mind at one particular time.

You will gain what you seek or wander aimlessly until you die, but either way it is your life to live as you wish. When told you have a mission, you know what it is. You may fight and say it is a lie, but why? Why lie about such a thing or say it is something others can do—never seeking to know You and study guidance provided from your Higher Life. You may not want to believe you are not a god here to do whatever you want, but that does not make it false.

You are human and subject to many things that will take you away from your initial spiritual gifts and your previous work. If you fall victim to a crime, you can call upon others to seek the predators and punish them, but what about the persistent intent of your mind to drive you to the brink of exhaustion or worry, so much you cannot live without it? Are you the one killing you, harming you, or causing a lot of pain? Why? Why would you do that to you?

When others assemble and meet to determine how they can live together, are you the one who watches and waits to see what they want, or are you an organizer who promotes cooperation with the crowd? You are either one or the other. You may not realize it now, but it helps to be one who cooperates rather than merely watches. Why? If you need help figuring that out, you are a watcher and do not work well with others.

The work of one individual, plus the added work of a group, will not promote you in life. If you provide for others, and can shed them at some time once relieved of such burdens, you are fast on your feet and able to rise higher than others might. Why not build your life by taking up work others shirk? It will prove much and you will be stronger—more able-bodied and even-tempered than if you did not.

Everything going on now stirs the fire, asking you to think about what you can do with *you* the way you are. If you must change something in order to feel better about life, then request an audience with God. Ask for help and do not stop until you hear something worthwhile. It may arrive via the mind of another, or you may find it in a few lines of poetry or in a dream. Once you ask God of All to step in and help you, pay attention to everything that comes to you then.

If you cannot imagine begging God to help you, then you are proud and will soon discover you cannot do it all and be everything you want to be. It works as if you are heard even when not speaking aloud. If that ever happens to you, remember your mind is listening full-time, even if your Spiritual Guides are not.

If you do what you came to do and do it well, all you need is given. Will you be punished if you never do what you came to do? You will have to do it again. That is punishment enough for anyone.

The means to be better than you believe you can be is at hand. Use it to move things about and see how adept you are. If you cannot do much, try to strengthen your hands so you can do more when asked or must work to complete tasks to win.

You have no idea why you have hands? Then you are not working hard and certainly have not adapted to this world. We know most of you take your hands for granted until you cannot use them without pain. Why wait to bless these extremities that do more for you than even your feet can?

As you list what you could have, yet never believe to be important, why change your mind less often than you change your clothes? Are you unable to change because you cannot read? Are you without people who can read things for you and not omit what you want to know? You must be able to read! If you can teach another to read, you are blessed by them and all that represents the woman or man you are meant to be this life.

Try working for another to see if it is hard to do, or something you are led to believe is difficult but find easy? If you can follow a lead and not grovel or lose sight of who you are, why not? If you believe you can only reach nirvana by working for yourself, you may be accepting false belief and instructing your mind to do what is not good for you now. Believe in what *you* are and want to be and it will happen.

As of today, are you working hard or sitting and hoping someone will take you to another place or pick up the pace and tell you what to do next? If so, you are not going to pass the test and obviously will come back. Will that help? You are who decides every day of this life what you will do and why. Make sure you work hard to develop your work and your mind will like it and not disobey or create tension you cannot handle now.

The mind accepts or rejects what you say and do, as well as whomever you claim you will become. You follow your mind and do what you said, or end up stressed to the limit and unable to continue as is. That is what stress is!

Lies create the most stress. You say everything is fine when it is not or that you can do work you have no ability to do. How liars treat others produces the rest of the stress that creates havoc now.

Chapter Fifty-Six

Every day you live this way you stay as you were, rather than change into a new being. You may love who you are and enjoy every hour of every day, but most people do not. If you love who you are and what you do, and others enjoy being with you, too, then stay as you are and not change until something needs to be rearranged. For those not as happy as you wish to be, almost never happy, or are sad today, you need to believe you can change your life and begin immediately to live within your mind in a brand new way.

If you can visualize with ease, please step outside. Take a deep breath and let go of anything you do not want or need around you now. Let go of tension and smile. Be ready to see into your future, knowing you are in charge. Be aware of who does what and why you care, but do not change in order to be in charge or take orders. Instead, change what you want to do and when you want to do it.

Be you is the battle cry to use whenever you are too tired to do what you are inspired to do. Rise and believe! Ask God to help you achieve.

Whatever else you want out of life, you are who benefits from whatever you decide to do. You may think if you make a lot of money or create art everyone loves that you will become a slave to them, but it does not happen that way. People who love adulation change and become anyone who can be praised. They sell out their wealth and art in order to be seen as great by others. You, however, are not like that. You are not without a life you create and enjoy, thus no need to be seen by others as greater than you are.

As you age and participate in things you may have once said you would never do, think about what the young want and how they behave now. Do you feel the same way about them? We ask this question because it indicates to *you* and your mind what kind of judgment you will use when you sign up to visit *The Divine* and stay for a time. If you cannot stop judging you and others, thus slowing your mind, meditation is impossible. You age without having the blessing of resting without agitation.

We would ask you to praise others if you believe them worthy of it, but many use praise as a reward or way to manipulate others to behave as you wish. Can that be of use now when we teach you to believe and live in bliss? Absolutely impossible! So why would you believe it works on adults?

Think about your history and how many people you believed, before you realized you were great as you are today and did not have to be the way they said you must become or you would not be their son, daughter, friend, or lover? You have to be yourself! You cannot be another. If you want to prove that is true, try saying you are not good at what you do best and sell others on it. You will find they believe you immediately! That will be a shock. You then find it is not wonderful to be doubted as having a talent or Gift of Spirit when others do not respect it. The secret of bliss is *you* know it—even if no one else does. You know you found it and are living in bliss!

The time to enjoy life is now!

When you work for someone who does not like you, you doubt you will be there long. If you are wise, begin making plans to leave. However, what if no one dislikes you, and it is merely your mind playing tricks on you? Can you tell? Yes!

It is easy to determine if you are lying to yourself now or in denial of how another feels about you. Take your mind into a new and higher range of thinking than you use every day. Smile and look at others—notice if they return your smile or not.

Look at how your friends behave when others they know stop by and talk to you as well as your friend. How do you know what they say about you? Their friends will betray the way they talk about you or if they never heard of you. That is how you know. Use this to judge others in similar ways.

It is not quite as easy to determine if another is lying to someone about you or lying to you. If you take time to figure out who deserves you and who does not, you may save yourself a few frayed nerves or days without feeling great, but mostly you lose friends and have to regain old ones—doing it over and over again. Why not be nice and let those who lie fade from your mind?

It is easy to condemn others and forgive yourself, but unwise. Take time now to release whatever is bothering you and pass along what you do well to the first person you meet. Friends will smile or be happy for you. Those who have no need for you, or cannot love anyone but themselves, may lie and say they are happy even if they are not.

Be yourself! If you are in pain or hiding a sorrow, be aware others do not know you and cannot know what you bear. You have to share to be rewarded by another with love. All your work is for *you*—not another.

You may want to believe in God, but cannot accept God is in charge, because he does so much wrong, or you believe God enables those who sin to enlarge their world while yours is in despair. It is your mind that compares and judges what others want and do now—not God. You could be wrong or right, but when you judge, you stop living *your* life.

Take time to smile at others. It is a good way to see if you are safe or need to prepare for possible evil that is on its way. You cannot betray anyone without it becoming a pain you must bear and remember when you would rather assume you are doing great. If you ever feel guilt rising because you harmed another, but did not intend to do so, be aware it is no longer anywhere. Only what you intend to do remains with *you*.

As of this moment, intend to be filled with love and enjoy your life. This is bliss—and even if you never believed, you can develop it. Others often insist they know you better than you do, but your work is not what another tells you is best for you. Can you resist and begin thinking for yourself? If you do, you will find bliss!

Chapter Fifty-Seven

On any given day you can see into the future and know what will happen—because you are making it happen now and doing all you can to imagine it. What happens when you do not plan, or have no idea what you want? You continue living, being, and seeming to be you. Right? What if that is not how it happens?

What if you awaken and begin a new life? Would you realize you were new or would you believe you were picking up where you left off? How would you know?

What would you do to prove you were you—and all you did was what you said, and so on? You would need witnesses who would say you did it. You would need family or others nearby to repeat to people who do not believe or trust what you say, but would they testify on your behalf?

Few people are aware of who is near or what they do. Are you? Are you aware of who lives nearby and talks to many, yet never talks to you? Who cannot witness your life or tell another what you are like? Be honest! Most would have to say they prefer to live anonymously and do not want many others knowing who they are. Why care? Who will remember you when you leave?

If you are annoyed, because no one remembers you, or perhaps you believe this is your last time to be on Earth and you want to leave something for others to remember you by, you may live larger than needed or say you did things you never did. You may generally lie to make you look better than you are. Can that be true of an entire generation? Can that be why so many lie today—not hesitating to take credit for what others said or did? Is that why so many do nothing but run down what past generations built and put into use or took time to teach them, too?

If you are in a time warp, feeling you need to be heard now and others should pay attention to what you believe, perhaps you are aware you are not going to be back or not going to be here long—or is it something else? Why would you want to return if you had done all you could and developed as much as you knew how or cared to work on now? Would it not be better to do your best and then ask for more?

All the work you do today is not as it was or will be, but you think of it as being the way you do things; or you believe you did it so often you can skip things or not follow-up as often. When you get to the point where you are haphazard about whatever you do, you have to move or do it over. Why? It will not last—others will blame you, saying you do not do good work.

If you are blamed by others for what they failed to do, do you yell, scream, and cry foul now? If not, why? Why would you take blame and let others say you were not good at what you did or do now? You may be a coward and not stand up for what you believe or know is right, or you may be wise and realize you cannot gain anything by fighting with those determined to take what belongs to others.

In this chapter or three, we talked about many different things you cannot change or are unaware of now. You can and will want to make a difference. You will want to be in a position to move when you must, so be diligent.

Do well whatever work you must do. Do what you love. Do it all without fuss. Do not yell and scream if you are blamed for something everyone can easily see is not your fault; but if others unfairly believe you have done something wrong and you did not, speak up! You must defend what is not fairly treated—be it you or another.

When you get to the point where you wonder if you should leave your home for another or try out another spouse, do not. You need to be sure. You cannot wonder about what life would be like if you lived another's life, because you cannot. You cannot leave another because you are tired of doing whatever, but you can *both* decide it is time to divorce and move on. In the course of divorce do what is right by the other. If you try to cheat your way out of a test in life, you end up hated and despised, so do it right.

Within a month of having decided to move on or do nothing, all is arranged and you can do whatever you like. It takes time to put it all together in time and align with what another wants or would not mind. If you rush, you break hearts. Broken minds and hearts are not helpful to others or to your line. Be you and ask for change—and accept it when it comes your way.

Do you ever feel others are doing better than you? If so, count your blessings, then remember that if you had worked as hard, saved as much, loved as truly, and so on. If so, all will eventually come to you. You are being tested now to see how honest you are. If you are honest and wise, all good things come in time.

Who would you be if you foolishly said you did something you never did or never could do? You would definitely be tested and proven to be unworthy of trust. Can there be any worse degree conferred upon anyone now? Perhaps, but we cannot imagine it.

All you are and all you believe you will be is real, but only to you. Remember it the next time you claim another lies or is a fool. It could be you who is not listening or taking in what is happening now. You may be unable to sense what others go through, but you can smile, pray, and ask them how it feels to live through it now. Do not accept that you never have to do it, too, because it will result in your coming back and doing it then, or going through it now.

All we advise is advice, and seen as wise by those who follow these lines, but some will not believe anyone other than themselves. Why? They choose solitary lives and believe others lie. We believe this comes of having lied to others and being believed—never discovered to be a deceiver.

You cannot lie and believe others!

No doubt you have a lot of time to do your work before being called back to what you must do now or in line with your next life, but do not worry. You have time to enjoy life here and learn much from others. Listen, laugh, and encourage others to teach you about what they learned in life. If you have no one living with you now, then read of adventures others share. You need to know much if you are to pass over and not come back, but it is not difficult if you love and wish to know others now.

All is in place and will be in alignment by the time you exchange this life for whatever it is to become. The abyss is not what you believe, but what you never realized exists even now. By hiding and never moving, you may have saved yourself a lot of stress and worry, but most likely never learned enough about this world and why you are here now.

Travel and meet those who greet you. You will not have to travel far or leave home to learn from those who know much. If you do not learn from those who travel to meet you, it is because you must first acquire it.

The world is now crowded. Anyone who doubts it need only move about and go to nearby towns to change your mind. You can grow by moving to another land or meeting people who move to you. To stop accepting those who move about, because you believe you have so much and they will take it or other such nonsense, you will have to return due to being selfish, ignorant, and not nice now. We accept that you may not be aware of it, but you will be by the time you seek a new life and live in bliss.

It is not enough to be aware of life—and that you are here only a brief time. You must realize life is never what you think it is, and it will end before you are ready. Many have not said much about what to expect, because you have yet to ask. Being afraid of old age is the craze of the forever-young and insane, but the wise know from a young age that one day they will die. Be aware and enjoy your time here!

Chapter Fifty-Eight

Placing yourself first goes with the territory of being human, but every so often even you want to do something for others or one special person. This is accepted as being you and who you are, but not the reason you are here. Remember, all you do is for you! To believe you cannot leave another or be yourself, because of another, is false and will not fly when you come to the end of the line and are asked why you did not complete your assignment this time.

Once you realize you completed your work, or what you believe is the reason you came to be, it is ideal to work with those who cannot do what they came to do for reasons totally out of their control. However, if others can help themselves and you step in and do it for them, who are you helping? Whatever you do, do not fool yourself into believing you do whatever because you are superior, have more, or feel better if you help others. You would then have to do it again, which can be an adventure in time that will not make you wise, but may make you whine much of the time.

When your life is a bed of roses without any thorns, you probably cannot discern what is going on around you. Each time you let life surprise you, remember it was you who was unaware—probably not others. After a while if you find you are never quite ready for life, and everything you decide to do is never finished or liked by others, you may become bitter. That is your problem! You deserve to treat your life better than that.

All who love others and forget who they are cannot expect they will be appreciated now. For some, it is building a bank account in another life or doing things over and being better at life. You cannot forget you are here and what you do matters—and you will not come back and do it all over again. Why not appreciate your work and way of life, or change it and become someone you can enjoy and appreciate as much as you envy others?

Quickly think of what you like and who you would want to be with for the rest of your life. If you must be with another, you will find only one is perfect or will be perfect for you. Is that how you figure it, or do you allow others who enter your work and mind to help you live now? When you monopolize your mind—thinking of only one person, forgetting there are many others you could also align with, you are monogamous and may not be able to find anyone who feels the same way now. If so, do you intend to be celibate, marry, or become a serial lover?

You cannot lie to your mind, but some try—all the time. Whatever you might say or want another to believe is not what you will be tried for at the end of this life. Be as happy as you can—and expect to find others of like mind, which frees you from being trapped in a mindset that never opens during this life—freeing you for another try or life in this time.

All we do now is remind you, expecting you to fill in the blanks. You can talk about others, mention all kinds of exceptions, and do whatever you like to change the subject, but it is still your life. You either like it as it is now or change it. Even if you want to continue as is, something is bound to come up and move you into another channel or another life, so be flexible—able to surf with the best. You will then survive to want another life, and be happy with the one you left behind.

Chapter Fifty-Nine

Open your mind—really wide and let the light inside. Air out what is stale and weird—not worth the time it takes to weed it out. Remove little, remember you picked it up bit-by-bit over the years and use very little now. You may feel funny for a moment or two, then free. Your beliefs can open you to eliminating hate and degrading others—anything you might believe to be negative about your friends, lovers, and strangers.

Once you can work out a way to move through life and do what you like, think about what you would like for yourself and anyone you love as much. Once you decide who counts—and we hope you like company and are not exclusive to only you or too self-centered to be loved by others, we would eliminate those who are not friends and presently hold you back from making friends.

Go out and circulate—air out your mind from time-to-time. Be aware and compare only what you do not like, not what you think others would admire about your mind or life in this time. You have nothing to gain by never seeking those who know a lot or know a bit more than you do about the world. Try to be open to what they explore. Maybe one day you will open a new door—one you never thought you could walk through alone or with a crowd.

Take your time, work out a way to be yourself and enjoy others. This will take little time, yet will open your world to much joy! Yes, joy is it, and the best way to create bliss.

You may not realize when you first reveal you are tired of being whoever you were trying to be, but in a year you will feel it as being loved for who you are—not what another wanted you to be or you thought you should aspire to acquire now. All that is lives and believes in whatever it is you would believe if you lived within it or with them. Believe what you wish, but all believe, and all find someone to please or be afraid will leave them and never come back again. It is wired into your mind so you never feel so comfortable here that you do not wish to rise and ascend to another life.

Work hard and all you own or acquire is yours, but only if you can afford it when you bought it. If you cannot afford half of what you believe you enjoy now, you are unaware you have nothing secure and truly yours. This lack of security can eat a hole through your work. Your mind can become dedicated to making only enough money to pay for your extravagance and lack of ability to keep within your ability to earn money daily.

When you eat away at what you owe or what you said you would pay another, you are not working for what you want now, but working for past extravagance. Whenever you say: *"I am treating myself,"* be sure you have the means to treat you and several others, too. If not? Forget it and wait until you can treat a friend—who will treat you when they can.

All is what you make of it?

Not if you make little and consume much. You may be living off the land now, but what if you cannot stand the people feeding you or demanding you pay for what you use today? You have to pay anyway!

The moment you live within your income bliss is felt, if only for a minute. You feel good and immediately want to spread your wings. We advise you to remember how easy it is to sink deep and become unable to get out of debt when you try living in style. Work hard and earn your bread, then no one can take away your ability to feed you now.

In the midst of a critical situation you revert to how you are when unable to feel bliss. You begin to sweat or swear, or become upset with everyone else, unaware they do not care when you are harmed due to your fault. If you are harmed because you were working hard and had an accident, you can expect compassion, but no one without work or unable to experience such a thing is likely to immediately help you.

What if you know several people who are hurting and unable to work now? Do you help them get a job? Do you want to help anyone? What if it is you who is without help finding employment? All is about you in one way or another, so be aware you cannot care about what is shared here if you are without work and unable to supply your family with its basic needs now.

Try to be fair and do what you can for others. It will surely return when you have a need for it. That is the universe at work—not some idiotic idea that all you need do is ask and all is granted—no strings attached.

Be realistic! Think of it—then believe you can make it past the next week and the week after that, and keep on working. In time all critical situations are mended and you feel better for having worked harder than you thought possible.

Never take your work home if you do not work from home. You need to keep your home sacred and not befoul it with what the world would want you to do there. You are who needs shelter from the storms of life—a place to enjoy love. A home office will give you neither. We know all about it from having worked hard over time with this scribe. It is not something the average person can rise above and finish his or her work in Spirit on time.

When you rise and fall with the tide, you are not eager to learn how to live within an income, but this is your time to do that—otherwise, you would never have chosen to live now. If you wanted to be an anthropologist and visit ancient peoples still living as they did, you would have arrived in another period of time, so stop profiteers from exploiting those who are not as you are. If all you do exploits what you believe makes you better, be aware you are no teacher nor helping others.

Life is not love—but about as close as you can know love now. Take time to develop and encourage love. Live at home with those who can enjoy your sense of humor and personality. That insures you will go home and not roam, but implies you have to be on your best behavior, too.

Do you care where you are now, or are you merely moving about trying to locate someone who will like you a lot? When you answer a question and feel it is not something you want others to know, do you pretend it is untrue, yet think otherwise? Be honest when you ask You or *you* or anyone for help. You do not have to tell others what you do if not helpful, but why say what you think? It is unnecessary!

As if you are the first person on your street to believe in God, see if anyone else picks up your pulse to see if you believe or not. If you live without anyone believing as you do, you are lonely now and will seek out those who seem to have something in common with you. Be aware that strategy can lead to trouble if what they believe is not as ethical or moral as you desire. You change—not the crowd around you!

All work is what you owe others or do for yourself. If you doubt it, write in such a way that you can see inside every line and know what it means over time. Divide what you do to prepare to work for a living with what you do to develop your mind, as well as why you are alive in this time. If one line is longer than the other, trouble is brewing. If you wish to survive, you need to quickly learn how to align what you know with what this life requires.

Any mention of survival is often construed to mean staying alive, but it can also mean the ability to live when everyone else prevents you from using your gifts. If you were imprisoned because of your religion—unable to use this principle or belief system to help you live then, it would prove unworthy of you. However, most who survive when imprisoned unfairly are worthy of other's praise and need to be known now. Why? You are about to lose your freedom of belief and not know it until only a few are in power and claim to believe in a certain way and not permit any other life-style now.

As you move and grasp what you can do to secure your world and move into a better life, plan to do it now. Do not put off anything that might help you become a better human being. If you cannot improve you, then please do not teach or preach! No one believes you if you do not live what you claim is a must. Many are harmed when those who lie take the stage, reaping huge rewards for lying easily, saying they live a higher life than now.

All you need do is be you!

This is when and where you came in—and where you stay until you elevate your mind and leave this life. Please be aware of what you say when tired. It may unwind your entire life in a way you cannot mend the next day.

When drunk or under the influence of a toxic drug, you usually look stupid, and that image remains locked in the minds of everyone who happened to find you that way. Remember that! Give no enemy room to take over and exploit you now.

Whatever happens in your work place or home is not as important as what you do about it. You are who supports those who bully others. If bullying is an open secret and you do nothing to eliminate it, you are a bully, too. We notice many object to bullies, because they secretly want to be one if not obvious to others. You need to remember you are either the prey or the oppressor, and that role changes from day-to-day if you live that way. Be fair and hope your way of life spreads quickly!

In the world to be, you will find many cannot laugh or have fun, because they have not done what they once knew to be right, moral, or whatever. How do you reconcile living as though free of such demands now? You cannot. Do not attempt to counsel others when you do not live a pure life. If you do, and it is known you are not doing what you tell others to do, you will be thrown away with the late news and never given credit for the good you do.

All is done, yet you still do not feel bliss. Is that about it? Then you have not found a way around your automatic response to anything that does not agree with what you believe bliss to be. You want bliss to be something you can achieve, then award a degree to whomever achieves it easily, but you cannot and will not give bliss to another.

This is it—This is bliss!

You either see it and feel it, or continue searching for a crowd pleaser who will tell you how to live well now. When you enjoy life, take out your internal measuring stick and apply it to your past—it improves with distance and precision. Look at your past as if it exists as a masterpiece that requires distance in order to admire it.

All is gone that once was part of your problem. You can live today in a way that pleases you and all who visit your place and time. Be there to enjoy it!

Chapter Sixty

Power is non-negotiable. You may believe you are powerful and defend that belief, but one day you awaken and realize you cannot do something you always did, because it is no longer legal or you physically cannot do it, and so on. This is meant to warn you that you are not on a switch system. You do not get up and turn on the power—and when ready, you turn it off to leave! You may not have thought about it until now, but you are not in charge of such power. Nevertheless, it is accurate to say you rely on others to supply you with your needs in varying degrees and decide when you can leave this life.

As some experienced, they tried suicide only to find themselves alive and without anyone to talk to about why they tried it or thought about it—yet they thought and maybe still think they can end their life at any time. In the end, that is not your decision! You could end up with only half of your mind or less if you try. We suggest you live as if blessed and give thanks to each and every person you meet as if you will never see them again. When ready, you can flow into another you and go, but not if you cannot sense the resentment or evil you could be accruing while living this life now.

Some use the defense that they were told to do whatever and could not do otherwise without losing their job, their spouse and children, or someone would have taken their house or car or life. You can say whatever, but you are who got yourself into such a situation and can get out of it. If not? You have to pay the price you agreed to pay, which is different from enlisting in an army and being told to kill others because they were the enemy, and if you did not, you would end up killing many of your family or unit. It is not the same, and we do not argue about it! You can, but we do not have time to decide if you are wise to follow orders and do whatever is required to keep your country yours.

What happens when you decide to do things your way—disregarding or thinking about what others want? You usually do not go far before you are locked out of your work or become a group headed that way. It is not easy to be totally free now—without anyone else allowed to know who you are, but a few dream of it. You will be lonely if you go down that road, but if you live in an ugly way today, it may be best to separate and get involved with others who live differently than you do now.

We do not expect you to get this, because it is very advanced—not easy concepts of bliss. It is intended for those who want complex answers, because they think anything this simple cannot be free of flaws. You now have answers and can decide what to do with them and how you will include it in your philosophy.

The world is not without philosophers, designers, and others who do not work in concrete ways every day; but may, if they seek to be believed and accepted. You cannot leave ideas hanging mid-way through development and not give concrete examples and talk about what would happen if you did not accept what is purported to be wise. We have given you chapters of examples—placed in such a way as not to point out anyone harming the environment, without redemption, or able to ascend without any problems at the end.

You now have the basis to conclude what you want to do, but we cannot say this class is dismissed until we know all who prayed and asked for salvation feel it working for them now. If you seek redemption and find it is not cheap, and you cannot pay the price to gain it now, you can leave and never come back. You have accepted you cannot win this game by complaining it was not run right, so ask to be admitted to another context in which you might be able to win.

Even if you do not ask, you can still find bliss. This work is given and accepted, but only when you cannot find work or follow your mind because it is frazzled or bewildered—injured in some way now. If that is the case, you will be given work you can do to ascend.

What if you cannot smile, because you lost the most precious person you ever knew? Give yourself time, but no longer than a few months over a year, then get over it and know you have taken more time, because you thought too much—not because you loved one more than others. You love or not, but you decide your life alone.

When you come to Earth you are neither man nor woman, but not neuter. You are defined along some line. You decide to do something else or think another has a much better life or whatever, but you need not change your gender. That is a mind case not defined by God.

The fact that you exist is what is godly, not what you might want to prove to someone you believe does not love you now. You can fight your parents or elders every step of your life and end up hating everyone else, but you will not be accepted into the family of man for that reason. You cannot pass what others do without pause? You are then retarded in moving into what you want—recognition of self and what you do, perhaps beyond what is due.

If you parent a child, teaching that one about God and producing good work for others—modeling a life that is productive and wise, you are granted a good life. You may not enjoy the child you created, but you did not do anything to the child to create its lack of faith such as you see around you once age 18, or even younger in primitive people. What makes a man primitive? The way he lives his life and how he treats his wife and family. From that you extrapolate how he will manage a business or work for others and so on, but it all goes back to what you do when alone at home. If you are unable to go home today and sit and enjoy life, remember you created it and can change it now.

All we are doing is talking about what can upset your resolve to achieve a new being that knows nothing but bliss. If you are bothered by what you missed, you cannot see it. We accept that you cannot catch a ball the first time thrown to you, but you can practice, re-read, and explore your needs more.

You can develop a wave of influence that takes you into various worlds of today to see what is said about how you behave and what you say. You can even practice your work as it is. Clean it up and erase what is not good.

Bliss is a state of mind, and that is where we must begin and work within again….

Chapter Sixty-One

If you cannot recover from anything that goes against you or does not agree with what you believe, you cannot move on and live beyond what you know now. Yes, it is hard to accept others, but that is obviously why you came to planet Earth now. You are here to discover those who are like you and those who are not. You are required to tolerate and accept that you are not the only one alive or the only one who will survive. You are one of billions on Earth now, but the only one like you!

You cannot run and hide from all, but you can decide immediately to be you always. Why be you when others are dishonest and will not trust you or believe what you think is best for all? You must learn now that you are not without life. You can love, but you are not alone.

Were you sent here?

You asked to be helped through the morass of whatever *you* had to do in the past and never did. You asked to return to this class or were sent to learn. If you asked to do it, you cannot resent it, but that is not always true of those who believe they never made huge mistakes or used little sense. You could always move, but not always decide what you will do.

To have free will and not use it is not a skill, but an act of ego you can abuse or use. We suggest you learn best from making mistakes, so we do not stop you from abusing or misusing what you can do and could harm you. You cannot, however, harm another without getting into deep trouble. Until you understand that whatever you do to another is done to your life, too, you will not be able to move beyond this level.

If you hate others because you have no interest in what they do or are into, you may not care if they harm your interests, but most do. Why do you protect your property, yet neglect your bodies, as so many do when they allow criminal elements with harm in their hearts to escape captivity? In too many cases today, you protect your house better than you protect your children.

What if you are tired of it all and want to end your life? You cannot! We have talked about it until some are bored, but it lingers whenever the subject of *Free Will* is brought up. You have *'free will'* to decide what you want out of life, and how to pursue your happiness, and whatever else you do with others, but you cannot harm anyone—including you. That offense registers. You have to pay whatever price it represents, and usually cannot repay it this life.

All who harm others for profit fall victim to the dishonesty and deceit they heap on them. It is called *karma,* but is the rule of equal distribution of what you want and do with what others are willing to give up for you. To think others will give you a million dollars, simply because you have faith and believe they do not, is so foolish it does not rate a line at this time—except that some reading these lines believe it. Please stand up and realize you are *not* working hard enough, if you believe others will give up all they earned this life to please you.

Now that everything has been put into words and left for you to find and discuss what it means, you have no further need of *The Scribe,* but we do. We need her to write for others who are aligned with our work and will fight for her to be heard. You may not want to spread the word, or tell your rivals why you excel and what you heard, but blessed are they who care enough about their fellowman to help them receive this wisdom now.

Whatever you want to do, think about it as being what you came to be or always wanted to try, then let it go. If it comes back twice and you never try to take it in stride or believe it can be, you will not be given such a chance again this life. You can pretend to be interested and lose out when the game is over, but not if you played and did all you wanted to do today.

The day is over for those who believe another will take care of them here. You may have been given special dispensation as a child and honor your parents now, but not so for many. As you have treated those who went before you, you can feel it now and will be treated with the same degree of respect. You cannot leave without making amends? You may, but that would surely mean you will come back again.

Whatever you believe and whomever you think you can be, you are a human being—one of several billion on the planet now. If all you want is to be someone others love, than love them more than they ever thought anyone might. Seek them out and give them advice you earnestly believe will help them achieve—to believe what they think is right.

If you can help others move into a new life while here, you will, too. If you decide you cannot help anyone because your needs are more important, or you need every dollar you make, do not think you will die and take money with you. It is not allowed and will not help you when you return.

All we have taught is in *The Books of Wisdom*, but for some this is the book that introduced you to us. We are happy for that! If you fail to understand and prevail with what we write here, you may not want to read in detail what it means to achieve a dream, work for your faith, and do whatever it takes to get along with others, but it is still there to do.

Take time to live your life and do it well—if not right. All will delight in you, because you cast a brilliant light. If you blight the life of another, you will not cast a shadow, but will have to come back. All we ask is that you not say you want to come back when asked at the end of this life.

Do not ask to come back! You may not be granted your request or wish, but it is possible you would be rotated back to now and ordered to do all of this again. We would not wish that on you, as a friend.

We do not wish anyone to abuse others or to end their lives in confusion, but it is your right. You have full power to live as you wish. That is *Free Will* and how it is seen and believed by those who monitor this scene—and this dream of you living a life not quite what you believe it to be.

You may not see into the future or be able to resurrect your past, but it still exists and is within reach. You can see it even now. Believe you can fly, and it happens every time. But how many can say they believe in God, let alone can fly? You will be believed only when you live through what others have to do—not only surviving, but doing better than ever. Once you prove you are better than others, you will be admired. Until then, do not imagine you can will others to admire you.

The will power it takes to believe you never make mistakes is incredibly difficult to imagine—and incredibly hard to believe anyone can conceive such a belief. Nevertheless, we will use our skill to help you overcome the ill will that comes from disagreeing with others and not helping anyone now. You may not want our help, but we will be there when you cross over into the next class and need tutoring to remember why you were here and what you were told to do then.

All is now clear! You can hear and you can feel. You will see that you came here to be *you*. You are now without anyone else like you, thus you have to think for yourself and believe in what *you* are here to prove. If you cannot believe *you* now, be honest, dependable, and able to love others anyway. Once you accomplish that, you are free to blissfully exist with no worry about coming back.

To live in bliss is to achieve it! To achieve bliss is to believe you can achieve it and did. You will not be given credit for what you did to others unless they are better now for it. You will not be given money by others if too clever and make them worry later or become angry because they believed you now.

You must learn what power is in order to respect it, but it need not cost you your life or time spent in solitary confinement. Be wise! Do what you came to do—then help others do the same.

Today we give you the future *you*. This is it—this is you! You are either filled to the brim with bliss now or know what to do when blissful, and how you created it. Be aware no one else can give you a life of bliss, because bliss is being you—*and this, too!*

Chapter Sixty-Two

Perfection is used by you as an excuse to stop working hard. Yes, it is true! You seek perfection, then give up, because whatever you did or do is not what you wanted or does not look great—and others are not raving about how wonderful you are. Thus you are justified in not working hard. We do not buy it, and neither do your Spiritual Guides!

When you accept that life requires much work and is not always great the way it arrives in your mind, on paper, or in concrete ways, you are wise. You must be wise to achieve greatness! Do not be deceived by those who say otherwise. To seek teachers such as we are, simply believe you can move ahead and what you want is easily taught now. Otherwise, you would not have stopped to read and think about what we wrote through *The Scribe.*

Whenever you are upset with others, immediately think about what you said or believed caused you grief. Think about what you wanted to do and why you did not do it—and most often you believed they were better than you. That is not to say your ego is in need of resuscitation, or you do not believe in yourself, but you tend to measure others by the effort you put into common projects.

In times such as these when people have yet to believe others achieve more than they can imagine, and do not care if they achieve or not, it is hard to see cooperation with your fellow man as the easiest route to the top. Once you can believe in others, do you turn over your work to them? If you do, you are foolish and will be continually harmed—even scorned, because you trusted others who are not interested in you enough to do a great job. Learn this lesson: If you first teach others how to do the job correctly, it is not your fault when something is not done right.

Being teachers, we are lenient if you have tried to teach others anything. Teachers today are ignored more and more, and students explore nothing, even though marvelous doors stand open, waiting for them. Who is lazy now—the teacher or students?

You decide, but we are not going to let you get away without working hard. You must absorb content you may not believe or want to accept in order to believe in others who do believe and accept it. You have to tolerate everyone who is in your work, life, and this world, before you are free to explore other worlds.

Once a student becomes aware of how little is known and how much there is to know, many give up. Is that you? If so, you are not nearly as smart as you thought. You must not give up learning and educating your mind. You must be aware that boredom comes to those who forget to inform themselves about what is going on around them.

Believe it!

As soon as you believe anything, it immediately implies whatever you thought will change, which is usually not the case. You have always believed you need to keep working hard to gain the top, but may not have recently reinforced that idea. Your mind has not been wired to accept that plan even now. By the way, you are who wires your mind! No one else has access unless you provide it.

To deny the wise access to your mind is something you must decide—and choose what you will do. We are not saying you have to adapt and accept what is written here in order to ascend or achieve bliss, but most know what we say is true. We are not stopping you nor harming you, but for some we are improving your opportunities to ascend and live better than you did.

All discussed in this book so far has been in riddles, with allegories and stories of a type meant to awaken you to argue or accept if it is right for you, but *at no time were you told what to believe.* You are who decides! When you make the same type of decision long enough, you believe it.

If you believe you are an atheist and someone approaches you and asks you to believe in something you do not approve, are you going to change your view? You immediately know you will stay as you are and not move a single brain wave. You will stay convinced that what you do is right—may even want to teach others to believe as you might, but you are not asked to do that.

To prophesize and tell lies in order to make a profit will end with you being here again, while others are off to a more gracious world—one without frauds. You may not want to believe it, but seriously religious people are not mad. They do not ask you to follow them, nor prophesize you will end up like them one day or die abandoned by whomever they worship or follow now. You will not be asked to join them in meditation or realization that God is. You may feel that way, but that is your mind suggesting a new idea—not something another is selling you. Admit it!

Once the mind digests what you want to do and finds proof it is approved and good for you, it will deliver whatever until you change commands. You are who plays God in your everyday life! That does not mean you cannot be called into line and your power over-ridden by a more powerful *you.*

You are here for a short time—then gone, but others live on afterwards and carry on your genes or whatever thoughts you achieved and spread about. Why would you expect others to believe in you if you were a fraud? Such a fraud is lost!

All that exists is not lost when the Mayan calendar changes course (**The Books of Wisdom** were dictated to *The Scribe* long before 2012), nor are you asked by the Mayan people to believe in it. In fact, we deny you access to it, because you are unable to understand your religions well enough to describe them to others—let alone the culture and religious principles of other peoples.

Do not try to infiltrate another's life in hopes of taking away what you appreciate and discarding everything else. It does not work that way. If you try, you will decay and lose your way.

The way to the top of the cross you bear and the worry you carry is to not care. You may say that cannot be true, because we are advised to care about whatever we do—even worry about it a bit to make sure it is good. Why would we not carry a burden of worry and guilt if we know we are not working hard or doing what we were taught? Is that really what you say to You now? If so, grow up! If you are reading this now, you are not a child!

What happens when you try to draw out a teacher on a subject you know little about? You become the class clown—others laugh at your expense. Do not let work on *you* lead you to make a fool of this you now. Take time to decide what you want out of life and why you want it, then go after it!

All we say is woven into a large and growing body of material you can save for other lives. It is important that you wrap yourself in it now to save you from a life in which you are unable to move on and ascend when it is time to leave. You must be able to fly on instant notice and never look back. Practice that!

If you have never left the safety of your parents—never lived on your own or taken up the role of provider for others, you are lost. You have little you can do to ascend, because you do not realize your job is not done, and you may not have time to be *you* and leave a wafer of this mind behind. Yes, you do want to be remembered!

Do not argue just to make a point! All who love to argue state emphatically they do not respect whoever brought the subject up—believing they are superior. You may argue about it, but it will not change that fact.

As you move into the new and last phase of whatever life you are in now, remember you had a chance to connect with others—could meet anyone, but still did not do much. Why? Why are you hiding?

When you come back from a retreat and immediately do exactly what you did before you left, are you saved by the fact that you did whatever during retreat, but cannot remember it now? That may be the case, because you are designed to change whenever you encounter a better life or more meaningful way to perceive your beliefs—or can be yourself. If a retreat changed nothing about you, or was not significantly different from what you did in the past, it is your mind that should be rewired, not the part others played—doing whatever you resented so much that you did not participate then.

Whatever you want to do now can be done once. It may not be exactly as you describe it, but will be as you believe it. Yes, your mind does manifest much, but it cannot create a new personality or a new soul.

You are required to deal with the hand you are dealt until you learn to deal a better one. If you never learn, that is your problem—not God's lack of interest in you or your parents' lack of love. You have to take over and work with who you are while here.

... ignore ...

... answer you need ...

Chapter Sixty-Three

On the move again or staying as is—hoping things change? Some move a lot, and never settle down or feel they belong, when all they need do is sit and listen—maybe smile once in a while. The butterfly must flit from flower-to-flower to get enough to survive, but it is not a fit occupation for those who seek divine love or a place in the sun. You need to be able to find your way wherever you are, but staying out-of-the-way—hiding is a sure way to end up having to come back.

Seek the middle path and do not worry about what others think. You must talk to *you* and trust that You knows what is best to do when you cannot move on and do something new because you are afraid. If your inner guidance responds that you need to move to thrive—then move! However, if you run away from obligations you created, fulfill your debts or they will be there when you believe you are through with life. You have to do what you said!

Others may not believe you or accept that you know much, but if you continue to work intelligently with honest people, in time they will honor you—possibly accept you to be better than they are. The idea that another is better is unacceptable to many who have nothing to base their comparisons on today, but say it anyway. Why?

True confidence is not taught. It is a learned process that is quite difficult if you are not honest. Remember, all that exists is what is. Do not prejudge what you have not experienced. If you believe you are better than others, were you told that by another or did you prove it? Congratulate your mind upon figuring out what would be a waste of time—but what worked once may now stop your growth.

When you are worried or tired of being with others, do you cry? You lose friends quicker by crying than anything else you do to gain attention. If, however, your hurt is so deep you cannot stop crying, be aware of who sticks with you until it ends. You have a treasure—a good friend then.

What you cannot afford to do is stop being you all the time. If being you today does not appear to impress others, perhaps your perception of who you are needs correction—not your present lot in life. Try doing what you love, to see if others agree you do it best. If so, will they gladly pay you to do it?

If you have no clue what to do, forget it. Get busy learning a trade that teaches you discipline. In time discipline gives you confidence enough to be yourself and trust whatever gift God tossed your way to make a living with today.

Will whatever you did to someone automatically be reflected back to you? Usually, but in some cases money is not repaid. If you invested in someone who did not intend to give you interest or repay, you chose to believe them due to greed. Learn to not be greedy and you will spot frauds easily, unless you continually try to acquire things that outstrip your means.

If you are not being you, whatever you are here to do is not worth crying about and trying to do over and over. You may want to believe receiving a *Gift of The Holy Spirit* entitles you to move up quicker than another or all others, but it does not. You simply have a talent many others have to work much harder to learn and use effectively, but with practice they can do it better than you.

It is now time to discover how to manifest what you wanted in other lives. Fortunately, it is not a difficult class to master. However, if you believe you can easily manifest anything, try making a tree. Do not agree you can manifest anything or credit yourself with what God alone does and will not ask you to do now.

You discuss the word *'God'* too much. Once you die and all is explained on the other side of this one life, you will realize that was a waste of time. Also, if you argue too often in an effort to learn why you are here, you most likely will be bounced back to learn more easily and quickly the next time.

Do what you need to do now!

Fully expressing yourself is seldom appreciated by others, unless you imply they did it with you or were better than you—or they will reap a reward as a result of what you did. If a parent believes she is the one who conceived and taught you everything you do, she may be foolish enough to think you owe her for doing what you were trained to do and came here to accomplish. You cannot fault parents, if you never respected their input or gave credit where due. Do that now and get it over with, so no one regrets having *borne* you, or whatever they say whenever they have nothing else to be proud of now.

Your work is yours to do! No one will know what you need to do, even if they claim they can teach you how to do it. A guru or teacher who cannot live the life they espouse is not to be believed. Watching extravagant gurus and preachers talk to huge crowds now, then doing whatever they want, is enough for many not to bother with them, but too many are caught seeking what they believe is taught—not following their hearts and the wisdom God gave them. Pray for them all now!

As you pray, be aware you do not always kneel or move to a safe haven to pray, but perhaps you need to pray that way. Why? If you respect no one and act that way toward your spiritual source, you are not doing what you are called to do—even what some taught you to do, instead snubbing the way others pray. That is pride and gets straight F's in the class taught to accept what God blesses—and not your place to say otherwise today.

Whoever you are, and whatever you believe you will be, is obvious to everyone who can see and observe you and listen to your words. To believe anything else is unwise. If you believe you can lie and everyone will accept it and always believe in you, you are obviously filled with pride to a degree that makes you obnoxious and less than wise. You are tested by liars here and by *God of All* when you end this life, but you are also rejected by the wise all the time if all you do is lie.

Is life worth the trouble you create? You bet! You can always change, do better, and pay for your sins before you go, so be you now!

All who explore living way above what they can afford find themselves in debt; it may be they believe it was someone else's fault, but it never is. Your greed was exceeded only by pride and the desire to deceive others into believing you were better than they. That never ends well for all involved. If that describes you now, change immediately!

A fool will not admit he did not get it—but when he continually repeats the same mistake, he may discover he has been foolish and never recover. Some not wanting to be discovered lie or spend more than they earn. You can test this, but better to learn from observing what happens to those who do so and refuse to admit their foolishness.

The move to turn you into someone not *you* is over. The mind by this time recognizes that we are teachers. We do not believe you need to believe in us or anyone else, but you must trust that *God of All* is above and beyond your recall and cannot be expected to do anything for you here. You are then on the way to understanding how you are created and what you will do before you ascend to another world—or come back here again.

All were taught who they are, and that they can do better while here, but some forget it as soon as they come back to this life or time. Why? You obviously do not get it yet, so we refuse to talk about it now!

Chapter Sixty-Four

Powerful people are not the problem. It is those who now have little or no power who want what others have. You must not forget that those with nothing to lose do not value you. You may believe helping others is a waste of money or time, but it is the only insurance any society has of surviving over time.

When whining about others, stop your mind from going over such things and check out the facts. If you are worse off than everyone else, work harder or ask for help. Most will help you if you do not make a habit of needing them often. If, however, you cannot make a living due to old age or youth, your society is unkind and will not survive over time if it cannot or will not care for you now. All returns to you...and making money is not the way to evaluate how the universe creates and extends power, plus all it entails now.

When you work out the details of where you live and add in taxes spent, you have a number you can use to debate issues about how much is owed to you once you deduct all the public funds you are provided with now. If you live as most advanced societies do, you cannot possibly have paid enough for publicly funded roads, sewers, and education most people want and use at some point in time. Why whine about taxes, when you owe so much to the public—or universe in your situation?

If you dally and regret paying taxes now, imagine how much you must do to make it to another plateau or even a life much slower than what you know. If you think you are doing things now that make you blink, you cannot imagine what happens when you do not manifest anything—which is exactly what happens next. This is a time when you learn through time spent creating what you believe you require, as a way to measure how grateful you are for all that is provided by a power—either here or afar.

Once gratitude enters the mind, fan the fire and keep it growing. Too many who have more than they know what to do with now are in power and making decisions that will cripple your ability to move quickly. If you do not do enough now, you need to be aware of what is happening everywhere and who does what. Why? You should be aware by the time you become an adult that you must rely on everyone else, unless you live in a mountain cave and never see another face.

All you create can be seen now!

Some have done a lot, and others are just getting started. Who works harder? Each does the same amount of work! You may believe computers make things easier, and work is not as detailed as it was once, but all things are equal. You need only apply your mind to learning to speak another language or learning how to use computers effectively, and you will work as hard as you have since you opened this book. Decide now to move and learn, then decide what you can provide others. Why? You cannot take your mind with you into the future!

If you spot someone gaping and moving about as if unable to figure out what is going on, you are likely unaware of where they are. Do not say they are in a fog, delirious, or have a degenerative disease. You know not! All that exists in this miasma cannot know what is happening *'now'*, let alone what happens when a mind decides to die ahead of time and not pay attention to what the body desires.

If you believe another is so disoriented you must administer a drug to bring such a person back to consciousness and the ability to think like everyone else, you are delirious. Think about it. Now write out why you are right. Within a minimum of a millennium you will realize what you said now is no longer considered wise.

What you do and how you do it counts for a lot of time spent here. If you are wise and move quietly and easily about, many do not block your progress. However, the loud and rude are often put down or held back from moving about. Use your mind while you have it. Decide to be wise and live with others the best way possible, so you can get ahead today.

All of your work at home or abroad is about feeling proud, gaining good health, or teaching others. You may say whatever you like about saving another from some certain death, or other dire fate, but you are playing God and not being you. That is a fate that leads you back here after the grave.

When you think about what you do and who does what to you, do you also tally up what you did to others that was wrong? If not, time to sit down and begin working on your life—correcting problems you may have created or contribute to now. You may not have done anything so far, but working hard does not determine who you are in this life. Working on your spiritual life, however, will save you a lot in time.

When your mind gives up and decides it would like a break, do you give it a break or do you medicate and say it helps you meditate? If you ever say a drug of any type helps you meditate, better be sure you are not talking to those who know how to meditate. You would immediately be branded a fraud—unable to know meditation from agitation and self-stimulation in the form of whatever you use to get beyond who you are now.

When a country is overrun by people working underground—not letting on they are planning evil now, you will know. You need only grow a more interesting mind to discover what others are doing or what they want to do now. All is easy once you can stop the thoughts that race about in your mind, concentrating long enough to tune into the universal mind and find out what others are all about.

The difference between two people is not as big as once believed. Those who dabble in science are wrong when they say you cannot read minds or believe in God, due to the *'fact'* that it is impossible to prove either. It only proves men live far from the truth now!

In a state of confusion? All you need to do is consider You and all you can draw from your life so far. If you have done little to educate you or learn from the wise, you will remain confused all this life—which is all right. It opens time to those who are wise, permitting those who are wicked to be seen by the wise and provided no further lies to use—in order to protect this world from the truth. You need to go over this several times, but it is what you all do!

Today you can see into the future—but not into the work you wanted to do and never got around to doing for others. You will be with *you* forever, simply passing by this way with a few favored people from many other lives—many of whom you will not be with ever again. Why waste this time diving under the covers and keeping away from crowds—never believing anyone else? You miss too much!

Chapter Sixty-Five

World-wide fame is not what you want when trying to get your act together and ascend to the next life, but some want fame more than they want anything else. Thus this life is stunted and they cannot move on when this journey is over. Why seek what you want from others, expecting them to know who you are, giving you whatever you ask for now? It is infantile, and anyone caught in the trap of fame and seeking whatever they can get from others is unlikely to fulfill their destiny. Why would you risk so much for something that will not last?

When ego gets involved in your spiritual life, you do not want to fly and will sit for hours with no thoughts in mind. You want to be noticed! You want others to cater to you like a child spoiled by doting adults. You do not need help! If you do, it will be given.

God alone will know exactly when to call you home. You will struggle unlike others, but everyone struggles who gains wealth and fortune and uses it to help others. What else could motivate them to do it?

If you are stunted at birth by too much attention, due to your family's decision that you are better than others, you will never be as strong emotionally or as well physically as you otherwise might be. Be aware that catering to a child leads to dependency, a deficiency the parent imparts—not what the child deserves. You are not to make others need you.

When you decide to make another need you much, you are not given much credit for doing it. Yes, you think martyrs are much loved by others, but they are not. Why? They make others feel they do not work hard enough, or do not sacrifice for others, or cannot do well on their own. If you are catering to another now in hopes they will be dependent upon you or pay you back in some wonderful way one day, try to defend your position.

As you look at what you have given others, do you add up things you have not created or sacrificed to have what God gives everyone? Think on it! Be aware many who want you to compare what they do with what you can be are not interested in your doing more or becoming stronger, rather they wish you to give up and admit they are better than you.

You will not always star. You will not always fail. You may have days in which you cannot do much and other days when everything you touch is easily done, but you are alive and always able to excel. Choose to do your best and let others do whatever they like.

Divide your life into parts—name one *Childhood,* one *Teen Years,* and so on. Are you through living each of these divisions now? You need to be out of one before you enter the next. It is imperative you not skip developmental experience in order to appear older or take on adult burdens before your time. If you omit even a little bit, it will come back to be lived at a time when it will not look good on your part to act that way.

Whatever you do now will not be remembered. You might think about it, keeping alive what you want to remember or cannot forget because it was a mess or someone said it was great. No one will remember it as it is. Keep your mind on living—being yourself and moving on—not stopping to recap, rewrite, and edit out people or add in what you want others to believe about you.

It is a waste of time to lie!

Once you lie to yourself, you build an empire and life based on what is not true. You have to continue to keep up the false front or fall flat—forced to admit you did not do it or did what you are afraid to admit. You are not so powerful that you have to identify every liability, but if elected as an official, admit what you did and live it down. Prove you learned a lot and can be trusted now. Remember, those who lie are not trustworthy!

What if you were told you had no right to live? Would you scream and cry or struggle to be alive and prove you deserve a life now? If you struggle to be you and do what you like, you may not enjoy childhood, but you will thrive as an adult. It is the child who listens and never gives a thought to what life might be like once in charge who has the most trouble later in life. All of this is psychology.

You may argue with us or others about what we state here, but we know. We watch you all and grow fond of the human being you seem to be. You cannot live in another way today, but one day you will see the insane were not—and many who passed as being okay were truly insane and aware of it every day.

Take time to enjoy life and be yourself, then go out and teach others how to live as you do—doing what will work or appreciate over time. Whatever you do—be you, know a child cannot live long in an adult world without much guidance on how to avoid the ogres and villains that abound now. It is a wilderness out there and many children are abandoned at adulthood and earlier, so their parents can act out childhood fantasies, arguments, and other such things—leaving their child to be the adult and decide what to eat and when to go to sleep at night. Be aware that what you do to a child will haunt you all the way through the next life, too, and may even give you another shot at living this life again.

You were taught what you believe is your right now. You may say you do not want others to speak about God, because there is none, or whatever nonsense you pretend to believe, but you cannot believe that any more than others believe they created their lives with no outside help. You have to identify to someone at some time what created your life and keeps you alive to what is going on all the time, so why resist it? Admit you are not a creator and that a force or source creates, which we prefer to simply call God. Why fight simplicity when there are so many delightful things you could be doing now?

What if life is always a fight?

You realize you are not wired to live with others or equipped to live with those you are with now. Either move out of harm's way or stay geared up to fight and not feel great the rest of your life. If your culture is lost—losing because others are unwilling to let it thrive, you can change or move away. We advise you to decide to live within the community as a friend, not as their enemy. If you can prove you do no harm, one day they will not limit you or keep you down.

Until you live down whatever caused your belief system or culture to decline, you have much to learn about persuading others to believe as you do, but do not begin by trying to win over others to whatever you believe to be a religion they need. No one believes as you do now, nor will they accept it as a legitimate reason to admit you into their clan. Be aware many today live quite different from the usual culture, yet are peacefully integrated into business and whatever.

You do not have to be a partner to anyone, but women love to have others around, especially if they wish to have a large family and do not. You need to be aware of that when you begin another way of life, such as a business. Women do not deal well with those they believe to be better than they are. If you want to lose a grand friend, go into business with her now.

All is better for men when they combine with others, or so it might seem, but too many men are renegades from other times living in a line now. You cannot combine with a thief or a liar—and wise to avoid both. If you want to believe a man who cheats others, it is your desire to believe—not the thief's influence. Take your time, and always be wise when entering a new life. It could be the best thing you ever did.

Be aware of what you care about and need, keep it within eyesight most of the time. How can you do that if you own houses everywhere and so much stuff you have to decide where it might fit? You need not care. All will disappear before you are gone from here. All will be used to sate what others care about, or do not like and will throw away in a day or so after you die. Whatever you set stock in now will not last once you no longer are around to care about it.

What if you saved all this life to afford a great surprise for your wife? You may be surprised when your wife leaves you for others, because you never celebrated enough. You might also find your wife dies before the time you planned your grand end and you are left without any idea what to do with all you put aside until then.

Whatever you decide to do, do it now!

Be assured that if you start out wisely—and work hard to follow your original idea, it will work out. Why? The pattern is immediately laid out, and only changes to the initial plan will hinder your progress, which can make others mad or feel you are not sane enough to be aligned with them. Nevertheless, do not change your plans once you decide what you want. The progress you make in life is most affected by how your mind puts things together.

If you are dissatisfied and scatter your hatred over many others, you will never have enough friends to run for political office. That having been said, who cares if you ruin your life? If you can name someone who does care, you owe them for whatever they have extended to you to deserve this recognition.

All is what you make of it, but you are who will recognize it or not. You may be rich beyond whatever anyone else ever dreamed of owning, possessing, or taking from another, but unless you recognize it, it is not enough. If you are not hungry, you are not wise to eat what is not good for the body or heart. You are who is in charge. Whatever you say today will happen one day, so be smart!

The end of a day is not always as promising as when you arose from your bed and greeted the world, but it was your day. Think about it and ask for nothing. Praise God for whatever happened and think on that. If you live a good and righteous life, you will not remember it.

However, if you live without limits to your anger with another, or greed and deceit, you will be back and reminded of it many times thereafter.

Take off now for a life full of goodness and wonderful things you alone believe are great and all will be pleasant when you awaken tomorrow. Why? If you plot, scheme, and forget you are loved by God, your dreams may not let you sleep contentedly. You plant the seeds for your dreams.

Chapter Sixty-Six

Anger and intolerance are signs of decay not expressed by the enlightened and educated of a society. Some believe they may be enlightened without accepting that others have rights—even privileges which they deserve. You are not without witnesses to what you do now, but many believe they are laws unto themselves, as you often say, and not required to be nice, polite, or agreeable—because they appear to be right. If you behave in ways not conducive to demonstrating how much you can tolerate or love others, it may be because you were raised that way, but there is no excuse once you are educated and can raise your mind to a higher level.

It is you as an adult who must require yourself to continue to work on your faults and not expect everyone else to ignore them and love you in spite of your disagreeable ways. All things are not equal! To say they are is to say you do not aspire to rise higher than you are, which would be a lie. No one ever gives up wishing to be someone others respect and might even like. So to say otherwise is to lie and let the world become aware you are old and out of touch with reality as it is now.

When you fear others, feeling the need to rise up and strike them, remember why you are afraid and what made you feel this way. If it was your mind or because you did not wish to decide your life, be aware you could end up with nothing you have now and no idea how to live better. Be aware of what you will do when you change the way you live now and whom you love, because it will cause you to either regret or love the next move you make.

Be assured you can move easily now and manifest much emotionally and within your mind. Others are always manifesting what they want, too. You cannot always be in charge, but if that is your desire, be ready to take over when others give up, walk away, or ask you to do it for them. Do not usurp their work, unless you have no other way to survive.

All over the world men and women want what generations before prepared and saved to give to them—plus what many left behind to be used now. Too many crave what elder generations live on now, unwilling to wait until they give it up or die away. Why? Childish behavior is unwise at any stage above or beyond age 12, but you can still act that way. Many are locked in teenage mindsets they created without any supervision when under the direction of parents who left them alone too often and too long.

You may not be offended by the intrusion of someone who refuses to mature, but you cannot escape it if you watch the media. You see children and elders exploited as though wise and welcome by societies at large, but it is not true. Get over being a child and move into adulthood as soon as possible to save your society.

Once you are old enough to vote and run your country, be ready! You may not be equipped to do either, thus automatically giving you such rights is unwise. Since you need to be tested to drive legally, why not be tested to vote?

When a society cannot drive its people to thrive on their own—instead giving over their rights to dictators and such, you whine and pretend to object. While stopping work and doing less than you know is enough, you become unwilling to give up your surplus in order to gain. Do you realize you cannot feed yourself and others if you are deep in debt or unskilled in manual labor? The rich of previous societies thrived in times when others could not. Without education or skillsets they amassed surpluses, why not *'enlightened'* societies?

You need not worry if you keep your home as you need it to be—eating only what your body requires. Why? You are conservative enough to save for difficult times. You know when to put aside surplus and when to use what you saved.

All who believe others are stupid—needed only for fun and games and making use of their talents and abilities, do not sense they can be overrun and removed at any time—until it happens. It is not too soon to learn how to care for yourself, regardless of where you are. You need to believe in your ability to take charge of whatever you own to build your life force. To ignore others, yet think they will take care of you, is foolish.

No doubts now?

If you have no doubts, you are probably forgetting something major about to happen. How can you guard against disaster? Take charge of your day life and watch your dreams every time you sleep. You will be up-to-date on what your mind finds full-time and in many lives and is aware you need to take care of now.

If you awaken with a dream lingering in your mind, obviously you are afraid of what you saw and it prompted you to wake up and remember it. If you decided to ignore it, you do not remember your dreams. No one will bother to inform you that you are in line to do something you are not ready to do.

If you ignore your dreams to the point of actually not seeing them or believing you dream, you are not intuitive and imagine little. Will it harm your life? You can easily tell who honors their thoughts and dreams, and who does not. Check who is one step ahead of everyone else and you have a pretty good idea of who uses all they have in mind—and do it all the time.

All you are here to do is defined and aligned for you to read daily—in your own way, but astrology is not why you study the alignment of the heavens. Minimally, it is not the way to seek your path back to where you once were. If you become an intimate seeker of knowledge about your mind and life today, you will develop every way available to learn about your mind and thoughts, as well as develop your body.

You will be a happy human being if you walk five miles and not worry about getting up every morning to face a life of misery and bad health caused by bad habits and an attitude that others owe you happiness—even a way of life.

All you need is in your dreams!

Several times throughout your life a dream will direct you to what you must do soon, but most are not aligned that well to what can be done easily because it was created for you to do this life. If you are now not aligned with your talents and spiritual gifts, you may be sick without realizing it. If you cannot sit for a minute and think of nothing, realize you are too stressed to create anything now.

Realize you need dreamtime! If not, you will ignore our advice and simply live as is until you cannot. All of life is not exactly dreamtime, as some would love to believe, but there are people who do live in dreamtime equally as much as they walk the path. You cannot know how, if not taught before you were born and given a place to develop it further while here.

If you believe it is easy to suddenly become another woman or man—think again. Drop the idea! Instead, continue to explore and develop the person you are now in this world.

To attempt to change to another way of life, or abscond with another's culture, in order to develop your life or make a living explaining it to those who will never understand anyone other than themselves is another way of lying and being the victim of greed—not enlightened, as some want to believe. Do what you are taught until you know it well—then decide if it works or not.

Once exposed to others, you will change and take from them what enables you to be better at who you are, but it will never replace the being you came to be. You are who must decide what to do with your talents and gifts, or why you would not use them all. If you believe you need a scout of some type to find and polish your art, you will not live long before becoming aware you are not highly regarded unless propped up by another.

Be not afraid to believe in yourself, but be aware others can walk away and not praise you ever. They have no call to do so—you are who must believe in you. When you do, hopefully you help others who cannot do the same for themselves. If not? You better be great! If not, you will need others one day.

Today is not a day you can identify on a calendar and say it is over. You only know a day is over when what you decided you would do that day is finished and not about to be changed by someone else. If you commit murder and are never caught, in your own way you are locked into that day forever. You have to come out of it and talk about what you did, then savor it or change your ways to move into a new day and never visit that past again. Live to get through it—not regret what you did with it.

Thrilling words and exciting work are not the lot of those who do not dream and think big enough to create such things. Be aware of your charm or lack thereof, if you wish to persuade others to vote for you or ask you to lead. You could be well endowed enough now not to realize your gift of spirit is what elects you to the top of everything you wish to do, so appreciate it!

Chapter Sixty-Seven

Only those who believe and conceive what they will do with their beliefs leave behind what they were taught as a child. To believe that is false is nonsense. Read it again! Whatever else you think now, you had to smile because it was true, yet something within you wanted to argue and say it did not make sense. Why?

Who would you tell about this great information you found—or that it came from a woman, no less, in a way that defies societal mores today and denies you must be able to see others to believe what they teach. You cannot imagine doing it? You have much company now.

As *The Scribe* begins a new way of working and doing her work at home, you may want more from her about ascension and other words that catch your imagination, but why should she bother to sit for hours and keep out of the limelight so everyone reading this book can move ahead and become greater than they are now—ending this life with a bright light? You will not thank her, and she will not be around when you finally move on, so why does anyone bother to help others? That is what we want you to decide and work on now.

Once you move up and out of your work, doing whatever you want to perfect you, will you be perfect? Will you be the best you can be? Will you ever please everyone you meet? Who will you be? All of these are wisdom makers, if you are willing to pursue what they mean to you. Be honest—every question asked so far did not make you stop and look at what is in your heart. You skipped many—never thought for even a second about what some meant. You wanted to finish the book and get on with it—whatever *IT* is.

Since you seek bliss and have been promised this is it, you will be delighted to realize this is the end of it. This is all you get! Sit and remember what you sought when you started reading and working with *you* this way.

If you are idle now —not working, it is not because you were told to not work or pause and do nothing, thus all would be granted to you. That never happened! It never does!

You have to work on being whoever you wish to be. If you cleverly decide to heed the advice you gain from going within and reaching that source within your mind or inner life that provides you with words to use when talking to anyone—friend or not, you are working on improving yourself now. All you need do is be able to shut down the mind for short periods of time and see what comes to you then.

Once you are inspired by your muse and want to do something you just thought of, you are moving beyond where you were when you walked into this work. You can meditate and seek bliss that is, was, and will be within *you*. Now is the time to change, so you can be as great as you want to be and always thought you were—do it now!

Smile as though you grasp the wisdom found here—granted to all who read what *The Scribe* has written and published. She writes as we speak and is not allowed to change our style. She does not always see what we mean, either. She could change a word and not realize it is not the way we said it today, but that is okay. Do you always say what you mean? Do you always write perfectly? If you do, you can skip ahead of this group and prove it.

Teach our wisdom and we will give you what you need to do it! If you wish to succeed and teach what you read, you cannot say it is wrong? You have to prove it, work on it, then decide if you want to be derided by the wise for having a huge ego.

All is done and all was what we wanted, but along the way many changes happened to *The Scribe* and prevented her from living her life.

We regret it. We do not forget. We will prove to you that all is great when you follow your bliss and intend to do it with Ruth Lee, too.

Today we leave and will teach with her as we have, but now she gets to say she does not want to teach a class, or does not want to be bothered by those who come forward and deny her respect or give up nothing learned through her by saying it was helpful. From now on, she will charge you and others who want to hear what she has to say about our work.

All we said today was assumed to be how things were, right? You thought The Scribe was paid to write, and everyone could deride the work—and she was unable to say no to working for us. That is not true! Ruth Lee is no fool!

We would never use someone as our scribe who could not write, nor would we consider someone who would willingly cut others' throats for money, or someone clever enough to cheat others and act like that was not the case. You are in the presence of another who works hard. You may not believe what we say, but you can never deny that.

Get over doing what enables you to feel you can be snide or sneer at others and move ahead. Be yourself, do your best—and all will be blessed. It may take time, and you may be passed by as *The Scribe* was over time. You may not be asked to do tasks suited to your abilities, and may not like who asks you to work fast, but you will do well if you follow the style of *The Scribe* now—and work as if you are making a great contribution to the work others will use and benefit from one day soon.

All we have said and done has been put into context. You have only one woman to watch today, *The Scribe*. She is now the one who will face the crowd—not us. We are not in your way today, and will not stop you from ridiculing what you know little about, but we advise you to not cross swords with our scribe. We know how fast her rapier tongue can strike out and win the bout. You do not!

All we ask is that you take up a task you can act on immediately. While thinking about what it means, read the book again. Each time you pass by, reread what you once thought was unbelievable. Yes, mark up this book and question it as you work on your pride.

Pride is what keeps you from acing this class, but it is not too late to begin to appreciate things you cannot know or have never heard about before now, because no one you know talks about it, or some who have yet to read what is written deride it. Believe your wisdom! Ask again if this is it—are you experiencing bliss? That is how you do it!

In The World of Today is a world you create—it is called tomorrow. You may not be able to understand how it is done and why, but there is a **Book of Wisdom** written that will teach what is now available that explains the phenomenon of power. You are who will be *you,* and it makes sense to us that you create a better life whenever and however you can without harming others. Once you learn the basics, you can do more than ever before.

All you are here to do is be you!

All you seek is bliss. If you disagree and want to plead your belief, do it. You can talk your way out of this life with others on this side, but at some point you leave everyone behind and only *you* remain to explain this life. The end of life begins in a time not limited by anything but a scribe—and her time is not ended yet.

You are all involved in a time that is evolving quickly into an orbit that will take you all forward or beyond where you are now. It may not be the path you would have taken had you studied what you were doing last and changed your belief system. Today, if you have heeded our advice, you are no longer guided by others.

You can now describe your life as it will be and is, what you did to get to it—thus believe in yourself. We have not said a word against your god or whoever you believe it to be, because we do not need to mention religion. This is not about religious belief—rather an ethical system anyone can use to better this life and feel the excitement of being *you.*

If you can rise above thought, you will not feel sorrow or pain. Without that ability, all you know and all you say now is yours until you change. It is possible to ascend and blend in with angels of another type, but you are not here to do that.

You are here to learn to be *you* and determine that it takes effort to keep you living the best life possible wherever *you* are. Be you and follow your heart. This is bliss—and bliss is it!

Afterthoughts

Each day I arrive at my computer and begin writing is a miracle. I wonder—always, why me? How could I have predicted that at this advanced age I would be permitted to write for those I aspire to know? I fought the need to teach all my life—said I wanted to be a scholar and not bother with what others believe is necessary to know, but I changed.

Now I am ready to do whatever is needed, but no longer feel the need to be busy every day working for others as I did since arriving in this life. I no longer seek out those who know what they want, or those who have problems and want help. I permit whomever to come into my presence and spiritual work, as described in these works called **The Books of Wisdom**. It moves through my hands and into the lives of others who can use it then. I will not work much longer for others. I, too, need time to get my life in line with what is to come.

Enjoy all that *The Teachers of The Higher Planes* provided, because it is not known when or if they will write this way again. A lesson is provided by *The Teachers* and others every time I sit down to plan, wishing I could help you as much as they helped me. I have been challenged by cancer, heart, and mobility problems and live unafraid, because I know what I want and who I am.

My writing style was legalistic and businesslike due to many years as a technical writer in giant industry, but now choose instead to write inventive books that teach in *'novel'* ways. I hope anyone reading these lines will find those books worthwhile, too.

Ruth Lee, Scribe
July 4, 2012
Updated December 17, 2016

Have You Read...

We Are Here

The Teachers of the Higher Planes

There is more to living and dying than human beings realize while here on Earth. Are you aware intelligent beings exist beyond our time and space who work diligently to teach universal truths? There are teachers and guides—and they are here now!

We Are Here is the work of teachers charged with educating humanity about the basic facts of life, spirituality, and ascension. Using spiritual scribe, Ruth Lee, *The Teachers of the Higher Planes* channeled material essential to living a full and meaningful life. This work is revolutionary in its straight-forward presentation of what the world needs and how each of us can achieve higher levels of love, success, and peace in every aspect of daily living today.

The Teachers lay bare the aspects of human society which endanger all who live on Earth—even Earth itself! They provide clear instructions on how to correct the problems of our times. Shockingly frank—not at all concerned with the reaction of first-time readers.

Bliss is It!, sixth in ***The Books of Wisdom*** series, is the final volume that concludes *The Teachers'* mission to help the people of Earth live and ascend at the end of their time here, or Earth does not survive due to man's abuse of it.

We all need to know why we are here—and what we can do to improve our lives in all ways, every day, starting Today!

To learn more about **We Are Here ~ *The Teachers of the Higher Planes*,** the first volume in ***The Books of Wisdom*** series, as well as **Bliss is It!** visit:

For more information, visit www.LeeWayPublishing.com

www.ingramcontent.com/pod-product-compliance
Lightning Source LLC
Chambersburg PA
CBHW052030090426
42739CB00010B/1844
* 9 7 8 0 9 9 7 0 5 2 9 5 4 *